D1524294

TWENTIETH CENTURY WARRIOR

Major General Edwin D. Patrick, New Guinea, 1944
(Courtesy of Joseph A. Castagnetto) Photo taken in 1944.

TWENTIETH CENTURY WARRIOR

THE LIFE AND SERVICE OF
MAJOR GENERAL EDWIN D. PATRICK

BY

WILSON ALLEN HEEFNER, M.D.

FOREWORD BY

GENERAL BRUCE PALMER, Jr., USA

(RET.)

 WHITE MANE PUBLISHING COMPANY, INC.

This White Mane Publishing Company, Inc. publication was printed by:
Beidel Printing House, Inc.
63 West Burd Street
Shippensburg, PA 17257 USA

In respect for the scholarship contained herein, the acid-free paper used in this book meets the guidelines for permanence and durability of the Committee on Production Guidelines for Book Longevity of the Council on Library Resources.

For a complete list of available publications please write:
White Mane Publishing Company, Inc.
P.O. Box 152
Shippensburg, PA 17257-0152

Library of Congress Cataloging-in-Publication Data

Heefner, Wilson Allen, 1931-
    Twentieth century warrior : the life and service of Major General Edwin D. Patrick / by Wilson Allen Heefner ; foreword by Bruce Palmer, Jr.
        p.   cm.
    Includes bibliographical references and index.
    ISBN 0-942597-81-8 (alk. paper)
    1. Patrick, Edwin D., 1894-1945.   2. Generals--United States--Biography.   3. United States. Army--Officers--Biography.
4. United States. Army. Infantry Division, 6th.   5. World War, 1939-1945--Biography.   I. Title.
U53.P33H44   1995
355' . 0092--dc20
[B]   95-12915
                                                                    CIP

PRINTED IN THE UNITED STATES OF AMERICA

TABLE OF CONTENTS

LIST OF PHOTOGRAPHS

LIST OF MAPS

FOREWORD

This book is the appealing story of Edwin D. Patrick, an old–fashioned hero in the traditional American mold. His earliest known paternal forebear was born in 1757 on the Eastern Shore of Maryland, his progeny migrating westward to Ohio, and eventually settling in Tell City, Indiana, located in the true heartland of America. His great–great–grandfather served in the Maryland Militia during the Revolutionary War, while his father fought on the Union side in one of the bloodiest battles in the western theater of the Civil War as a rifleman of Company G, 81st Regiment, Indiana Volunteer Infantry, a forerunner of the Indiana National Guard. And so volunteer military service was part of Patrick's heritage.

Born in 1894 in Tell City, and growing up there, "Ed" Patrick graduated from high school in 1912, and entered Indiana University the following year. While in college, he received a commission as a second lieutenant in the Indiana National Guard, joining Company I, 2nd Indiana Infantry, in 1915. About this time, fate intervened in the immediate form of trouble with Mexico when President Wilson mobilized most of the National Guard, and Lieutenant Patrick found himself with his regiment in southern Texas, near the Border. Up to this time, he had dabbled in law and had shown an unusual aptitude for journalism, indeed pursuing the avocation of writing throughout his life. But now the time had come to make up his mind about a military career and he seized the moment, earning a regular commission in the U.S. Army and taking the oath of office on March 26, 1917, on the eve of America's entry into World War I. Thus began an unusually varied and successful career in the Regular Army which was to span a period of almost twenty–eight years until he was wounded in battle on Luzon, Philippine Islands, during World War II, and died as a result of those wounds on March 15, 1945. He was one of three U.S. Army division commanders to die of battle wounds during World War II.

General Patrick served during some of the most momentous years of our Republic—a period that saw two world wars, in each of which he was cited for bravery in battle. Only a very few men in the U.S. Army saw action in both wars, and only a handful were cited for valor in both—a rare achievement indeed. The inter–war period, the 1920's–1930's, were formative years for "Pat" (as he was known in the Army) Patrick. They included years of troop duty with famous old U.S. infantry regiments: the 23rd at Fort Sam Houston, Texas, and the 15th in Tientsin, China, as well as years as a student and, later, instructor at the Infantry School, Fort Benning, Georgia, the Command and General Staff College at Fort Leavenworth, Kansas, and the Army War College in Washington, D.C. Patrick was also selected to attend the Naval War College at Newport, Rhode Island—another rare distinction given only to a very small number of army officers.

However, the important thing about these various assignments was not so much learning more and more about one's chosen profession both in school and in the field, but forging lifelong friendships with one's military contemporaries. Ours was a very small peacetime army—officers knew practically every other officer, either personally or by reputation, particularly in his own branch. Whether at school, or with troops, or on staff duty, an officer could size up his contemporaries, both professionally and personally. Because it was peacetime and funds for training were scarce, schools were extremely important in the professional development of the army, and so only the very best and the brightest were chosen to be instructors and run the schools. But equally important were the real soldiers who truly wanted to serve with troops and were not bashful about it. At any rate, the sheep could be separated from the goats, and the "bootlickers" and the impostors could be spotted a mile away. This is how men destined for greatness, such as General George C. Marshall, without question the most outstanding American leader of this century, could, unerringly for the most part, fill the big jobs for an army that expanded twenty–five–fold in a little over a year's time—he already knew who these superb leaders were.

And so Patrick served in a very tough league of "old pros," and was not found wanting. He was known to some of the crusty "old pros" in the Pacific, such as General Walter Krueger, who had come up from the ranks and went all the way to four stars. One of Krueger's favorite expressions was "The trouble with the Army is the officers"—what he meant was that the best officers were the leaders who didn't "sit on a high horse," but knew their men, and shared their hardships and dangers without hesitation. Krueger knew Patrick well and liked what he saw—"a man's man." This is why Krueger, commanding Sixth Army in the Pacific, had Patrick assigned to a combat command as soon as he could. Krueger knew that fighting in the Pacific was for the most part quite different from combat in Europe—the rugged jungle country of New Guinea and the Philippines was no place for large armor formations, but was close–in infantry fighting country where closing with the enemy had a special meaning. And Krueger knew that Patrick could handle it.

But Patrick was also a bold, hard–charging leader who could have been a great cavalry–armor leader in Europe. He strongly felt that "Fortune favors the BOLD," and he was always willing to take the chance to prove the old adage. Had he lived longer, he would have gone on even higher in the U.S. Army; but his luck ran out on Luzon in March 1945.

Twentieth Century Warrior is more than just a fine biography and the gripping account of a fighting U.S. infantry division—the 6th—in the Southwest Pacific during World War II. The book also paints a warm and insightful picture of the "Old Army" during the days of the American Empire in the Pacific and the Caribbean that existed during the first decades of the Twentieth Century. But most important of all, the book is a compelling testament for a man's full life in the U.S. Army—an institution that Edwin Daviess Patrick loved and admired.

Bruce Palmer, Jr.
General, USA (Ret.)
The Fairfax
Fort Belvoir, Virginia
May 1992

PREFACE

On May 15, 1950, I was in a long column of enlisted men of the U.S. Army and U.S. Air Force standing on a pier at the Oakland Army Terminal, waiting to board the USNS *General Edwin D. Patrick*. We made up the advance party of the contingent of troops that would depart two days later from Fort Mason, the Presidio of San Francisco, on a thirteen–day voyage to Yokohama. Little did I suspect that the voyage on the *Patrick* would, almost forty years later, launch me on a quest for information about the ship's namesake, a quest that would last more than three years; take me on trips totaling more than twenty thousand miles to libraries, archives, and private homes throughout the United States; and lead to correspondence with scores of institutions and individuals from California to New York, from Nebraska to Texas. During that time I interviewed former army personnel who ranged in grade from private to general, and had the privilege of meeting Patrick's two surviving sons and two nieces. The nieces allowed me to read many intimate and revealing letters that he wrote to his mother, brothers, and sisters during his twenty–eight year military career. I also met with one of the few men still living who were with Patrick east of Manila on that fateful morning of March 14, 1945.

This book was conceived, quite unknowingly, during that fifteen–day "liaison" between the troopship and me on my voyage to Yokohama. The product of this conception was to undergo a lengthy gestation of more than forty years, the gestational period to be marked by only rare feeble stirrings of the developing fetus within the cerebrum of its procreator. The first pangs of labor began in 1988, and after a labor period extending over more than three years, the product of this union finally saw the light of day in January 1992.

When I began my search for information about Patrick in 1988, I knew only that he had died on March 15, 1945, of combat wounds received the previous day while he was commanding the 6th Infantry Division on Luzon, Philippine Islands, and that his widow and three sons were listed as living in Ruidoso, New Mexico. Just beginning my graduate studies in United States history at the University of Hawaii, after retiring from a twenty–eight year career as a pathologist and nuclear physician, I was unsure how to proceed in obtaining information about his life and career.

I began by inserting requests for information about him in such publications as *Army Times*, the *American Legion Magazine*, the *VFW Magazine*, and publications of the Reserve Officers Association, the National Guard Association, the Retired Officers Association, and Masonic bodies. I also contacted the National Personnel Records Center and the U.S. Army Reserve Personnel Center in St. Louis, Missouri, hoping to review Patrick's service record. This latter hope was crushed when I learned that his service record was one of some sixteen million service records that had been partially or completely destroyed in a 1973 fire at the National Personnel Records Center, where those records had been stored. That loss of his service record tremendously complicated my reconstruction of his military career.

However, I did receive scores of letters in response to my requests for information in the aforementioned publications. Many were from men who had served in the 6th Infantry Division or in the 158th Infantry Regiment, or who had sailed on the *Patrick* during her nearly twenty–two years of service. Others were from people who had only heard of Patrick or who had relatives who had served with him. More than 99 percent of these letters conveyed very favorable and even laudatory opinions of Patrick, confirming my belief that the life and career of this man were truly worthy of a formal biographical study.

Still, after several months of these efforts, I had been unable to locate any surviving immediate family members. Not knowing how to proceed further, I placed a telephone call to "Information" in Ruidoso, and found that indeed a Patrick family still lived there. When I telephoned the family, Mrs. Patrick told me that her family was not related to Edwin Patrick, but that another Patrick family had previously lived in Ruidoso; she thought that Mr. Patrick had been a lawyer.

I next consulted the *Directory* of the American Bar Association, and found the name "Thomas Patrick," listed as residing in Terre Haute, Indiana. I knew that Patrick was a native of Indiana, and that he had a son named Thomas, but the age of Thomas Patrick, the attorney, precluded his being Patrick's son. However, it was possible that he might be a relative of the general. Contact with this family confirmed that Mr. Patrick was indeed General Patrick's nephew. Mrs. Patrick placed me in touch with the general's two nieces in Tell City, Indiana, Mrs. Mary Margaret Goffinet and Mrs. Ruth Anne Werner. Those two ladies, who have been of tremendous help and a real encouragement to me, responded immediately to my letters, supplying me with the addresses of his sons, and offering me the opportunity to visit them in Tell City, to review letters, photographs, and other memorabilia that they had in their possession that pertained to the Patrick family.

This contact was the key that I had been seeking to unlock the door of Patrick's life. My more than five years of subsequent research have culminated in this book.

I should like to dedicate this work to the family of Major General Edwin D. Patrick, to all those men who served with him in World War I and World War II, both living and dead, and to those men and women, both living and dead, who sailed on the USNS *General Edwin D. Patrick* to their rendezvous with destiny on the Korean peninsula during America's "forgotten war."

I should like to express my indebtedness to Martin K. Gordon, Ph.D., Executive Editor, White Mane Publishing, Co., Inc., and Barry W. Fowle, Ph.D. Historian, U.S. Army Corps of Engineers, my editors. They challenged me to become a critical winnower of my manuscript, that I might cast out the chaff, and look at Edwin Patrick as a "whole man," not only acknowledging his strengths and successes, but also his foibles, peccadilloes, prejudices, and, yes, even his failings.

I must acknowledge the incalculable debt I owe Patsy, my wife of more than thirty-five years. She has been a constant and unwavering support during the lean and difficult years of medical school and residency, and during the demanding years of my medical practice, enduring lonely days and nights when it was necessary for me to be at the hospital. She has guided our son, Jay, and our daughter, Annette, to become mature, responsible, and loving adults, imbuing them with her unwavering Christian faith. She has, without complaint, indulged my love of military history, trudging battlefields from Guadalcanal and Tarawa to the Ardennes, from Gettysburg to Vicksburg, from Okinawa to the beaches of Normandy. She has lovingly sustained me and encouraged me during my career in the Army National Guard and the U.S. Army Reserve, despite the fact that my duties frequently required me to give up weekends and vacation time that I am sure she would have preferred I spend with her and our children. Finally, this book could not have come to fruition without her, for she typed the entire manuscript.

LIST OF ABBREVIATIONS

ABN   Airborne
AC   Attended college; no record of graduation
AD   Armor division
Adm.   Admiral
AEF   American Expeditionary Force
AGO   Adjutant General's Office
AP   Troop transport
APA   Attack transport
AWC   Army War College
Ariz.   Arizona

Brig. Gen.   Brigadier General; in "Appendix F": BG
BN   Battalion
BR   Branch

Ca.   California
CAC   Coast Artillery Corps
CAV   Cavalry
CDG   Commanding
CE   Corps of Engineers
CG   Commanding General; in "Appendix F," in-
                    dicates college graduate
C&GS   U. S. Army Command and General Staff
                    School
Colo.   Colorado
COMSOPAC   Commander, South Pacific Area
CP   Command post
Corp.   Corporal
Capt.   Captain
Col.   Colonel
Conn.   Connecticut

D.C.   District of Columbia
Del.   Delaware
DG   Distinguished Graduate
DIV   Division
DOB   Date of birth
DUKW   Amphibian, $2^1/_2$-ton, 6x6 truck

ED	Post-high school education
ESG	*Ecole Superieure de Guerre*
FA	Field Artillery
Ga.	Georgia
Gen.	General
GHQ	General headquarters
GPO	Government Printing Office
GSC	General Staff Corps
HG	Honor Graduate
ID	Infantry Division
Ind.	Indiana
INF	Infantry
Kans.	Kansas
Ky.	Kentucky
LCVP	Landing craft, vehicle and personnel
LS	Letter signed
LST	Landing ship, tank
2nd Lieut.	Second Lieutenant
1st Lieut.	First Lieutenant
Lieut. Col.	Lieutenant Colonel
Lieut. Gen.	Lieutenant General
LVT	Landing vehicle, tracked
Maj.	Major
MC	Medical Corps
Maj. Gen.	Major General
MG	Machine Gun; in "Appendix F": Major General
Minn.	Minnesota
MTN	Mountain
NA	National Archives, Washington, D.C.
N.C.	North Carolina
Nebr.	Nebraska
NG	National Guard
N.J.	New Jersey
N. Mex.	New Mexico

NRC	No record of college attendance
NWC	Naval War College
Okla.	Oklahoma
OP	Observation post
ORC	Officers' Reserve Corps
ORD	Ordinance Corps
RCT	Regimental combat team
Reinf.	Reinforced
Ret.	Retired
RG	Record Group
R.I.	Rhode Island
SO	Special Order
SOPAC	South Pacific Area
SRC	Source
SSC	Senior Staff College
SWPA	Southwest Pacific Area
Tex.	Texas
TL	Typed letter
TLS	Typed letter signed
TMs	Typed manuscript
USA	United States Army
USAFFE	United States Army Forces in the Far East
USAMHI	U.S. Army Military History Institute
USAT	U.S. Army Transport
USMA	United States Military Academy
USMC	United States Marine Corps
USMCR	United States Marine Corps Reserve
USN	United States Navy
USNA	United States Naval Academy
USNS	United States Naval Ship
Va.	Virginia
V. Adm.	Vice Admiral
VMI	Virginia Military Institute
Vt.	Vermont
WD	War Department
WW II	World War II
Wyo.	Wyoming
YR	Year

CHAPTER 1

THE FOREBEARS

In 1757, in the small Eastern Shore town of Snow Hill, Maryland, John Davis, the "earliest [known] paternal ancestor" of the Patrick family of Tell City, Indiana, was born. He was the great–great–grandfather of Edwin D. Patrick. In 1778, John married Mary Hodge, and this union produced nine children, one of whom was Edwin's great–grandmother, Elizabeth Parnell Davis. Nothing else is recorded about John Davis' life, except his service as a captain in the Maryland Militia during the Revolutionary War.[1]

Elizabeth Davis married Thomas Patrick on March 7, 1805, and bore two children, one of whom was John Davis Patrick, Edwin Patrick's grandfather, born in Snow Hill on February 10, 1805.

John early in life developed an interest in boating and water transportation because of Snow Hill's proximity to Chesapeake Bay on the west and the Atlantic Ocean on the east. Migrating westward, he acquired a boat and began plying the Ohio River with his store boat, carrying on a barter trade of foodstuffs and condiments, housewares, cloth, and livestock with farmers along the river.

In 1837, John tied up his boat at a levee in Cincinnati, and went to a local boarding house to secure room and board for the time he would be restocking his boat in the city. Working in the boarding house was Mary Elizabeth Powers, who, at the invitation of her cousin, the owner of the boarding house, had recently moved to Cincinnati from Baltimore, Maryland, where her parents had died during a cholera epidemic. Since John had arrived at the time of the evening meal, Mary's cousin sent her into the dining room to take his order, admonishing her that "he's a single man, Mary. ... You might catch you a fine husband." On her return to the kitchen, Mary informed her cousin that she "wouldn't have that fellow on a Christmas tree." But just six weeks later, on Au-

1

gust 23, 1837, she and John married, and started down the Ohio on their honeymoon in their well–stocked boat, stopping at all the landings as they came down the river, and restocking at intervals.

They eventually docked near Leavenworth, Indiana, in the spring of 1838, where John decided to sell his boat, feeling that a boat was no place to raise a child. John was successful in trading his boat for a small farm some ten miles west of Leavenworth, where he opened a store and a post office. Several children were born on this farm, including Edwin's father, John Thomas, born on April 6, 1842. A few years later the family relocated to Leopold, Indiana, a thriving little community of French farmers. Here John Thomas Patrick spent his youth and early manhood.

Following the outbreak of the Civil War, John T. Patrick enlisted on August 22, 1862, in Company G, 81st Regiment, Indiana Volunteer Infantry. Just four months after their enlistment, these raw, untrained recruits of Company G saw their first combat in one of the bloodiest battles fought in the western theater of operations, the battle of Stones River, December 31, 1862–January 2, 1863. It was "the most deadly battle of the war in proportion to numbers engaged," the Union forces suffering casualties of slightly less than a third of their troops, and the Confederates losing more than a third of their forces. One of the Union casualties was Patrick, who, near sundown on a snowy December 31, suffered a gunshot wound of the right lower leg, which fractured his tibia and fibula. He was evacuated to a hospital in Nashville, where a "young intern" received permission to care for the soldier, and saved his leg, though for the rest of his life John would suffer episodic infections of the leg, with the expulsion of small fragments of bone from the old wound.[2]

On July 21, 1863, John returned as a civilian to Leopold, where he worked for several years in his mother's store. He began traveling back and forth to nearby Tell City to study German, and there met Margaret Menninger, whom he married on December 5, 1869.

They settled in Cannelton, where John, after a short time as a traveling furniture salesman, was elected Clerk of the Circuit Court. Several children were born to the couple, but only two, Clara Elizabeth, born December 2, 1876, and Alice Augusta, born May 2, 1880, grew to adulthood. Margaret died on March 8, 1881.

On September 17, 1882, John married Margaret's younger sister, Anna, and they settled in Tell City, purchasing a home on North 9th Street, between Jefferson and Fulton Streets, and bringing John's two daughters from his previous marriage into their home. John Patrick opened a law practice in Tell City, and founded the Citizens National Bank of Tell City.

John and Anna had six children, two of whom died in infancy: Edwin was the youngest of the children, born on January 11, 1894. He had two brothers, Charles and Herbert, and one sister, Alma.

John continued his practice of law and served as president of his bank until his death on June 15, 1915. Anna died in Tell City on March 5, 1952.

Edwin D. Patrick, five years, and Alma Patrick, eight years
(Courtesy of Mary Margaret Goffinet and Ruth Anne Werner)

The Patrick Family, ca. 1905. Front row, L. to R.: John, Alma, Anna, Edwin. Back row, L. to R.: Hebert, Alice, Charles, Clara.
(Courtesy of Mary Margaret Goffinet and Ruth Anne Werner)

CHAPTER 2

THE FORMATIVE YEARS

Patrick was the youngest child in a large but very close–knit family.[1] He was particularly devoted to his mother and would remain so throughout his life. In looking back some years later on his youthful years in Tell City, Patrick told his niece, Ruth Anne Werner, that "the things that were most important in his parents' home were family, church, and education." He especially remembered with fondness the lively family discussions that took place around the family dinner table, discussions in which young Patrick took an active part. Although Ed[2] was "the baby of the family," when he spoke during these family discussions "in his deep bass voice of authority—there was complete silence and everybody listened."[3]

Ed and his sister Alma were particularly close. When it was time for them as young children to go to bed, they would go to their bedrooms, which were just across the hall from one another. With the doors of their bedrooms open, they would be able to see each other from their beds. Ed would ask Alma to tell him a bedtime story almost every night, and Alma always complied with his request, often improvising stories, the telling of which would sometimes extend over several nights. When she would finish the night's story telling, Alma would always say, "Good night, Ed," but would never receive a reply, since her brother invariably fell asleep while she was telling the story.[4]

When Ed's widowed paternal grandmother came to live at the Patrick home, she occupied a room on the first floor where there was a fireplace in which there was always a fire during cold weather. This room was a favorite play area for Ed and Alma, and they kept their toys and games in the bottom drawer of their grandmother's wardrobe. They loved to lie on the floor in front of the fire to read

5

or play together while their grandmother knitted, or told them stories of her childhood years in Baltimore.[5]

During cold weather Ed and Alma had the responsibility of closing all of the outside shutters on the windows of their home at dusk. They would always do the dining room window shutters last, so they could look into the dining room and admire the dining table set for supper and the lamp that hung over the table. Sometimes Ed would say to his sister, "Alma, we've got the prettiest house in the whole world."[6]

Ed was charged with several household chores, but the one he disliked most was having to keep the brick walks around the house free of grass and weeds. Every Saturday, he had to get down on his knees and, using a kitchen knife, dig the grass out from between the bricks. He also had the responsibility for watering, feeding, and grooming the family horse, "Dolly," who pulled his father's buggy on his trips to the courthouse in nearby Cannelton.[7]

He and his friends, including his best friend Jack Kreisle, would often go to the nearby Ohio River during the summers. Although their mothers forbade swimming in the river, the boys ignored their orders. Sometimes they would take corn, watermelons, and cantaloupes from nearby farmers' fields, roast the corn over a campfire, along with any fish they might have caught in the river. On one occasion Ed and Jack were caught stealing a watermelon, and their fathers made them repay the farmer and apologize for their deed.

Often the boys would row across the river to Kentucky, where they would explore the countryside south of the river. His niece states that "they knew all the back roads and country trails in Perry County, Indiana, and Hancock [County], Kentucky."[8]

One summer Ed acquired a straw hat, which he wore constantly. On one particularly hot summer evening, after playing outdoors all day, he went in for his bath. When his mother looked in to see how the bath was progressing, she found him sitting in the bathtub with his straw hat still on his head.[9]

Ed showed an interest in vocal music during his childhood and youth, singing at picnics of his church, St. John's Evangelical Church, in which he was confirmed at the age of fifteen. In high school he was a member of the Senior Male Quartet.[10]

During that same year, Ed visited his sister, Alice Patrick Zoercher, in Washington, D.C., where her husband, Louis Zoercher, was serving as secretary for their congressman.[11] This was apparently the only trip young Patrick made outside the immediate vicinity of Tell City during his youth.

His niece described Ed as "a very forceful and dynamic young-ster," who, even as a youngster, "showed his leadership ability and his interest in other children ... [and] always had a following of the boys in the neighborhood."[12] George Ress, one of his boyhood friends, told Patrick's mother, in a letter written after her son's death, that Ed "was just a little smarter than the rest of us [and] was the best liked and in our kid ways—[best] respected of all the group."[13]

He attended the Tell City public schools, graduating as salu-tatorian from Tell City High School in 1912. In high school Ed served as the manager of the high school baseball team. He was described in his high school yearbook, *The Rambler*, of which he was the editor–in–chief, as follows:

> Noisy when awake but not awake much. Open to arguments on any subject and always imagines he is on the right side. Gets to school on time when not tardy or absent. Because he doesn't like to walk, he makes it a point to be invited as the partner of the hostess at all social affairs. (Owing to Pat's be-ing Editor–in–Chief, we didn't permit him to write himself up for fear he would use up too much flow-ery language.—The Staff.)[14]

Following graduation from high school, Patrick entered Indi-ana University in the 1913 fall semester. During his first two years at Indiana University he completed courses in the Romance lan-guages, German, English, mathematics, hygiene, economics, his-tory, and journalism. His grades in these courses were mainly "B's" and "C's," but he did achieve several "A's" in English and a "B+" in journalism. A note on his transcript indicates that he incurred a penalty of one hour for failure to take Physical Training during 1913. Patrick was a member of the debating team that represented the university in the Indiana State Triangular Debate.[15]

Ed's fraternity, Phi Delta Theta, had a mascot, a huge mas-tiff. This dog had no name, and was universally referred to by the fraternity brothers as "that damn dog." Each summer vacation it became the lot of one of the chapter members to take the dog to his home for the summer, and in time this job fell to Patrick. When he arrived at his home with the dog, Ed was faced with a dilemma: since his mother allowed no profanity in her home, what name should he give the dog for the summer? He hit on the idea of tell-ing his mother that the dog's name was "Dan." When Ed and Dan prepared to return to the fraternity house in the fall, Mrs. Patrick told her son that the dog was "really not an intelligent dog because he didn't even answer to his own name."[16]

In his third year at Indiana University, Patrick attended only the fall term of 1914, taking Law. In October 1915, he began studies in the Department of Law of the University of Michigan, where he was in regular attendance from October 1915 until June 1916, when he was called to join his National Guard company for active service.[17]

During his time at Michigan, Patrick was employed in the University Printery. He also worked at nights, on weekends, and during free hours to repay tuition loans.[18]

Mr. A. P. Fenn, a businessman of Tell City, in a letter to Congressman William E. Cox, stated that Patrick had "always been a leader among his boy friends, [had] good character and splendid habits and was one of the best students in Tell City High School." Although rather quiet in demeanor, he was a forceful public speaker.[19]

Congressman Cox indicated to the Secretary of War that Patrick possessed no bad habits, had an analytical mind, and was morally upright. In a subsequent letter, Cox stated that Patrick was "as fine a young man as ever walked this earth, ... large in physique, broad in mind and of a naturally military turn of mind."[20]

Reflecting on Patrick's desire to be an officer in the Regular Army, Mr. Louis Zoercher, his uncle and the editor of *The Tell City News*, stated that "he has military blood in him," referring to Patrick's father's service during the Civil War, and that he was "ideal timber for an army officer." He closed his letter by stating that Patrick was "a M–A–N, every inch of him."[21]

Although the judgments of these men may be somewhat hyperbolic, they do appear to indicate the genuine high regard in which Cox, Fenn, and Zoercher held Patrick. He was certainly industrious, working at numerous jobs to earn money to attend college. Although his college grades were at best average overall, they do indicate that he possessed considerable skill in the use of the English language, which would be reflected in his personal correspondence, research papers, and newspaper articles written during his career in the army.

He was also loyal to and supportive of friends, as demonstrated by a loan he made to a friend for the latter's college expenses, using part of the money that he had himself borrowed for his own tuition. A man of integrity and honor, Patrick repaid the entire loan, even though the friend to whom he had lent the money had not yet repaid him.[22]

The only fraternal organization that Patrick joined, other than his college fraternity, was the Tell City Lodge of Free and Accepted Masons. He petitioned the lodge on February 25, 1915, and was duly elected on March 25. On April 8, he was initiated as an Entered Apprentice Mason, was subsequently passed to the degree of Fellowcraft Mason on April 22, and was raised to the degree of Master Mason on May 13, respectively.[23]

CHAPTER 3

SOUTH TO THE BORDER

On February 11, 1915, Patrick, who listed his occupation as a reporter, received his commission as a second lieutenant in Independent Regiment #1, Indiana National Guard, and then became one of the original three officers of Company I, 2d Indiana Infantry, organized in Tell City on February 7, 1915. The unit trained weekly in Tell City under the command of its officers, and performed its two weeks of annual training at Fort Benjamin Harrison, Indiana.[1]

Beginning in 1911, a series of events had occurred in Mexico that would produce marked changes in the lives of the Tell City Guardsmen, particularly Lieutenant Patrick. Internal conflicts in the northern part of Mexico led to recurring incidents along the United States–Mexico border that posed a serious threat to peace, and led to President William Howard Taft's strengthening of the American army patrols along the Mexican border. In 1913, General Victoriano Huerta deposed and replaced President Francisco Madero, who was assassinated shortly thereafter. Full–scale civil war then broke out between Huerta's forces and those of Generals Venustiano Carranza and Emiliano Zapata, the chiefs of the radical elements. President Woodrow Wilson, who had succeeded Taft, refused to recognize Huerta's government, and imposed an arms embargo on both sides. But in early 1914, when Huerta's forces had halted those of Carranza and Zapata, Wilson, in a move to help Carranza, lifted the embargo imposed on Carranza and Zapata.

Huerta's followers retaliated by arresting American sailors in Tampico in February 1914. Although Huerta soon released them, Rear Admiral Henry T. Mayo, commander of the American fleet in the area, demanded a public apology; Huerta refused. This event led Wilson to order a contingent of sailors and marines to occupy

Tampico. By the end of the month there were nearly eight thousand troops ashore, under the command of Major General Frederick Funston. With war becoming a distinct possibility, Wilson and Huerta accepted mediation, and Huerta agreed to resign in favor of Carranza. Francisco "Pancho" Villa, a former ally of Carranza, rebelled, however, and proceeded to gain control of most of northern Mexico.

After Wilson extended diplomatic recognition to Carranza's government, Villa initiated a series of border incidents, culminating in a raid against Columbus, New Mexico, on March 9, 1916, where his troops killed a substantial number of American soldiers and civilians before being driven off. On March 10, Wilson ordered Brigadier General John J. Pershing to enter Mexico and assist the Mexican government in capturing Villa.

For the next several months Pershing's troops pursued Villa over hundreds of miles of Mexican territory, but Villa eluded capture. The prolonged presence of American troops in Mexico led to clashes between the American troops and Mexican civilians and government troops, leading to the deaths of scores of Americans.[2]

In May, at Funston's urging, some five thousand officers and men of the National Guard of the states of Texas, New Mexico, and Arizona were federalized to reinforce the troops along the border. In case of a full war with Mexico, however, which seemed increasingly likely, those forces on the border were deemed to be inadequate for defense, and certainly would not be able to undertake any offensive operation into Mexico. Therefore, on June 18, 1916, President Wilson ordered the National Guard of all the states except Nevada, which had no National Guard, into federal service. By the end of July, no less than 112,000 men were in assembly areas in San Antonio, Brownsville, and El Paso, Texas, and Douglas, Arizona.[3]

Responding to Wilson's order, Indiana officials ordered mobilization of the state's National Guard, including Tell City's Company I, 2d Indiana Infantry. Patrick, along with his unit, was mustered into federal service on June 28, 1916, and signed a six-year oath of service. He then went with his company to Texas, where the company and its parent regiment, the 2d Indiana Infantry, were garrisoned at Llano Grande.[4]

During the months following their arrival in Texas, the Hoosier National Guardsmen trained intensively, the training culminating in November 1916, when some 23,000 Guardsmen took part in twelve days of field maneuvers between Camp Llano Grande and Port Isabel.

During this period of federalization of the National Guard, the Regular Army, in order to implement provisions of the recently-enacted National Defense Act of 1916, began a course of instruction designed to prepare promising National Guard officers to take the competitive examination for appointment in the Regular Army.[5]

The commanding officer of the 2d Indiana Infantry recommended that Patrick attend the prescribed course of instruction in preparation for his taking the examination to compete for a Regular Army commission. Patrick was then attached to Company D, 28th U.S. Infantry, at Fort Ringgold, near Rio Grande City, Texas, for that schooling.[6]

Patrick completed the examination on that date and achieved the grades (actual percentage multiplied by relative weights) of

1.	United States History and Constitution	83.5
2.	Geography	79.0
3.	Elementary English	91.0
4.	Algebra	78.0
5.	Geometry	66.5
6.	Trigonometry	57.0
7.	Elementary German	72.0
8.	General History	84.5
9.	Elementary Surveying	88.8
10.	Advanced English	186.0
11.	General Average	80.57[7]

Although he had attained an overall satisfactory general average, he had failed in two subjects, geometry and trigonometry.[8]

On October 16, at Harlingen, Texas, two physicians found him physically qualified; they recorded that Patrick was seventy-three inches in height, weighed 149$^1/_2$ pounds, and was "Erect. Muscular. Well developed." On the same day a board of three Regular Army infantry officers determined that he was fully qualified for appointment in the Regular Army.[9]

On January 16, 1917, Patrick received notice that his examination was being held for action by the Secretary of War. On the following day the secretary waived the academic deficiency, clearing the way for Patrick's provisional appointment.[10]

As border tensions eased, a phased release of National Guardsmen began in September. On November 24, the United States and Mexico agreed upon a peace protocol. By mid-February 1917, virtually all Hoosier Guardsmen had been mustered out.[11]

Patrick was mustered out of federal service at Tell City on February 21, 1917.[12] On March 25, he received notice that he had been accepted for appointment in the Regular Army as a second lieutenant, effective March 21, 1917. He immediately telegraphed the Adjutant General: "Commission received[;] accepted[;] letter with oath follows," and sent off his "Oath of Office," dated March 26, 1917. Patrick resigned his Indiana National Guard commission, effective March 19, 1917, and prepared to report to his first active army station, Fort Leavenworth, Kansas.[13]

CHAPTER 4

OVER THERE

Second Lieutenant Patrick reported to the 21st Infantry at Fort Leavenworth, Kansas, on April 15, 1917, as a student in the Army Service Schools, created by the 1908 merger of the Army School of the Line, the Staff College, and the Army Signal School. Coincident with his reporting to the Army Service Schools, Patrick received his promotion to first lieutenant.[1]

In 1916 the War Department established a three–month course of instruction at the Army Service Schools that was designed to prepare newly–commissioned second lieutenants, other than those who were graduates of the United States Military Academy, for duty in the Regular Army. These officers were to complete the course prior to their joining their regiments, and successful completion was necessary for their obtaining permanent commissions. Patrick was a member of the second, and last, class of provisional second lieutenants to attend this course; the course was discontinued in July 1917, because of the entry of the United States into World War I.[2]

In his opening address to the students, Lieutenant Colonel James W. McAndrew, Acting Commandant, stressed that the course of instruction would provide "an insight into the duties of subalterns and above all ... give [the students] a safe and solid foundation upon which to build [their] future efficiency." He indicated that "the Army is no place for the time-server or the dilettante," and that the course would demand their undivided time and attention. Although the course was of shorter duration than that for newly–commissioned officers of the British Army, McAndrew assured the new officers that if they responded to the efforts of their instructors they would join their regiments "with a knowledge of [their] duties that it might not be possible for [them] to get in a year's service with troops in the field," and that they would be transformed from a liability to an asset in their regimental organizations. He further admonished the lieutenants that "the greatest efficiency in [their] profession [could] be attained only by complete abstinence from the use of intoxicating liquors or drugs," and that they should avoid financial indebtedness.[3]

Following McAndrew's opening address, the students began their study. They attended lectures covering such subjects as "Estimating Tactical Situations and Composing Field Orders," "Messing of Organizations," "The Customs of the Service," "Company Administration," and "Military Art," the latter course covering such topics as small infantry problems, minor tactics, and terrain exercises.[4]

Completing the course on July 13, 1917, Patrick received the following evaluation:

Conduct .... Excellent
General Bearing .... Very good
Studious Habits .... Very good
Physical Training-Swimming .... Very good
Care and Management of Rifle and Equipment .... Excellent
Small Arms Firing Manual (Theoretical) .... Good
Battle Fire Training and Hasty Landscape Sketching . Fair
Military Art .... Good
Drill Regulations.. Very good
Army Regulations .... Very good
Field Engineering .... Fair
Military Law and Rules of Land Warfare .... Good
Sanitation .... Good
Manual of Interior Guard Duty .... Good
Signaling (Semaphore) .... Very good
Equitation .... Good [5]

Lieutenant Colonel Charles Miller, Acting Commandant of the Army Service Schools, stated that Patrick had made "good progress" while a student, and that "in time [he] should make an efficient officer."[6]

Patrick reported to Company C, 21st Infantry, Linda Vista, California, in July 1917, and was assigned to Calexico, California. His company commander, Captain John H. Page, Jr., rating him during his time with Company C, stated that he had formed a very favorable opinion of Patrick, and concurred in Miller's judgment that in time he would become an efficient officer. Page also agreed with Miller that in the event of outbreak of war Patrick should be given a troop duty assignment, and gave him "very good" ratings in "attention to duty," and "professional zeal," and for his "intelligence and judgment shown in instructing, drilling, and handling enlisted men."[7]

Patrick then served brief tours of duty at San Diego, California, and Fort Sill, Oklahoma, prior to reporting to Camp Greene, North Carolina, in February 1918. During these assignments he was promoted to the grade of captain (temporary) on August 5, 1917, and to the permanent grade of captain on December 11, 1917.[8]

At Camp Greene, Patrick joined the 14th Machine Gun Battalion, 9th Infantry Brigade, 5th Division, eventually assuming command of Company A of that battalion.[9] On April 7, 1918, the 14th Machine Gun Battalion proceeded by train from Camp Greene to the port of embarkation, Camp Merritt, New Jersey, arriving there at 0630[10] on Tuesday, April 9. Two days later the unit entrained for the trip to New York City, where, at 1530, the troops boarded the S.S. *New York*, which sailed immediately for Liverpool. Arriving in Liverpool on April 21, Patrick's unit entrained for Southhampton the following day, where they moved into a rest camp. From Southhampton the unit embarked on a tramp steamer on April 23, arriving at Le Havre the following day. On April 25, the 14th Machine Gun Battalion, with the remainder of the 5th Division, less the division engineers, artillery, and trains, moved by train to the 13th Training Area at Bar–sur–Aube, approximately 120 miles southeast of Paris, arriving on April 26, to embark upon a planned three–month training program to prepare its troops for commitment to combat.[11] The 14th Machine Gun Battalion, including Patrick's Company A, began its training in Baroville, seven kilometers south of Bar–sur–Aube.[12]

The first month of the pre–combat training would be devoted to instruction of the units of the division in areas to the rear of the front lines; following this, units of the division would affiliate with Allied units deployed in the front line; during the third month the division would participate with the division artillery and aircraft in field training in the tactics of open warfare. It would then take over a section of the front line trenches under its own commanders. One highlight of the training period occurred on May 26, when General John J. Pershing, commander of the American Expeditionary Force, inspected the 14th Machine Gun Battalion.[13]

At Baroville additional officers joined Patrick in Company A: First Lieutenants Homer P. Peters and James W. Thomas, and Second Lieutenants Jens H. Frostholm and R. W. Thomas.[14]

After completing its month of training at Baroville, Patrick's company moved to Bar–sur–Aube to rejoin the rest of the 5th Division.[15] On May 31, the division received orders assigning it to the French XXXIII Corps, French Seventh Army, in the Anould Sector

east of Epinal. This sector straddled the principal range of the
Vosges Mountains, about fifty kilometers east of Epinal, and secured the Bonhomme Pass through the Vosges Mountains. Now
affiliated with the French 21st Division, the 5th Division's service
in this quiet sector would complete the greater part of its pre-
combat training program.

On June 1, Patrick's company, accompanied by Headquarters Company and Company D, left Baroville for Bar-sur-Aube.
The companies then moved on to the village of La Houssiere in the
Vosges Mountains, arriving there on June 3. Two days later Patrick's
company began its final phase of training prior to entering the
front lines.[16]

While serving in the Anould Sector, Company A was attached
to the 1st Battalion, 61st Infantry for training from June 12 to
July 3, and served variously at Anould, La Croix aux Mines, and
St. Leonard within the Vosges Mountains. On July 4, the company
was assigned to the 9th Infantry Brigade, and on July 13 was
attached to the 3d Battalion, 60th Infantry, in preparation for its
move into an active sector of the front lines.[17]

Near the end of this training period the division received orders to relieve the French 62d Division in the St. Dié Sector, beginning the night of July 14–15. The St. Dié sector lay north of the
town St. Dié, joining the Anould Sector near La Fave Rivière, extending northwest for about twenty-five kilometers, and controlling the Saales Pass.

On July 3, the 9th Infantry Brigade was relieved in the Anould
Sector, and moved to the Arches training area southeast of Epinal.
During the night of July 14–15, the brigade began to relieve the
French 62d Division in the left (northern) portion of the sector. On
the following day the 10th Infantry Brigade moved from the Anould
Sector to the St. Dié Sector, and continued the relief of the division
in the right (southern) portion of the sector. The 5th Division com-
pleted the relief July 19, and assumed command of the sector.[18]

When the 5th Division assumed responsibility for the sector,
the Germans controlled No Man's Land and exercised aerial supremacy. However, the Americans soon developed a successful
sniping program, which kept the Germans concealed and under
cover within their own lines. The division's machine gun battalions actively engaged the enemy in No Man's Land and within the
enemy lines, wresting control of No Man's Land away from the
Germans, and also were used in an antiaircraft role, markedly
reducing the number of German flights over the division lines.
When the 5th Artillery Brigade joined the division after July 28,

the artillerymen immediately began their missions of barrages and harassing, counterbattery, and interdiction fire.[19]

From that date until August 16, the sector was quiet and the division covered its front by frequent raids and active patrolling, and was itself subjected to a number of enemy raids. The only other combat began on August 15, when the 10th Infantry Brigade relieved a French army unit, and mounted an attack against a German salient in this sector. By August 20, the brigade had reduced this salient and consolidated its positions. The 9th Brigade, and its assigned 14th Machine Gun Battalion, did not participate in the action. On August 19, First Lieutenant Harold F. Ammerman was assigned to Patrick's company.[20]

On August 23, the American 92d Division relieved the 5th Division, and the latter moved to the Arches training area for rest and further training, where it remained from August 23 through August 29. Patrick's company was relieved from its attachment to the 60th Infantry, and rejoined the 14th Machine Gun Battalion at Dounoux in the Vosges Mountains on August 26.[21]

During this time the troops rested, cleaned up, and drew new equipment, and the division received replacements of men and animals. Training to fit the troops for movement warfare began, including schools in gas warfare, liaison operations, and machine gun, mortar, and rifle firing, and practicing of movement of companies and battalions across difficult terrain. The division carried out this training in preparation for joining the newly-formed American First Army, whose first mission was to be the reduction of the St. Mihiel salient.[22]

The St. Mihiel salient was one of a number of German bulges in the Allied lines that interfered with railroad communications essential to further offensive operations. The First Army was directed to reduce the salient, which was roughly triangular in shape, with its angles near Pont-à-Mousson, St. Mihiel, and Verdun. It extended approximately 25 kilometers into the Allied lines and

> cut the Verdun–Toul railroad and allowed the Germans to interrupt traffic on the Paris–Nancy railroad with artillery fire ... and would seriously threaten the flank of any allied operation which might be undertaken in the Meuse–Argonne region.[23]

The First Army planned to remove the salient by three coordinated attacks: the main attack against the southern face by the United States I Corps and IV Corps, a secondary attack against the western face by the United States V Corps, and a holding action against the tip of the salient by the French II Colonial Corps.[24]

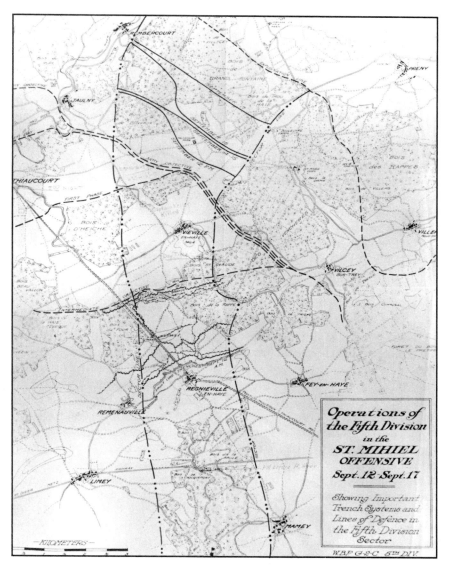

Operations of the Fifth Division in the St. Mihiel Offensive, Sept. 12 – Sept. 17, 1918

(*History of the Fifth Division*, opposite 120)

On August 26, Pershing ordered the 5th Division to join the First Army as part of I Corps, and move to an area southwest of Luneville on the Moselle River. All division units had closed on their new locations by August 30. On that date Patrick's company was attached to the 3d Battalion, 60th Infantry, and would remain with that unit throughout the upcoming training period and the subsequent St. Mihiel operation, except for reassignment to its parent battalion from September 11–12.[25]

Training emphasizing open warfare methods resumed, with particular emphasis on the advance of companies and battalions across terrain using only maps and compasses. In anticipation of the employment of gas by the Germans, all officers and enlisted men were required to wear their gas masks for one–half hour daily.

Beginning on September 4, the division moved by forced night marches a distance of fifty kilometers northwest to the town of Martincourt, all units closing on that town by September 10. On the night of September 9–10, the division relieved elements of the 90th Division in the Villers–en–Haye Sector, on a line extending "from a point 1 kilometer east of Regnieville–en–Haye to Remenauville, exclusive." The 9th Infantry Brigade, including the 14th Machine Gun Battalion, took up its position on the Mamey–St. Jacques road.[26]

The German positions facing the 5th Division troops were well suited for a defense in depth. There were four successive heights, the first, second, and fourth of which contained well–organized systems of trenches; the third defensive position consisted only of lines of wire. The fourth defensive line was the formidable Hindenburg Line, and consisted of a double line of trenches reinforced by concrete dugouts and protected by a double line of wire.[27]

The 10th Infantry Brigade would lead the division attack, with the 9th Infantry Brigade in reserve. The battalions of the attacking brigade would be supported by the companies of the 15th Machine Gun Battalion. Patrick's company was to be part of a separate group formed by the 13th and 14th Machine Gun Battalions, commanded by the division Machine Gun Officer. These units would deliver long–range supporting fire from the support trenches in the Bois dit Jolival and Bois de la Chambrotte just north of the St. Dizier–Metz highway.[28]

At 0130, September 12, the greatest artillery bombardment yet mounted by the Americans began, extending around the entire salient, from Verdun around St. Mihiel and east to Pont–á–Mousson. With the 10th Infantry Brigade in line, the 5th Division attacked as the left center division of the I Corps at 0500 on September 12. Although the 11th Infantry on the right initially encountered heavy machine gun fire, it and the 6th Infantry on its left had gained the intermediate objective at the northern edge of Bois St. Claude and Bois des Saulx by 0615. The support battalions of the two regiments swept through the assault battalions and were on the first day objective, the northern edge of Bois Gérard, by that evening.[29]

With the army objective line secured by the 10th Infantry Brigade, the 13th and 14th Machine Gun Battalions ceased their supporting fires and moved forward with their Hotchkiss machine guns, taking up strong positions against a possible enemy counterattack on a line running from northwest to southeast through Vieville–en–Haye. Patrick's company was positioned to the east of the town to cover a gap that had occurred when the 90th Division on the right of the 5th Division had encountered stiff enemy resistance and had not kept pace with the latter's advance.[30]

The 10th Infantry Brigade spent the morning of September 13 organizing its position, and that afternoon repulsed a German counterattack. The division continued its attack on September 14 and 15. On September 15, the 9th Infantry Brigade began the relief of the 10th Infantry Brigade on a line in the northern edge of the Bois de Bonvaux and just south of La Souleuvre Ferme, completing the relief the following morning. The brigade then advanced against intermittent resistance, shelling, and gas attacks into the southern edge of Bois de Grand Fontaine, a portion of the First Army exploitation line.

This action, during which the division advanced approximately seven kilometers, and the actions of the other divisions of I Corps and those of IV Corps and V Corps reduced the St. Mihiel salient, removing the threat posed by it to the upcoming Meuse–Argonne Offensive.[31]

During the St. Mihiel offensive, the 14th Machine Gun Battalion suffered 17 dead and 32 wounded: included among the dead was Private Patrick J. McGuinness of Company A.[32] One of Company A's wounded men was Corporal Charles E. Zanzalari. In a 1945 letter to Patrick's son, Thomas B. Patrick, Zanzalari related that while he was showing Patrick his gun position,

> a shell exploded close to us wounding me. After giving me first aid and bandaging my wound he made me comfortable until I was taken to a hospital.[33]

On September 19, Patrick's company reverted to the command of its parent battalion, and moved with the rest of the division to the Pagny–sur–Meuse area west of Toul, where the division resumed training for the upcoming Meuse–Argonne offensive, which would include three Allied converging offensives: an American attack between the Meuse River and the Argonne Forest on September 26, a renewal of the British–French attack between the Oise and Scarpe Rivers on September 27, and a combined Allied attack in the north, east of Ypres, on September 28. The objective of the American attack in the south was to seize the Carignan–Sedan–Méziéres railroad, the severing of which would cut the principal German lateral line of supply, rendering the German positions to the west and northwest of Sedan untenable.[34]

On October 5, the infantrymen of the 5th Division moved by truck to the Blercourt–Nixeville area west of Verdun, and later that night continued on to the Foret de Hesse, fifteen kilometers west of Verdun and twenty kilometers south of the American front lines. For the next five days the men of the division pursued an intensive training program in preparation for entering the fighting.

On October 10, Company A was once again attached to the 3d Battalion, 60th Infantry, and during the night of October 11–12 moved to Malancourt, in preparation for the 5th Division's relief of the 80th Division in a narrow sector east of Cunel and five to six kilometers west of and paralleling the Meuse River. The front line lay just south of the Cunel–Brieulles road.[35]

The 60th Infantry occupied the left half of the division sector, with the 61st Infantry on the right. Immediately after occupying the front lines three companies of the 3d Battalion, with a section of Patrick's company, advanced up the narrow gauge railway east of Cunel. They immediately met heavy enemy machine gun fire, but, inspired by the heroic actions of Company M's First Lieutenant Samuel Woodfill, the patrols reached the northern edge of Bois de la Pultiere and occupied the town of Cunel. However, an enemy barrage forced the outlying patrols to withdraw to the Cunel road, where Patrick's company took up its position. On the right the 61st Infantry had advanced to the northern edge of the western portion of the Bois de Foret. The night of the 12th, the 3d Division began the relief of the 9th Brigade in order that the 5th Division might be re–formed for an attack in a sector to the west, between Cunel and Romagne. Patrick's company remained in the Cunel region.[36]

On October 14, the 10th Brigade, 5th Division, making the main attack, passed through the 3d Division west of Cunel, in the direction of the Barricourt Heights, drove through to Le Grand Carré Ferme, and assisted the adjacent V Corps in the reduction of Bois de Bantheville. The 60th Infantry, on the right of the 10th Brigade, attacked to seize the Bois de Pultière. Almost immediately the assault elements encountered heavy machine gun fire from the wood to their front and from Romagne and the direction of Bantheville. By nightfall the troops of both brigades had advanced approximately two kilometers, and dug in.[37]

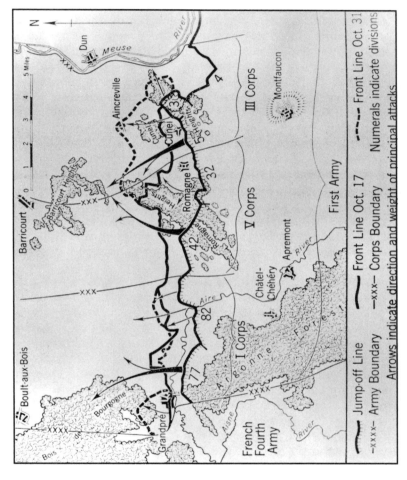

Plan of Attack of First Army, October 14, 1918

(American Armies and Battlefields in Europe, 180)

The division continued the attack on the 15th, and by night-fall the 60th and 61st Infantry Regiments had succeeded in clear-ing Bois de la Pultière. However, enemy fire from the Bois des Rappes held up their advance into the wood. Following a $2^1/2$ hour barrage by the American artillery, elements of the 60th and 61st Infantry entered the wood, and some even succeeded in reaching its northern edge. Initially ordered to hold within the wood, they later received orders to withdraw. However, some of the troops did not receive the withdrawal order and remained in the wood until the following day. Since the seizure of the wood was felt to be necessary for the further advance of the 10th Brigade, the latter did not attack on the 15th. At the close of the day the 60th Infan-try, including Patrick's company, was withdrawn to reorganize. Company A moved to Montfaucon, where it remained until Octo-ber 19. Among the casualties suffered by Company A during this action were the following: Second Lieutenant Jens H. Frostholm and Private First Class William Amrhein, killed, and First Lieuten-ant James W. Thomas, wounded.[38]

On October 16, the 10th Brigade relieved the remaining troops of the 9th Brigade and continued the attempt to seize the Bois des Rappes, finally succeeding on October 21, in the process suffering over two thousand casualties. During the night of October 21–22, the 90th Division relieved the 5th Division, which moved into Bois de Malancourt and an area east of Montfaucon, where it reverted to corps reserve.[39]

During the night of October 26-27, the division relieved the 3d Division north and northeast of Montfaucon, just to the right of the previous division sector, to participate in the final phase of the Meuse–Argonne offensive, the cutting of the Carignan–Sedan–Mezierres railway and the crossing of the Meuse River.[40]

Still attached to the 3d Battalion, 60th Infantry, Patrick and his company moved to the town of Avocourt on October 19, and then, on October 26, moved into the line with the 3d Battalion at the east edge of Bois de Forêt and on Hill 281 north of the wood, where they would serve as the regimental outpost. On October 28, some of Patrick's machine guns displaced slightly eastward to take up outpost positions closer to the Meuse River.[41]

At 0530, November 1, Company M, 60th Infantry, with four machine guns of Company C attached, attacked, and, in four min-utes, had waded the Andon River, and seized the town of Cléry–le–Grand. Company M, aided by barrages of indirect fire from machine guns of Patrick's company placed on the forward slopes of hills south of Cléry–le–Grand, continued its drive forward, and by late afternoon had occupied the western slopes of Hill 261 to the north-east of the town.[42]

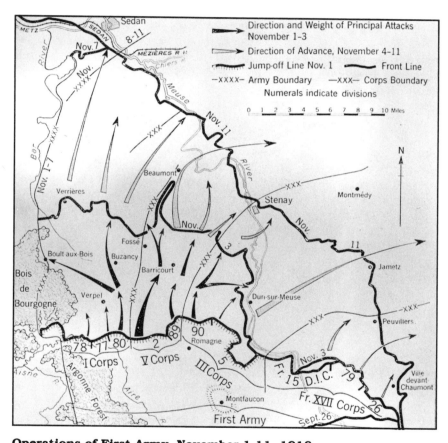

Operations of First Army, November 1-11, 1918

(*American Armies and Battlefields in Europe*, 186)

On November 2, Companies A and H of the 60th Infantry seized Cléry–le–Petit, and on November 4, Patrick's company moved to the vicinity of that village to provide supporting fires for the crossing of the Meuse River by the 60th Infantry.[43]

The 5th Division planned to cross the Meuse River and a canal just to the east of the river at two points: the 10th Brigade in the vicinity of Brieulles and the 9th Brigade in the vicinity of Cléry–le–Petit. The heights east of the Meuse River and canal were heavily fortified, and the crossing sites would be subjected to heavy fire by the Germans.

Units of the 10th Brigade finally succeeded, after several attempts, in crossing the Meuse on a footbridge east of Brieulles early in the morning of November 3, and by that evening the brigade had established a firm foothold across the river. On the following day two footbridges were thrown across the canal, and by dawn of the 5th the entire brigade was east of the canal.[44]

The 9th Brigade had initially hoped to bridge the Meuse just north of the junction of the canal and the river, but heavy enemy fire from the heights prevented this. On November 4, the third battalions of the 60th and 61st Infantry were ordered to bridge the river east of Cléry–le–Petit that night. The division engineers completed the footbridge under cover of darkness, and by the morning of the 5th, two companies of the 61st Infantry and the 3d Battalion, 60th Infantry, were across the river. Patrick's machine gun company provided covering fire during the crossing and some of his men with their guns crossed the river with the riflemen to assist them in their further advance. The engineers then bridged the canal under heavy enemy fire, and the two battalions and their supporting machine guns quickly consolidated the bridgehead.[45]

The 61st Infantry advanced northward and captured Dun–sur–Meuse in the early afternoon. Patrick's company moved with the 3d Battalion to a ravine just south of the town, remaining there until the 6th, when it accompanied the battalion to an area southwest of Mervaux, which had been captured earlier in the day by the 2d Battalion, 60th Infantry. Company A remained near Mervaux until November 10, when it left the 3d Battalion, and rejoined the 14th Machine Gun Battalion near Louppy, where it was when the armistice took effect the following day.[46]

During this phase of the Meuse–Argonne offensive, two men of Patrick's company were killed: Private First Class Nunze Gallo and Private Dale D. Maltice.[47]

For its action during the St. Mihiel and Meuse–Argonne Offensives, Pershing cited the 5th Division in "General Orders No. 11." He commented specifically on the division's crossing of the

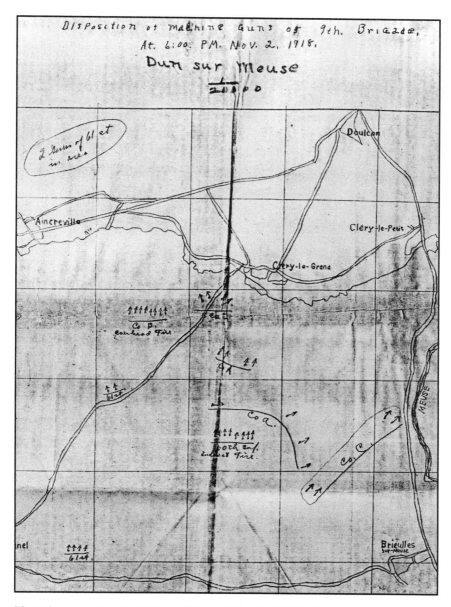

Sketch-map showing disposition of the 14th Machine Gun Battalion, November 2, 1918, vicinity of Cléry-le-Petit, in support of 9th Infantry Brigade during crossing of the Meuse River at Dun-sur-Meuse

("14th MG BnOp Maps," File 205-32.6, WWI, 5th Division, RG 120, NA).

Meuse River, rating it as "one of the most brilliant military feats in the history of the American Army in France."[48]

Patrick received the Silver Star Citation for distinguished conduct in action during the river crossing on November 4, when he went forward in the face of intense enemy machine gun and shell fire and administered first aid to one of his men who had been wounded while crossing the Meuse River near Cléry–le–Petit.[49]

On November 14, the 32d and 90th Divisions relieved the 5th Division on the line held on November 11, and the division moved to positions near Dun–sur–Meuse. The division, now assigned to duty with the Services of Supply, Army of Occupation, moved to the area of Longwy and Longuyon on November 22, and five days later took up its service–of–supply duties in the southern part of Luxembourg. The division also controlled circulation along the frontier between Luxembourg and Germany.[50]

The 14th Machine Gun Battalion arrived in Garnich, Luxembourg, on December 11, and moved to Oberkorn, Luxembourg, on December 18, where it remained on occupation duty until July 5, 1919, when it was shipped to Camp Pontanezen, Brest, France. The unit embarked from there aboard the USS *America* for the United States on July 13, arriving in Hoboken, New Jersey, on July 22. The battalion then went to Camp Mills, Long Island, New York, where it entrained on July 25 for Camp Gordon, Georgia, arriving there on July 28.[51]

Capt. Edwin D. Patrick, Oberkorn, Luxembourg, 1919
(Courtesy of Mary Margaret Goffinet and Ruth Anne Werner)

CHAPTER 5

THE POSTWAR YEARS

The 14th Machine Gun Battalion, with Patrick still in command of Company A, arrived at Camp Gordon, Georgia, on July 28, 1919. Patrick assumed temporary command of the battalion on July 31, while Major Jens A. Doe was on leave. After again assuming temporary command of the battalion on October 31, Patrick, in detached service status, left on November 15 to attend a machine gun school at Knoxville, Tennessee, where he was described as an "experienced M. Gunner."[1]

In February 1920, Patrick reported to Fort Lawton, Washington, where he remained until August, when he was assigned to Fort Benning, Georgia, as an instructor at the Infantry School. In September 1922, he entered the Infantry School as a student in the Company Officers Class, graduating the following May.[2]

After a brief assignment at Camp Devens, Massachusetts, Patrick reported to Camp Alfred Vail (now Fort Monmouth), New Jersey, in September 1923, to begin studies at the Army Signal School.[3]

Patrick was one of eleven infantry officers among the sixty–four officers who began their studies in the fall of 1922. The fifteen Signal Corps officers in the class would be students in the "Company Officers Course," while the officers of other branches, including three from foreign armies, would enroll in the "Basic Course" in signal subjects. Both courses were nine months in length.[4]

Both groups completed courses in the Department of Communication Engineering and the Department of Applied Communications. The major difference between the courses of instruction was the emphasis of the courses for the Signal Corps officers on "communication engineering," and the focus on "applied communications" for the other officers. Signal Corps officers also completed courses in such subjects as military sketching and map reading, subjects in which combat arms officers would already be proficient. In June 1924, sixty of the original sixty–four officers, including Patrick, graduated.[5]

After his graduation, Patrick moved to Fort Sam Houston, Texas, to join the 23d Infantry. In April 1925, he became Adjutant, 3d Infantry Brigade, 2d Division, and commander of the brigade Headquarters Company at Fort Sam Houston.

That month the 3d Brigade, along with other division units, began an intensive training program. The program centered about impending war between two hostile "states," the enemy "Red" state west of the Colorado River (Texas) and the friendly "Blue" state east of that river.[6]

The hostility between the "Red" and "Blue" states arose out of a dispute over the location of the border between the two states in the vicinity of Brownwood, Texas. On May 1, 1925, a "Red" division began to move from Fort Worth toward Brownwood. The "Blue" government ordered the 2d Division to move from San Antonio without delay to the vicinity of Brady, and be prepared to oppose any movement of "Red" forces across the Colorado River. The 2d Division moved out on May 4, and by May 9 had reached Fredericksburg, some 85 miles north–northeast of San Antonio. On May 10, in response to a concentration of "Red" forces that threatened San Antonio, the commanding general of I Corps, "Blue" forces, ordered the 2d Division to return to the San Antonio area to counter that move. The division did so, arriving at Fort Sam Houston on May 1, at which time the commanding general terminated the exercise.[7]

Patrick later told his stepsister Clara that the field exercise had been demanding, undoubtedly referring to the myriad activities for which, as adjutant, he had been responsible during the brigade's three weeks in the field: unit personnel records and reports, loss estimates, personnel daily summaries, requests for and assignment of brigade replacements, unit morale activities, postal services, religious activities, maintenance of discipline and law and order, exchange services, and internal arrangement and management of the brigade command post.[8]

On Saturday, May 16, Patrick began a leave of absence. On Monday morning, May 18, he married Nellie May Bowen Bouquet in Christ Episcopal Church, San Antonio. Following the ceremony, the Patricks went to Galveston for a ten-day honeymoon.[9]

Patrick had met Nellie May at Fort Sam Houston in the spring of 1924, when she came to care for her ill brother, a second lieutenant in the 23d Infantry. She stayed with her brother until the fall, when she accompanied him on convalescent leave to their parents' home in El Paso. On their return to San Antonio in December, her brother resumed his military duties, and Nellie May remained there, continuing to look after her brother. Patrick began dating her occasionally, and the two soon became "real companions." In April 1925, the two "real companions" decided to marry.[10]

Nellie May Bowen Bouquet, was the daughter of a prominent El Paso family. Her father, Judge James E. Bowen, had come from the Pecos Valley, where he owned land on which he hoped to discover oil. However, that hope did not materialize and, according to Patrick, the Bowens, at the time of Nellie May's marriage to him, were impecunious.[11]

Patrick described his new bride as a very attractive blonde with a very keen sense of humor. *The Tell City News* social editor wrote that she was a vivacious, clever, and charming young woman. She was a graduate of the Marlborough School for Girls in Los Angeles, and was described as a brilliant pianist who gave her finishing recital in the Little Theatre in Los Angeles, receiving an ovation. During World War I, she used her musical talents to entertain soldiers in the El Paso area. She had previously been married for almost a year to an army aviator, who was killed in an aviation accident just a few weeks after Nellie May had given birth to their son, Ulric.[12]

After their return to Fort Sam Houston, the Patricks took up residence in one of the old World War I barracks that had been converted into a house. Patrick described the house as follows:

> The house is unsightly from the outside, but real
> pretty on the inside, when the beaver board walls
> are worked on with a little paint and tasty draper-
> ies are hung around. Of course, when it rains, the
> roof lets in quantities of water and in the winter the
> wind blows right thru the house, but that's the way
> of the army and we are used to it.[13]

Patrick continued in his duties as the brigade adjutant throughout 1925 and the early months of 1926, when he received notice that he was to join the 15th Infantry in Tientsin, China. After a leave at the family home in Tell City, Edwin, Nellie May, and Ulric began their trip to the Port of Embarkation, San Francisco, first stopping at the Bowen home in El Paso.[14]

CHAPTER 6

ON A SLOW BOAT TO CHINA

While staying at the Bowen home in El Paso, Patrick began the first of five lengthy articles for *The Tell City News*. In these articles, "From Texas to China," he described his visit in El Paso and the nearby Mexican city of Juarez, his travels westward to San Francisco, the voyage to China, and his arrival in Tientsin.[1]

He particularly enjoyed his visit to Juarez, where he found every third house to be a saloon. He first went to the Central Cafe, a combination bar, curio shop, and slot machine casino. There he confronted the slot machines and recounted the struggle that ensued within him as each of his ancestral lines, German, Irish and Scottish, debated what he should do:

> The Irishman says: "Aw qwan wid ye, spind a quarter, ye moight win." To this the Scotchman says: "Hoot mon, ye canna' win—save yer quarter." What should I do? I already have my hand on the quarter and before the Scotchman can stop me I've dropped it into the slot. I pull the handle. There's a whirr, a click; a row of pictures appears and I hear a metallic cough and a jingle of coins. I look down and see a pile of quarters, eight of them. "Begorra," yells the Irishman, "I told ye. Now dthrop in inither and ye moight win agin." But the Scotchman yells, "Quit, mon, quit! Ye canna win anymore." Up to this time the German has been looking nonchalantly on, not saying a word. But now he speaks up, "Do vatever you vant, but do it quvick and den order a shtein of beer, I'm gettin dry."[2]

He then went to the local bullfight, which he found to be distasteful and a poor form of sport, comparing it unfavorably to baseball.

Throughout the recounting of his experiences on this trip to China, he frequently stereotyped other races, displaying a racial bias not uncommon among American Caucasians during the 1920's: he described them variously as villainous (Mexicans), half–civilized (Chinese and Filipinos), violent (Filipinos), poor workers (Filipinos), and shiftless (the Chamorros of Guam).[3]

Patrick and his family boarded the "Golden State Limited" for San Francisco on March 27. On board the train was Brigadier General Joseph C. Castner, Patrick's brigade commander in the 5th Division in France. Castner, who had been commanding Fort Bliss for two years, was also on his way to China, to assume command of the army forces there. The two renewed their acquaintanceship, Patrick noting that he found Castner to be "a very congenial companion besides being the very capable army officer I already knew him to be from past experience."[4]

Patrick provided vivid descriptions of the country as the train traveled to San Francisco: the desert of southern Arizona with its greasewood bushes and their canopies of bright, yellow blossoms; the ocotillo plants with their blossoms of flaming red; the giant cacti; the Colorado River, the Grand Canyon's "creator–artist"; and the San Joaquin Valley, with its

> fields of waving grain and blooming orchards, ... acres and acres of orange groves flecked with white blossoms and laden with golden fruit, dense forests of stately eucalyptus trees and in every spot where no cultivated vegetation grew, the wild California poppy enhanced the beauty of the scene with its brilliant orange colored blossoms. ... Nature has decreed that California be beautiful and there is little that man can do to prevent it.[5]

After arriving in San Francisco on March 29, the Patricks went to the Stewart Hotel, where they stayed until their transport sailed for the Orient. While in the city, the Patricks visited Golden Gate Park, the Cliff House restaurant, Seal Beach, and the Presidio.

On April 6, the family went to Fort Mason, where they received medical clearance, and were informed that they could board their ship, the United States Army Transport *Thomas*, at 0930 the next day. The *Thomas* was to sail at noon on that day, carrying Patrick to his new assignment "on China station."[6]

Patrick and his family boarded the *Thomas* the next morning, and Patrick discovered that he and the ship had at least one thing in common: they were both thirty–two years old. The *Thomas*, built in Belfast, Ireland, in 1894, was sold to the United States during the Spanish–American War, during which she carried troops to Cuba. In spite of her age, the *Thomas* was deemed the best Army transport afloat. However, Patrick felt that this was faint praise since "the worst passenger ships afloat in the world are U.S. army transports."[7]

Through the influence of Castner, the Patrick family was able to obtain a stateroom for the long voyage to China. The stateroom was on the upper or promenade deck, which provided them with "plenty of open deck space for walking all around the ship."[8]

After settling his family in their stateroom, Patrick reported to the dock to assume his assigned duty as the officer responsible for loading about 600 troops destined for the Philippines and China as replacements. The troops started boarding at 1630, and Patrick began his

> troublesome task. ... Through ignorance and care-
> lessness they are constantly going astray and get-
> ting lost unless they are carefully watched. Being
> for the most part recruits it is difficult to keep them
> in formation and alert at all times. ... [T]heir names
> were called and to step lively up the gangplank was
> a job indeed. However, with the aid of a few good
> noncommissioned officers I completed the job in
> about an hour.[9]

Because of a problem with one of the ship's boilers, the *Thomas* did not sail until the following morning. Standing on deck, the Patricks watched the dock disappear in the distance as they steamed through the Golden Gate. Passing Seal Rocks and Cliff House, the *Thomas* moved into the Pacific Ocean, where the ship promptly ran into a storm that lasted for two days. Patrick describes the dining room at breakfast the first day at sea as

> almost filled—I mean that it was filled at the begin-
> ning of breakfast. But long before the meal was over
> only a few occupants remained. The rest had either
> sneaked out quietly or they had jumped out of their
> seats unceremoniously and dashed out with their
> hands to their mouths.

On the afternoon of April 13, the *Thomas* sailed past the north shore of the island of Molokai, and approximately an hour later the passengers caught their first glimpse of the island of Oahu. After rounding Diamond Head as darkness began to fall, the ship docked in Honolulu at 2200, where an army band greeted the passengers by playing "Aloha." The docks swarmed with army friends and their families carrying leis. As the Patricks disembarked, their friends welcomed them in the traditional way, placing leis around their necks. This act confirmed to Patrick that "nowhere is hospitality warmer than it is among army people."

After a quick trip around the city, their friends took them to the Moana Hotel, where they strolled through the lobby to the court facing the beach, admiring within the court the large banyan tree decorated with hundreds of twinkling lights of all colors.

The family returned to the ship for the night, and the next morning, in a rented chauffeur–driven car, Patrick began a tour of Oahu; Nellie May did not accompany him because she had been in Hawaii before. He first visited the Pali ("cliff"), where King Kamehameha had succeeded in getting complete possession of the island of Oahu by driving the army of his enemies over the Pali. Patrick edged his way on foot to the edge of the cliff, and as he gazed down expressed his compassion for the "poor devils" forced over the cliff by Kamehameha, stating that they "must have had funny feelings in the pits of their stomachs as they started going over."

From the Pali, Patrick went to Schofield Barracks, noting the pineapple and cane fields along the road. Harvesting the cane fields was a long line of "Filipinos, Japs, Chinamen and some negroes and whites." Patrick quoted their superviser's comments on the quality of the laborers:

> The chinamen [sic] are the best workers, the Filipinos the worst. All of them are poorly paid and they are not much more than half civilized. ... It is a common occurrance [sic] for them to get into arguments among themselves while cutting cane and use the knives on one another.[10]

Patrick then returned to Honolulu. After a lunch of ice cold pineapple, Patrick returned to the ship, lamenting the fact that he would not have time to visit the island of Hawaii and see the volcano Mauna Loa, which was then erupting, since the transport was due to sail at noon.

The *Thomas* set course for her next destination, Guam, a fifteen–day voyage that Patrick described as taking first prize for monotony, broken in part by a single whale–sighting, one or two sightings of groups of porpoises, and the sighting of a few birds, most likely albatrosses, since, according to Patrick, "they seemed to fit exactly the description of albatross in Coleridge's 'Ancient Mariner.' "[11]

The heat became intense, making the staterooms unbearable during the day. However, the nights were quite pleasant. The ship's officers attempted to mitigate the discomfort and relieve the boredom by publishing a newspaper, carrying news obtained from the ship radio, and by holding three dances a week, with dance music by army Filipino bandsmen traveling to the Philippines on furlough. The band also presented several concerts, and the officers organized two amateur shows.

On the fifteenth day out of Honolulu, the *Thomas* arrived at Guam. As the ship was entering the harbor, the crew received word that the governor of Guam had invited the passengers and crew to attend a dance that he was giving in their honor. Because of the difficulties of transporting all of the enlisted men to the dance, only officers, warrant officers, and high ranking noncommissioned officers and their families would be allowed to attend.

Traveling to shore in launches, the Patricks traveled by automobile along a coral road that ran along the ocean shore for four miles to the village of Agana, the capital of Guam. The dance pavilion was in a coconut grove next to the governor's house, and an orchestra made up of American marines provided the dance music.

Instead of dancing, Patrick took the opportunity to explore Agana. He noted particularly the cleanliness of the village, comparing it to China, "the land of filth," where he was when he wrote the newspaper article. He also commented that Guam's population was composed of Chamorros, whom he described as "easy-going, rather shiftless but intelligent people."[12] He pointed out that the island was the only genuine colony that the United States possessed, and was governed by a retired U. S. Navy captain. The laws were very strict, and, since there were practically no violations of the law, there were no jails. Guamanians committing offenses received sentences of hard labor; foreigners who broke the law were expelled.

Patrick returned to the dance pavilion in time for the coconut milk ice cream and watermelon punch refreshments. The dance ended just before midnight, and the navy personnel assigned to the station at Guam returned their army guests to the *Thomas*, which sailed the next morning at 0700, bound for Manila.

In the conclusion of his newspaper article, Patrick made a prescient statement about the fate that Guam most likely would suffer in the event of war between the United States and Japan. In 1926, Guam was serving as the relay point for several important cable lines to the orient, but was not heavily garrisoned or fortified. Patrick predicted that if war were to break out between Japan and the United States, the forces on Guam would be able to protect our cables to the Philippines for only a short time. On December 10, 1941, following two days of air attacks, over eight thousand Japanese troops landed at multiple sites on the island, defended only by a garrison of approximately five hundred marines. Several hours later, the island surrendered.[13]

The *Thomas* set course for the San Bernardino Strait, the body of water separating the southeast tip of Luzon from the island of Samar. After passage of the strait, the ship entered the Sibuyan Sea on the night of April 30–May 1. Hugging the southern shore of Luzon, the *Thomas* passed between Luzon and Mindoro on the evening of May 2. On the following day, the ship anchored outside the breakwater of Manila Bay, to the east of the fortified island of Corregidor, which guarded the entrance to the bay. The Patrick family arrived at the pier that morning, and immediately went to the Luneta Hotel, overlooking the bay, where they would stay for the next five days.[14]

The next day Patrick drove about Manila and out into the surrounding countryside. He notes that the carabao (water buffalo) was still the most important mode of transportation on the island. He also commented on the native dress of the Filipinos; the uncomfortable heat in the islands; the "calesas," which are horse–drawn carts frequently used as taxis; the canopies of beautiful trees and flowers along the streets; and the cosmopolitan nature of the city.

During his stay in Manila, Patrick visited Intramuros, the walled city, garrisoned by the 31st Infantry. He also went to Fort McKinley, where a battalion of the 15th Infantry and the 45th Infantry (Philippine Scouts), a Filipino regiment with U.S. Army officers, were stationed. He remembered that there had recently been a mutiny in the 45th Infantry that had to be put down by United States troops, which led him to conclude that "one good white soldier is worth a dozen of the little brown fellows and the little brown fellows know it."[15]

The Patricks, while in Manila, spent most of their time at the Army and Navy Club, attending two dances and spending several hours each day in the spacious lounging rooms.

Preparing to leave Manila, Patrick expressed his feelings about the city:

> My feelings concerning Manila were a bit conflict-
> ing. I liked the free and easy life there, but I had the
> feeling that it was too much of a good thing and
> that in time it would be boring.

On May 8, the *Thomas* sailed for China, the last leg of the Patricks' journey. On the third day out of Manila, the ship passed to the east of Formosa. Three days later they passed Port Arthur in southern Manchuria, and entered the Gulf of Chihli on the last day of the voyage. The *Thomas* docked on the night of May 13, 1926, at Chingwangtao, approximately 175 miles east of Peking and 150 miles northeast of Tientsin.[16]

CHAPTER 7

ONE OF THE
OLD CHINA HANDS

When he and his family arrived in China, Patrick joined an infantry regiment that was part of an American military force in China that had its beginnings in the Boxer Uprising at the turn of the twentieth century. However, American involvement in Chinese internal affairs dated back much further, and a brief recapitulation of the history of American–Chinese relations is in order if the reader is to gain an appreciation of the mission of the 15th Infantry ("Can Do") Regiment in China when Patrick joined the unit.

The United States has a long history of interest and involvement in Chinese internal affairs. In February 1784, the 360–ton *Empress of China*, owned by a group of American merchants and bearing a forty–ton cargo of ginseng, a medicinal herb, and other articles, docked at Canton. Ten months later, the ship left on its homeward voyage to New York, with a large cargo of tea. Thus began commercial relations between the two countries.[1]

In 1786, Samuel Shaw, who had served as the officer in charge of the cargo aboard the *Empress of China*, assumed the position of American Consul at Canton. During the ensuing twenty–five years, trade between the two countries grew immensely, producing in 1912 the first American millionaire, John Astor. The trade, now consisting of furs from the Pacific Northwest bartered for Chinese tea, continued to flourish during the nineteenth century, culminating, on July 3, 1844, in a treaty between the two countries that granted the United States permission to trade in the newly opened ports of Amoy, Foochow, Ningpo, and Shanghai, in addition to Canton; consular representation; most–favored–nation status; and extra–territoriality.[2]

Western influence on China continued to grow during the remainder of the nineteenth century, accelerated by the Arrow War (1856–1858) and the Taiping Rebellion (1851–1864).[3]

Reacting to the increasing influence of Western nations within their country, many Chinese began to develop anti–foreign feelings, stemming from their anti–Christian sentiments, resentment of foreign economic domination, anger over imperialism, and the effects of natural disasters. These frustrations eventually boiled over and contributed to the Boxer Uprising of 1900.[4]

Finding encouragement from the royal court, the Boxers cut the railway line between Peking and Tientsin, isolating the capital city. In June 1900, the Boxers began to besiege the foreign legations in Peking. An international relief force, including American soldiers, sailors, and marines, struck out for Peking, and, by August 16, had defeated the Boxers and relieved the siege. The foreign governments, through the terms of the Boxer Protocols, gained even greater concessions from the Chinese.

When the American forces withdrew from Peking, the American commander, Major General Adna Chafee, left behind a reinforced U.S. Army regiment, which was to serve as a legation guard. Reduced in the spring of 1901 to a rifle company, that army force was replaced in 1905 by marines.

In January 1912, responding to the overthrow of the Manchu government the previous year, and fearing attacks upon foreigners, one battalion of the U.S. Army's 15th Infantry Regiment arrived in China from the Philippines to guard the railway from Tongshan to Lanchow. In March 1912, the 15th Infantry was raised to its statutory strength when the 2d Battalion was organized from the troops already present. Six of the regiment's eight companies occupied quarters at Tientsin, where the regiment remained until 1937, when it left China because of fear of the consequences of an accidental incident between the troops of Japan and the United States.[5]

In 1926, the year of Patrick's arrival in Tientsin, Brigadier General Joseph C. Castner, the new commanding general of the U. S. Army Forces in China, fearing that his forces could be easily overwhelmed in any serious encounter with the Chinese, deemed the original mission of the army in China to be outdated, and asked the Departments of War and State for new instructions. Although refusing to change the original mission, the two departments tacitly acknowledged the difficulty of keeping open the railway route to the sea, thus reducing the army's mission to protecting American lives and property in the Tientsin areas; the force was there for " 'a political purpose and [had] little military value.' "[6]

Patrick's correspondence with his family and his newspaper articles give no clue as to how much he might have known of the history of United States–China relations and of the mission of his unit in China as he stood on the deck of the *Thomas* in Chinwangtao harbor. However, he does recount his initial impressions of the Chinese people, the "dock collies" [*sic*] at Chinwangtao:

> I can't forget, however, the impression that their dirty ragged clothing made upon me, their animal–like gestures as they scrambled on the dock for cigarettes and pieces of food that were tossed down to them by the passengers and I certainly won't forget my feelings when I saw the ship's garbage thrown out on the pier and the fellows pounced upon it and fought over it like dogs over a slop barrel.[7]

The passengers stayed on the ship that night and most of the next day, when Patrick hired a rickshaw to visit the town of Chinwangtao. Pulling the rickshaw was "a little fellow, thin and a bit sickly looking." As his ride continued, Patrick began to feel "sorry for the poor devil … pulling a big hulk like me over that difficult road." He even entertained the thought of having the "Chinaman" stop and get in the rickshaw and rest, while he pulled the vehicle. But he rejected this, feeling that "somebody might laugh at me."[8]

After his return to the *Thomas* from his sojourn in Chinwangtao, Patrick and his family boarded a smaller ship, the *Kaiping*, for their trip to Tientsin, up the Hai River, which Patrick described as being crowded with sailing craft of every size. At about 1030 on May 15, the Kaiping docked at Tientsin.

Since Castner was aboard, there was a large body of troops assembled on the "Bund," the name given to the river front. To the right of the formation was the 15th Infantry band. Next to the band was the entire force of American troops standing at attention and "present arms," while the band played the "General's March." Patrick was impressed with the appearance of the soldiers, and stated that these troops were "enough to strike pride in the heart of anybody born under the Stars and Stripes."

To the left of the 15th Infantry was the British East Yorkshire Regiment. Then came a battalion of the Imperial Japanese Army, a company of French Colonials, a company of Italian marines, and a battalion of Chang Tso Ling's [*sic*] Chinese soldiers.[9]

Patrick was quick to point out that the formation and ceremony were not to welcome him and his family to China, but rather were for Castner. He stated that the foreign nationals in China used such displays to impress the Chinese by "making face, …

one of the principal pastimes in the orient." Patrick went on to define the term, "making face": "making somebody believe you are something you aint [sic]. Four-flushing is a pretty good synonym."[10]

The Patricks motored to a friend's house in Tientsin, where they stayed until they chose a house from several offered to them. Patrick selected a house located in a place known as "the Alley." It was one of a block of houses built and owned by a society of French Catholic priests. Although he noted that the rent was cheap, Patrick complained that the priests were miserly and refused to keep the houses in good repair. This necessitated his spending the equivalent of about one hundred American dollars to fix up the house. The house had a living room, a dining room, two bedrooms, pantry, kitchen, bathroom, and servants' quarters in the rear. The Patricks had five servants: a head servant, a cook, a nurse for Ulric ("Rick"), a "house coolie" (who cleaned and shined shoes and performed other household tasks), and a rickshaw coolie who took them "wherever [they] want to go at any time."[11]

The Patricks furnished their home with three of "the finest rugs made in China," brocaded piano and table covers, wicker furniture for the living room, and a secondhand dining room set. The total cost was approximately $195.00 in American currency.[12]

At this point it seems appropriate to provide a brief description of Tientsin and of the American Barracks in Tientsin.[13] Tientsin is situated in the southeastern part of the province of Chihli at the head of the Hai River, a waterway of great commercial importance, formed by the confluence of the Grand Canal and the Pei River. The city in 1926 had a native population of approximately 900,000, and a foreign population of about 4,400, approximately half of whom were Japanese. About seven hundred Americans lived in Tientsin, and, along with all the other foreigners, lived in the "Foreign Concessions."

The city lies in a vast alluvial plain, about seven feet above sea level. The climate was described as good, but the prevalent dust storms aggravated existing nose, throat or sinus infections, and were not conducive to good health. Malaria was also quite prevalent during the late summer and early fall months.

The American Barracks (or Compound) occupied one city block in the former German Concession. It contained three parallel lines of buildings, most of which were three stories high, running east and west, with some detached buildings on the south. These buildings divided the compound into three parallel courtyards, the largest 260 by 90 feet, in which regimental ceremonies were held. The buildings in the compound were built in 1917, but in 1926 were considered to be of poor construction quality and difficult to keep in good repair.

Assigned to the 15th Infantry(-) in 1926 were 39 officers and 747 men, assigned to the 2d and 3d Battalions.[14] The enlisted men were housed in two–company barracks, which had kitchen, mess room, and store rooms in the basement. There were also a hospital and a recreation hall in the compound, as well as stables, a corral, ice plant, bakery, veterinary hospital, and blacksmith shop. The troops drilled in the compound, on nearby vacant lots, and on a field about a mile away. Tactical training took place on two plains on the outskirts of the city.

Children of the troops attended the Tientsin Grammar School, which the "Local Examination Syndicate" of Cambridge University had sanctioned, and the North China American School, a high school in Tunghsien, about sixty–five miles from Tientsin. Both of these schools had tuition fees.

Recreational activities for the officers revolved about the Tientsin Club, with a well–equipped bar, the Tientsin Race Club, the Tientsin Country Club, the Tientsin Golf Club, the American Tennis Club, and the Tientsin Polo Club.

The enlisted men's recreational activities included athletic events, movies, amateur stage productions, dances, and band concerts. Nearby the compound were a club erected by a group of businessmen, a cafeteria and meeting place operated by the YMCA and the Knights of Columbus, and one post library and two off–post libraries.

However, other diversions competed for the enlisted men's off–duty hours: "liquor, fighting, and prostitutes." One former soldier recalled that immediately outside of the American barracks in Tientsin, the "signs saying 'Bar' seemed to stretch into infinity." One former officer of the 15th Infantry stated that at one time every other man in the regiment was infected with a venereal disease. Of course, not all enlisted men pursued such vices, and many used their off–duty time to travel, to learn more about China and the Chinese, and to associate with friends at noncommissioned officers' and soldiers' clubs, bowling alleys, and confectionaries.[15]

Patrick joined one of the most elite units in the U.S. Army. It was one of the few army regiments in which all of the troops wore tailored uniforms. The summer uniforms were of "Hong Kong khaki." The winter uniform "included 'rabbit fur caps as they used to wear on the great plains and turtle neck sweaters and sheep skin coats.' Even the enlisted men of the regiment carried swagger sticks while in uniform in Tientsin"[16] The training for the regiment was generally divided into two parts, one in Tientsin and its immediate environs, the other in the field at Camp Nan–Ta–Ssu, located along the coast of the Gulf of Chihli, 3 1/2 miles from Chinwangtao.

The training year, which ran from December 1 through November 30, usually consisted of eight segments that varied in length from 2 weeks to $2^1/2$ months. During these periods the units of the regiment conducted company–level and battalion–level training in such subjects as marksmanship; combat principles of the squad, section, platoon, company, and battalion; bayonet; and gas defense. Daily training ended at 1200, and in the afternoon the troops participated in schools, administration activities, athletics, and recreation, unless otherwise directed. There were also the usual inspections, reviews, and parades, as well as marches of up to ten miles in length. In addition, in 1928 all officers and selected enlisted men attended a course in the Chinese language.[17]

The field training at Camp Nan–Ta–Ssu occupied the months of June, July, and August. The two battalions alternated six–week tours of duty at the camp, where they conducted marksmanship and combat firing, as well as training in company and battalion combat principles.[18] Rifle firing was most emphasized during this training, utilizing 200, 300, 500, 600, and 1,000 yard ranges. The troops also fired pistols, Stokes mortars, the 37mm howitzer, and the machine gun during their field training.[19]

While at Camp Burrowes the officers were allowed to have their families with them. The officers and their families occupied tents on "Officers Row," located about three hundred yards from the main soldiers' camp; Chinese matting covered the tent floors. A mess hall provided meals, and tea was served daily in the quarters. A kitchen was also available.

About 150 yards from "Officers Row" there was an excellent bathing beach. There was also an Officers Club, where officers would congregate after the trying duties of the daily range work. For the adults there were riding, swimming, and hiking. The children enjoyed swings, see–saws, merry–go–rounds, basketball, and baseball.[20]

Noble describes those "trying duties of the daily range work" thus:

> Reveille was usually sounded at 4:30 in the morning, with the sergeants announcing a maskee uniform (wear what you please) of the day. The men were usually on the line shortly after sunrise. Firing generally stopped by noon and, if a soldier did not have guard, he was free the rest of the day. ... George C. Marshall wrote that "Bathing, riding and shooting occupies the time," while "riding in the picturesque country" was always a pleasure.[21]

While in China, Patrick held several assignments with the 15th Infantry: in May 1927, he assumed command of the 2d Battalion, vice Major Joseph W. Stilwell; in October 1927, he became the Post School Officer and the Regimental Machine Gun Officer. He commanded the Provisional Battalion in 1929, and for a time in 1927 served as summary court officer.[22]

Patrick also accumulated several honors in competitive events: a "308" in marksmanship. In March 1928, his battalion received the "Battalion Commander's Small Bore Trophy," and he was the winner in the "Officers Jumps" during the "Can Do Week" competition in December 1928.[23]

Patrick also organized or participated as an official in several competitions, including the Regimental Transportation Show, the 15th Infantry Military Tournament and Horse Show, and marksmanship competition.[24]

At 2330, July 9, 1926, Nellie May gave birth to Edwin Daviess Patrick, Jr. He weighed $10^1/4$ pounds, and, according to his mother, "looked like a steamed pudding$_x$." [sic]. Patrick reported to his family in Tell City that the baby had to be named "in a hurry, because records have to be filed with the American Consul General in order to keep him from being a Chinaman$_x$." [sic] While his wife was in the hospital, Patrick assumed the task of caring for their other son, Ricky, since even though they had "five Chinamen around the place [it didn't] mean much because they are a worthless lot$_x$." [sic].[25]

By June of 1927, the Patricks had spent all of their money furnishing their home, buying such things as silver goblets, compotes, coffee cups, and bread and butter plates; stacks of linen luncheon sets, napkins, tablecloths, and dresser scarves; ten or twelve Chinese rugs; carved wood and lacquer screens; wood and lacquer furniture articles; one wicker and two wooden bedroom sets. Nellie May had also purchased Chinese mandarin coats, Japanese Hori coats, a fur coat, and some Canton shawls. Despite these expenditures Patrick maintained that they had been "living in style at the same time."[26]

Patrick also reassured his family about the situation in China, apparently referring to the continuing fighting among the warlords of northern China, and the threat posed to them by Chiang Kai Shek's Nationalist army in the south, which in 1926 had begun its march northward to unite the country. He pointed out that Tientsin lay in the territory controlled by Chang Tso Lin, the northern warlord, but expected that the "Southerner [Chiang Kai Shek's Nationalists] will take over the northern country,... [but that] conditions [would] be exactly the same and soon afterwards somebody else will kick the Southerners out etc." He described the Chinese generals as "pirates," and indicated his belief that "no sincere nationalism exists in China or will exist for many years to come." He further stated that their "victories are won by propaganda, betrayal, lies and money." Patrick felt he was not exaggerating when he said that the "600 American soldiers here in the 15th Infantry could easily defeat the entire combined Chinese forces."[27]

Patrick subsequently reported the fulfillment of his prediction of June 23, 1927: the Nationalists had indeed driven out Chang Tso Lin, who had departed for Mukden, Manchuria, followed by his troops who were moving "as fast as they can." He also pointed out that the clash of Chinese forces with Japanese troops at Tsinan, followed by Japan's partial reoccupation of Shankung, had frightened the Nationalists "to death and taught them the futility of opposing a foreign army regardless of how small it is." Patrick stated that the Americans were not afraid of any trouble in Tientsin, having "much faith in the placidity of the oriental mind."[28]

Captain and Mrs. Patrick were an active part of the 15th Infantry's social life, with Nellie May serving as a member of a committee to plan a schedule of social activities for the 1928-1929 winter season. They hosted and were guests at numerous dinner parties, which were often followed by the playing of bridge and Keno (Lieutenant Colonel Joseph W. Stilwell noted in his diary entry of March 10, 1929, that he had attended a "crazy dinner at Patricks"). They went to numerous dinners and dances at the Tientsin Country Club, and on one occasion hosted a cocktail reception for two visiting dignitaries, a Mr. Forsythe and a Mrs. Ferguson, on the afternoon of November 26, 1926: "Cocktails were served and by eight o'clock the close harmony had reached a high state of perfections [sic]."[29]

While in China the Patricks became very much involved in amateur dramatic productions, "Pat" as an actor, and Nellie May as both an actor and a director. On February 22, 1927, Nellie May appeared as "Millie," a typical chorus girl, in the comedy, *The Best People*, put on for the enlisted men and their families. A reviewer declared this production "the best show, Amateur or Professional, ever staged in Tientsin." He went on to point out that "Millie" was "particularly good." In the playbill the actors acknowledged the "kindnesses shown the '*American players*' " by General Joseph F. Castner, Colonel Isaac Newell, and Lieutenant Colonel George C. Marshall. The Patricks also appeared in several other productions.[30]

The Patricks were also involved in the non-denominational religious life of the American Garrison: both sang in the chapel Vested Choir, and Nellie May also served as accompanist.[31]

Patrick apparently spent most of his time in Tientsin, although he did visit Peking on several occasions, noting that it was a "marvellous [sic] place to shop and also to sightsee." There is no record of his taking trips elsewhere in China.[32]

In February 1929, *The Sentinel* announced that Patrick, then commanding the Provisional Battalion, had received orders assigning him to duty as an instructor at the Infantry School at Fort Benning, Georgia, and would depart on the April troop transport for the United States. He was subsequently relieved of his duties as Provisional Battalion commander, and assumed the position of Regimental Machine Gun Officer. In March, Stilwell also received orders to report to the Infantry School for duty as an instructor.[33]

As Patrick's time for departure drew near, an article in *The Sentinel* commented on his contributions to the 15th Infantry:

> There's only one *"Pat"* and here he goes. We have reference to Captain Edwin D. Patrick, 15th Infantry, who has served in many capacities since he joined the American Army Forces in China, a few of them might be listed Commanding Officer of the Provisional Battalion, Regimental Machine Gun Officer, Summary Court and oh, so many more jobs. In every capacity he has functioned 100 perpcent [sic]. "Pat" is one of the most popular officers of the regiment and he leaves behind him many friends. His new station is Fort Benning, where rumor has it he will function as an instructor, a position he formerly held prior to service in China. "Pat" arrived in China in May 1926. All join in wishing *"Pat"* a successful and enjoyable trip home and all envy Benning.[34]

On Wednesday, April 18, 1929, the 15th Infantry formed in the compound to bid farewell to their departing comrades. The departing troops formed in line facing north, while the remainder of the regiment formed along the north side of the area facing south. After the regimental band played "Should Old Acquaintance be Forgot," Colonel Cummins, Executive Officer, 15th Infantry, addressed the troops and presented letters of commendation to several enlisted men. Colonel Taylor, commander, U.S. Army Forces in China, and commander, 15th Infantry, made a brief address, bidding the men "an enjoyable trip home and telling them they carry the reputation of the regiment back with them and to so uphold it." The departing troops were then dismissed and boarded trucks to begin their long voyage home.[35]

It appears worthwhile to look at the roster of officers who served with the 15th Infantry during Patrick's tour of duty with the unit. One of these officers, Lieutenant Colonel George C. Marshall, would rise to the grade of General of the Army, serve as chief of staff of the Army during World War II, and become President Harry S. Truman's Secretary of State and Secretary of Defense. He would also receive the Nobel Peace Prize. Stilwell would rise to the rank of general, and command the forces in the China–Burma–India Theater in World War II. Major Matthew B. Ridgway likewise would eventually receive four stars and serve as army Chief of Staff; during World War II he commanded the famed 82d Airborne Division and XVIII Airborne Corps, and during the Korean War he commanded the Eighth Army. Two officers would become lieutenant generals; thirteen, including Patrick, would rise to the grade of major general, and seven would become brigadier generals. I agree with Charles G. Finney, when he asked, "[W]hat other infantry regiment of those days can boast of such an alumni list?"[36]

CHAPTER 8

ONE OF MARSHALL'S MEN

In August 1929, Patrick and his family moved into on–post quarters at Fort Benning, Georgia, where he would begin his duties as an instructor in the Infantry School. Fort Benning is located nine miles from Columbus, Georgia, on ninety–seven thousand acres of land.[1]

When Patrick assumed his duties at the Infantry School, Lieutenant Colonel George C. Marshall, with whom he had served in China, was serving as assistant commandant of the school, a position he continued to occupy during Patrick's time at Fort Benning. As assistant commandant, Marshall was also head of the Academic Department. Given almost a free hand by the two commandants who served while he was there, Marshall was able to "mold the course and direct the teaching methods as he wished."[2]

His experiences at the Command and General Staff School, with the National Guard prior to World War I, and with the American Expeditionary Force (AEF) in France, had convinced Marshall of the need for simplicity in the techniques of troop leading. He had come to believe that the elaborate training and leadership doctrines that he had been a part of developing during World War I were of use for only a truly professional army, and not a mobilized citizen army led only in small part by highly trained professional officers and noncommissioned officers. Since future American wars would most likely involve a similar citizen army, the peacetime army must develop techniques and methods of combat leadership that the future citizen officers could readily grasp.

His experience as a commander in China had shown the validity of his conclusions. There he found his officers to be highly capable in the handling of weapons, target practice, and administrative work. However, they fell below those standards when attempting to solve tactical problems and leading troops in the field. The army schools to this time had focused on neatly laid–out tactical problems, complete with cut and dried solutions for the students to apply to situations they might face when actually leading troops, the "school solution." In these problems battle was organized and predictable, but Marshall's experience in France had shown him that in actual combat it was the unexpected that was normal. The schools had placed too much emphasis on *when* to make a decision, rather than on *what* decision to make in a tactical situation.[3]

Prior to Marshall's arrival, the Infantry School had been teaching tactics modeled on the American and Allied experience in World War I, i.e., relatively static warfare. He planned on revising the curriculum to emphasize and expand upon Pershing's concept of battle based on firepower and maneuverability, a concept that he had seen falter during the war because of the inadequacies of company–grade officers trained under the old rigidified system. To assist him in this revolution he chose a faculty of officers whose abilities he knew from close personal observation, who had recently served with and commanded troops, and shared his pragmatic approach to training officers.[4]

Marshall stressed that a well–trained troop commander should constantly have his eyes and mind alert to the salient military facts of any situation that he might face, e.g., terrain features; positions of adjacent units; capabilities of supporting or attached forces, such as artillery, air, and armor; and strength and capabilities of enemy forces. In field exercises Marshall would introduce the unexpected, e.g., enemy counterattacks when the student officer felt that the programmed field problem was at an end; a tank attack when he felt that the student had neglected to pay attention to an intelligence estimate that the enemy possessed an armor capability of unknown strength; requiring the students to use road maps, out–of–date maps, or foreign maps, rather than U.S. Army tactical maps. Recalling Pershing's insistence that the American Expeditionary Force move out of the trenches into open warfare, Marshall emphasized training for warfare of movement, agreeing with his mentor that "open warfare was better suited to the temper of the American soldier and that it was the one hope of forcing a decision in battle."[5]

Marshall did not stress theories of war in the curriculum, but rather the methods and principles of command. He firmly believed that in combat situations troop leaders would have to make up their minds quickly, often with very little information. He therefore stressed the art of improvisation, setting problems in rapidly moving situations where "even a mediocre solution arrived at in time was better than the perfect tactic discovered hours after the opportunity to use it had passed."[6]

He continued the course requirement for each student to complete a monograph on some aspect of military history, but added the requirement that the student deliver his monograph orally to his classmates, limiting the time of the presentation to twenty minutes. This was a device to force the officer students to come directly to grips with a problem and outline it clearly and briefly.[7]

That Marshall's observations about warfare were indeed valid was borne out by the experience of the U.S. Army in World War II. In the jungles of New Guinea and Luzon, the hedgerows of Normandy, the snow–covered Ardennes, and the forbidding Hürtgen Forest, Patrick and others would soon find that small unit actions conducted with little or faulty intelligence, inaccurate and inadequate maps, and often scattered and numerically inferior forces would be the rule, and that the success or failure of an entire operation might hinge on the ingenuity, drive, daring, and leadership of the company–grade officers trained by the Infantry School.

By the fall of 1930, Marshall had his own staff of instructors. Heading the First Section (tactics) was Lieutenant Colonel Joseph W. Stilwell, recently of the 15th Infantry in China. Marshall picked Lieutenant Colonel M. C. Stayer, who was a physician and not an infantry officer, to head the Second Section (logistics, supply, training, equitation, signal communications). He picked Stayer because he was blunt–spoken and a good judge of men, who could be depended on to say exactly what he thought. Major Omar N. Bradley, who would command an army group in World War II, serve as army Chief of Staff, and rise to the grade of General of the Army, headed the Third Section, which taught the use of weapons and developed weapons doctrine. Marshall brought in another of his old China hands, Major Edwin Forrest Harding, to head the Fourth Section, which was in charge of history and publications.[8]

In August 1929, Patrick joined this distinguished Infantry School faculty, assigned to the Second Section to head "Signal Communications." In all probability Patrick received this particular assignment because he had completed the Signal School in 1924.[9] Marshall described the faculty of which Patrick became a member as being "composed of the most brilliant, interesting, and thoroughly competent collection of men I have ever been associated with."[10]

During Patrick's tenure at the Infantry School, the number of hours devoted to signal communications in the company officers course increased dramatically, from the previous 30 hours to 137 hours. This occurred because many officers believed that the system of signal communications used in the infantry division of World War I had failed miserably. During that war Signal Corps personnel, augmented by some infantry troops, had operated the communications within the division. Patrick and others believed that below division level communications should be under the control and supervision of infantry officers.[11]

Based on the premise that an infantry communication officer must be proficient in the use of organic communications assets, the officers in this intensely practical expanded course learned to use Morse code; to operate, tune, and perform minor repairs on radio sets; and to utilize wire communications.[12] Patrick, because of his experience commanding a machine gun company in combat, his tenure as an infantry battalion commander in China, and his education at the Army Signal School, was admirably qualified to institute and direct such a course of instruction.

Only very scanty source materials covering Patrick's other military activities at the Infantry School are available. On May 5, 1931, Marshall commended him for the organization of the special communication personnel and special arrangements in support of recent corps area maneuvers, stating that

> the efficiency and fine spirit displayed by every member of the Academic Department concerned ... made a profound impression on all who observed and will do much to increase the reputation of the Infantry School in the Army.

In a field exercise conducted May 9–12, 1932, Patrick served as an assistant umpire for signal communications under the chief umpire, Stilwell.[13]

Even though little source material survives that pertains to Patrick's military duties at Fort Benning, there is considerable material relating to the Patricks' off-duty activities. Both "Pat" and Nellie May were active in the Dramatic Club of the Infantry School. Patrick served for a time as business manager of that club, and his wife served on the "Play Reading Committee," which was chaired by Harding, whom the Patricks had known in China. In addition, they both performed in several productions, and Nellie May directed at least one play.[14]

Nellie May participated in several amateur theater productions, including reprising "Millie" in The Best People, whom she had first played in the production of that play in Tientsin. A reviewer gave

> Mrs. Patrick most of the credit for setting the rapid comedy tempo of the second act [of The Best People].

... She showed a fine sense of climax and her abandon in the part is unusual among amateurs. The rollicking Millie will live long in the memory of her audience.[15]

Nellie May also directed several plays during her time at Fort Benning, including *This Thing Called Love*, in which her husband appeared.[16]

Patrick was selected to attend the U.S. Army Command and General Staff School at Fort Leavenworth, Kansas, beginning in August 1932. As he left the faculty of the Infantry School, Patrick joined a group of Marshall–era alumni who would occupy positions of high command and great responsibility during and after World War II: Bradley, Collins, Ridgway, Stilwell, Van Fleet, Bedell Smith, Terry Allen, Eddy, Cota, Huebner, Paul, Harding, Bolté, William Dean, and Almond. At least eleven of these alumni would join Patrick as commanders of divisions in World War II combat.[17]

CHAPTER 9

THE LEAVENWORTH AND WASHINGTON NATIONAL GUARD YEARS

As Patrick prepared to begin the intensive two–year course of study at the Command and General Staff School, the family moved into on–post quarters at Fort Leavenworth.[1]

In 1922, the Command and General Staff School was established at Fort Leavenworth, replacing the General Service Schools, which included the School of the Line and the General Staff School. The School of the Line was then renamed the Infantry and Cavalry School, the curriculum of which was structured around the duties of company–grade officers of the infantry and cavalry, with instruction also in international law and in military history; it was highly competitive. The General Staff School would train the best students graduating from the School of the Line for an additional year, for duty as General Staff Officers with tactical units and for higher tactical command. The Command and General Staff School, by contrast, would offer a one–year course emphasizing command and general staff duties in units ranging from reinforced brigade through army corps level. As such, instead of merely stressing general staff functions within tactical units, the faculty of this new school would place added emphasis on the aspects of command of these units.[2]

Because of the small size of the army between the two world wars, with its tactical units usually skeletonized, lacking essential equipment and frequently experiencing rapid turnover in key command personnel, officers had little chance to practice their profession under realistic training conditions. Army schools, therefore, provided the major opportunity for officers to gain professional experience. Attendance at the Command and General Staff School was a key part of that professionalizing experience. During the inter–war years, 3,677 officers graduated from one of the twenty–three courses offered at Leavenworth during that period.[3]

The faculty at the Command and General Staff School emphasized the solving of tactical problems, particularly at the division and corps operational levels. The aim of the instruction was to produce graduates with a common professional base, who were well–grounded in the basics of large–unit operations. The instructors required the students to solve increasingly complex tactical problems by detailed map study, and then prepare an "Estimate of the Situation" and, usually, a formal "Five Paragraph" written operations order.[4]

The first nine–month academic session consisted of over nine hundred hours of instruction, largely devoted to tactical principles and technique, command and staff procedures and principles, and logistics. The second academic session involved almost 1,400 hours, with greater emphasis on map maneuvers and problems. During this year the students also completed a research paper.[5]

The author has no record of the number of students beginning the course in 1932, but on September 4, 1933, at the beginning of its second year, Patrick's class contained 115 officers of the Regular Army and 3 officers of the United States Marine Corps. The faculty for that year included five officers who, like Patrick, would subsequently command divisions in World War II combat.[6]

Drawing on his own experience as an infantry company commander in combat in World War I, his time as a student at the Army Signal School, and his recent tour as instructor in signal communications at the Infantry School, Patrick completed a research paper entitled "The Training and Replacement of Infantry Signal Communication Personnel (Officers and Enlisted Men) in the Theater of Operations."

Pointing out that the World War I system of providing signal communications within the infantry division had failed miserably, Patrick argued persuasively in this well–written paper that infantry officers should receive sufficient communications training to enable them to coordinate and control signal communications in all units below division level.[7]

Patrick related his own experience at the Infantry School, where he had instituted an increase in the number of hours of instruction in communications for the Company Officers Class from about 30 hours to approximately 137 hours, based on the premise that the infantry officer must be as proficient in communications as he is in tactics and the employment of weapons. The Artillery School had emphasized this to its students prior to the war, and during combat the field artillery units had operated their own communications systems with organic personnel, and had enjoyed great success.[8]

In 1931, Patrick had begun an experimental communications course of 137 hours for the Company Officers class at the Infantry School. The course emphasized acquiring some facility in the use of Morse code, operation and repair of radios, and wire communications. By the end of the school year, a majority of the officers had demonstrated their ability to handle communications units by serving in various maneuvers as communications officers. Based on those results, Patrick recommended that the Infantry School give such a course in communications to all students at the school, and in time of war institute similar communications courses for new officers. The officer who reviewed Patrick's paper described it as "a most interesting discussion, of an important subject, of vital concern to the Army, and considerable educational value to all officers especially those of higher rank."[9]

During World War II and to the present day, the infantry division has utilized an internal communications system virtually identical to that recommended by Patrick. In division headquarters there is a Signal Corps officer who, during World War II, commanded the division signal company, and now commands the division signal battalion. At all lower levels within the division, an infantry officer detailed as the communication officer supervises and controls communication personnel and assets.[10]

The Patricks apparently continued their involvement with amateur theater while at Fort Leavenworth, as indicated by Nellie May's directing a comedy, *As Husbands Go*, on November 11, 1933.[11]

Patrick's class, numbering 115 Regular Army officers and 3 U.S. Marine Corps officers, graduated on June 15, 1934. Following his graduation Patrick received orders to report as an instructor with the 161st Infantry, Washington National Guard, at Spokane, Washington, where he reported on June 23. He initially was to have been assigned to Organized Reserves Headquarters in Hartford, Connecticut, but received a letter from the Chief's Office, offering him the position in Spokane. Although Patrick would have preferred to go to Hartford "for purely personal reasons, ... the letter put [him] in a position where [he] felt that [he] couldn't afford to refuse."[12]

The major duty of an instructor was to insure that National Guard units conducted their training in conformance with Regular Army doctrine, and that the units had met the standards that they were required to meet to maintain federal recognition. The instructors also served as resource people for the National Guard commanders and staff. Instructors were expected to attend the drills of the units for which they were responsible, and to accompany their units to annual training and command post exercises.[13]

In his "Annual Report" for 1933–1934, the Adjutant General of Washington wrote that the instructors assigned to his units were the finest soldiers available, selected by reason of special fitness for the detail. They consisted of commissioned and non-commissioned officers of long service and with wide experience, who had completed the courses of their respective army service schools, and were familiar with the latest technical and tactical advances of their respective branches. Many of the senior line instructors detailed for duty with the National Guard were officers who had served as instructors at the various advanced service schools and were particularly well qualified to bring the National Guard officers knowledge of the latest and most advanced techniques in the effective employment of manpower and materiel.[14]

Staying initially in a hotel in Spokane, the Patricks soon found a four–bedroom house, about $4^1/_2$ blocks from a school. On July 26, the day the family moved into the house, Patrick received orders to report to Camp Murray, near Tacoma, where the 161st Infantry was undergoing its annual training. Although the training period was almost over, Patrick did have the opportunity to meet the regimental officers. He returned home on July 30, but noted that he would have to return to Camp Murray in the near future for a two–week camp for division staff officers. At this juncture he commented that his new job would require a great deal of travel, "one thing I don't like about it."[15]

In the summer of 1935, Patrick, having been appointed Senior Instructor of the Washington National Guard in February 1935, attended the annual camps of the Washington National Guard and the California National Guard. A series of inspection trips followed these training periods. On completion of these inspections, Patrick participated in the Fourth Army Command Post Exercise at Fort Lewis, Washington, serving as a division umpire, one of the "pick and shovel men." He characterized the exercise as a "rather uninteresting fight [that] skipped the action of the covering forces and that made the entire play of the maneuver a series of frontal attacks." He believed that the principal value derived from the exercise by most of the involved officers was gaining familiarity with staff procedures. He also pointed out that little consideration was given to the logistical phase of the problem. Patrick stressed to Marshall that he would like to see a future exercise that emphasized logistics.[16]

Marshall replied that the latter's opinions on the recently concluded command post exercise were much in accord with his own impressions of a command post exercise in which he had participated in New Jersey, stating that these command post exercises were too often played out utilizing veteran troops, rather than using

> troops hastily raised towards war strength, men first under fire, supply and other service functions of Army Corps and Army conducted by improvised units. ... Tactics, and, to a certain extent, the strategy of handling these partially trained troops in the first campaign of a war is the great task of the Regular Army. ... This is not for general distribution.[17]

Few other records of Patrick's service with the Washington National Guard exist. On April 19–20, 1936, Patrick inspected Headquarters Company, 81st Infantry Brigade, Washington National Guard, Spokane, and recommended that the unit receive federal recognition.[18]

During the Christmas season, Patrick sent a Christmas greeting to his mother and his sister Alma and told them that he had been ill for a week with tonsillitis, and had been unable to do much Christmas shopping. He also revealed that he had been ordered to attend the Army War College in Washington, D.C., and that he and his family would probably leave Spokane in June or July 1936.[19]

CHAPTER 10

PREPARATION FOR HIGH COMMAND

Leaving Spokane in the early summer of 1936, the Patrick family motored across the country in a 1935 Ford. They stopped in Tell City to attend a family reunion, prior to going on to Fort Humphreys (now Fort Lesley J. McNair), Washington, D.C., where Patrick would begin his studies at the Army War College in July. The family established residence in a neighborhood close to Rock Creek Park in Washington.[1]

The Army War College, the motto of which is *"Prudens Futuri"* ("Providing for the Future"), is the army's senior service college, founded in 1903 during the tenure of Elihu Root as President Theodore Roosevelt's Secretary of War. The Grand Lodge of Masons, District of Columbia, laid the cornerstone of the War College building on February 21, 1903, using the trowel with which George Washington had laid the cornerstone of the nation's Capitol. Root gave the dedication address, beginning with a statement of the purpose of the Army War College:

> Not to promote war, but to preserve peace by intelligent and adequate preparation to repel aggression, this institution is founded.[2]

Root went on to describe that Army education was progressive, beginning with the post schools, then the various service schools, and finally the Army War College. From the graduates of the latter school would come the officers who would occupy the highest positions of leadership within the army. Candidates for attendance at the War College had to be at least captains, not be over fifty–one years of age, and have efficiency report ratings of at least "Excellent."[3]

The mission of the school, as defined in "War Department Regulation 350–5" (1927), was to train officers in field operations at the Army level and above, using the experience of the American army during World War I and to instruct them about the impact of political, economic, and social factors on the conduct of war, the duties of War Department General Staff, and the conduct of joint operations of the army and navy.[4]

The Army War College course of instruction was divided into two distinct phases:

> The first phase, "Preparation for War," required committees of students to prepare staff studies for various possible military operations, which the committees would then present to the assembled class, answering questions and defending their conclusions. The committees of which Patrick was a member during this phase prepared staff studies of the command system controlling operations in the Western Pacific as prescribed in Army War College War Plan–Orange, a War Department demobilization plan, and the organization of a communication zone in a contiguous theater. They also studied intelligence surveys of the major east European countries, and the national defense organizations of the main protagonists of World War I.[5]

> In the second, "Conduct of War" phase of the course, the class was divided into four groups. Patrick's group studied the IX Corps Area Mobilization Plan of 1933; the geographic, economic, political, and strategic effects of a war in the Pacific, including a map study of Alaska and the Aleutian Islands; and the organization of a theater of operations, developing a plan for the Southern Theater of Operations. The committee also wrote a hypothetical war plan.

In the concluding phase of the course, Patrick's committee joined the rest of the class in a strategic and tactical study of Civil War campaigns, including a "Staff Ride" to various Civil War Battlefields.[6]

The "Staff Ride" began on June 10, 1937, and included visits to Gettysburg, Antietam, Fredericksburg, Chancellorsville, the Wilderness, the Peninsula, Petersburg, Appomattox, the Shenandoah Valley, and Manassas campaign areas, and the Yorktown, Virginia, restoration site. The group returned to Washington on June 19.

At each of the battlefield or campaign sites, selected students presented features of the battle or campaign by oral narrative, in order to familiarize their fellow officers with the campaign or battle, and to bring out "lessons learned" from the action. Where possible, the students would make their presentations in pairs, one presenting a study to portray the Northern point of view, while the other officer would present his study from the Southern perspective. Patrick and his classmate, Major Wendell L. Clemenson, received General Thomas J. ("Stonewall") Jackson's 1862 Shenandoah Valley campaign as their assignment.

Clemenson covered the campaign through May 22, 1862. Patrick gave a detailed and comprehensive account of Jackson's decisive victories at Front Royal, May 23, and at Winchester, May 25. He concluded his presentation with a critical analysis of Jackson's tactics and of the strategic importance of the Valley Campaign.[7]

Patrick continued to display his dramatic talents while at the War College, playing the role of "General Skinnem" in the production, *A Morning in A.W.C.*, saluting the faculty, the wives, and the guests. The actors allegedly consisted of " 'Morons, Inebriates, and Aids [sic]' who, through the fortunate circumstances of comparatively 'chaste' E.R.'s [Efficiency Reports], have been priveleged [sic] to participate as students in the ARMY WAR COLLEGE COURSE, 1936–1937."[8]

Patrick graduated in June 1937, in a class of ninety–five. Fourteen of these graduates would lead divisions in World War II combat, and two, Patrick and Major James E. Wharton, would be among the three division commanders who would die in combat during that conflict.[9]

The Class of 1937 would join other Army War College alumni who came to fill practically all of the Army's high command and staff positions and many of those of the Army Air Forces during World War II. Indeed, fifty–nine of these men would become general officers, and five, Charles Bolté, Mark Clark, Muir Fairchild, Matthew Ridgway, and Walter Bedell Smith, would rise to the four–star grade of general.[10]

Since 1920, three army officers had been selected annually to attend the Naval War College at Newport, Rhode Island. The criteria for selection of those officers included a desire to attend the school, high academic ability, and "tact." Patrick was one of the officers selected to attend the Naval War College course of instruction that was to begin in July 1938.[11]

The Patrick family moved from the Rock Creek Park area of Washington, D.C., to Newport, Rhode Island, where Patrick began his studies at the Naval War College in July 1938. The family took up residence in a home on Red Cross Avenue there.[12]

The Naval War College conducted two courses simultaneously during the academic year: the Senior Course, which placed greater emphasis on strategy, and the Junior Course, which placed greater emphasis on tactics and minor strategy. Patrick became a student in the Senior Course.[13]

The staff and visiting lecturers presented the course material in a series of lectures, supplemented by exercises presented or conducted either by the staff or by the students themselves. Students were required to solve strategic and tactical problems, and then draw up plans to translate the military decision reached by this process into effective action. All students, participating in a command or staff capacity, would then play out the solution of the problem as a chart maneuver. The prime motive underlying these exercises was to develop in the students sound judgment and a firm grounding in the fundamentals of strategy.[14]

Visual presentations of the naval activities of World War I, particularly the operations of the Allied and German cruisers against the commerce of their opponents, provided further opportunities for the study of strategy and tactics.[15]

In addition to these naval studies, the students undertook studies in international law, economics, and foreign policies of the United States. Students of the Senior Class were required to demonstrate their familiarity with the latter subject by completing a thesis on a selected subject involving policy and international relations and their relation to strategy.[16]

Examination of the "Tentative List of Lectures and Presentations" reveals that lectures and staff presentations were held on a frequency varying from one day to three days weekly. The remaining class hours were presumably devoted to demonstration exercises, various operations problems, "quick decision" problems, maneuver problems, and thesis preparation.[17]

It appears that the year in Newport was one of the rare periods during which Patrick did not participate in any amateur theater activities, presumably because of the academic demands placed upon him. Nellie May, however, joined and became active in the "Torchbearers," a Newport theatrical group.[18]

Patrick graduated from the Naval War College in May 1938, and was ordered to Fort Sam Houston, Texas, to assume the position of Assistant Chief of Staff, G–3, Plans and Training Officer, Headquarters, Eighth Corps Area. On August 17, 1938, he received, by virtue of his position as Eighth Corps Area G–3, authority to switch the "crossed rifles" of the infantry branch on his uniform lapels to the coveted "star and eagle" of the General Staff Corps.[19]

CHAPTER 11

PRELUDE TO WAR

In June 1938, Patrick assumed his duties on the staff of Major General Herbert J. Brees, commanding general of the VIII Corps Area. As G–3, Patrick was responsible for all training plans generated at that headquarters, and for insuring that all subordinate units within the corps area developed and carried out their training plans in conformance with the directives of the corps area commander. The family moved into quarters on Staff Post at Fort Sam Houston.[1]

Shortly after arriving at Fort Sam Houston, Patrick found himself caught up in the planning for the extensive Third Army Maneuvers, scheduled for August 14–18, 1938. The maneuvers were to be conducted simultaneously at four separate locations: Camp Bullis, Texas; Fort Francis E. Warren, Wyoming; Fort Bliss, Texas; and Fort Huachuca, Arizona. The total of participating troops would be as follows:

1. Regular Army
   a. Officers: 731
   b. Enlisted men: 18,125
2. National Guard
   a. Officers: 1,529
   b. Enlisted men: 17,635
3. Reserve officers: 1,470
4. Umpires
   a. Regular Army
      (1) Officers: 178
      (2) Enlisted men: 154
   b. Reserve officers: 202

Patrick received orders to go to Fort Francis E. Warren, by way of Denver, on or about August 5, 1938, where he would observe the Third Army Maneuvers. No record of Patrick's activities at the maneuvers exists, however.[2]

Promoted to lieutenant colonel on June 12, 1939, Patrick continued a hectic schedule, traveling almost continually to observe the training of units within the vast area for which his headquarters was responsible. With the great increase in the strength of the active army in late 1940 as a result of the draft and the beginning mobilization of the National Guard, Patrick's responsibilities increased further, since a large share of the army was located on installations within the VIII Corps Area. He did express some concern over the frantic activities of his headquarters, stating that the plans for such a rapid expansion of the army and the training program were probably too ambitious, and pointing out that construction of the new camps was far behind schedule.

During his two years as G–3, he planned two large maneuvers, each of which involved from 50,000 to 70,000 troops, and for approximately half of whom Patrick and his staff were responsible for moving to and from Louisiana, where the maneuvers took place. During 1941, he was busily engaged visiting possible locations for future army installations in the states of Texas, Arizona, Oklahoma, New Mexico and Colorado. These sites were being chosen in anticipation of a full mobilization in case of war with Germany.[3]

In late 1940, Patrick learned that he was on a list of officers being considered by the War Department for appointment as chief of staff of the VIII Corps, activated at Fort Sam Houston on October 14, 1940. Although he did not receive the appointment, the mere fact that he was considered for this colonel's position while a junior lieutenant colonel indicated the high opinion of his abilities that his superiors held. However, on October 14, 1941, Patrick did pin on the eagles of a full colonel.[4]

Patrick's hectic schedule left him little time for his family or for recreational activities. However, on several occasions, he was able to get away for one or two days on duck–hunting and fishing trips.[5]

Patrick was planning to make a trip to Washington, D.C., in December 1941, during which he planned to visit briefly with his mother and other relatives in Tell City. However, the conference he was to attend was canceled at the last minute, and was rescheduled for January 12–17, 1942. Patrick planned to visit Tell City after the rescheduled conference, but the Pearl Harbor attack on December 7, 1941, and America's entry into the war, canceled that.[6]

Patrick commented that "this terrible deed the dirty Japs inflicted against us has put me into a siege of work such as I've never quite approached before." He and his staff were now working night and day, and, since December 9, had moved between seventy–five and one hundred trainloads of troops.

He told his mother of his family's Christmas plans, assuring her that despite his workload and the world situation they were "going to have a nice Xmas anyway." He lamented the fact that he and his family could not be together with his mother and other Tell City relatives that Christmas, but told his mother they would all get together "sometime after all this unpleasantness is over."

Patrick believed that he probably would be moved out for troop duty soon, and that older men would take over the jobs at Corps Area. This prediction soon became reality, when he received orders to report to Camp Barkeley, near Abilene, Texas, to assume command of the newly–activated 357th Infantry Regiment of the 90th Infantry Division.[7]

Patrick was not involved in any social or amateur theater activities at Fort Sam Houston or in San Antonio during his three and one-half years there. His hectic schedule and extensive traveling about the corps area most likely precluded his taking part in such activities. We do know that Nellie May busied herself with the "Gray Ladies," Red Cross volunteers who were working at the station hospital at Fort Sam Houston, and proudly told Chief of Staff General George C. Marshall of her volunteer activities, inviting him to attend her "Gray Lady" graduation ceremony on February 6, 1941.[8]

The 357th Infantry Regiment was activated at Camp Barkeley, Texas, on March 25, 1942. Most of the officer cadre came from the 6th Infantry Division at Fort Leonard Wood, Missouri, and the 33d Infantry Division at Camp Forrest, Tennessee. The enlisted cadre came entirely from the 6th Infantry Division.[9]

The regiment was brought to strength by recruits fresh from the reception centers. Destined to fight together, they would receive their infantry training together. Although they were from all over the United States, most came from the reception centers at Camp Wolters and Fort Sam Houston, Texas, and Fort Sill, Oklahoma.[10]

Patrick became the 357th Infantry Regiment's first World War II commander on the date of the regiment's activation. In April, he initiated an intensive basic training program for the 158 officers and 3,373 enlisted men of the regiment, requiring them to spend much of their time in the field. In addition to insisting on high standards of performance in military training, Patrick stressed physical conditioning, and within a few months the troops were taking road marches of up to fifteen miles with full field equipment. On September 15, 1942, the 357th Infantry was motorized, in conformance with an order requiring the conversion of a limited number of infantry divisions into motorized divisions.[11]

During Patrick's time as regimental commander, Major General Henry Terrell, Jr., the commander of the 90th Division, repeatedly asserted that the 357th Infantry Regiment was the "best in the division," and that Patrick was "his best regimental commander." In September, Terrell told Patrick that he had been recommended for promotion to brigadier general, but, unfortunately, had not been selected. When Patrick received orders transferring him to Washington, D.C., in November, Terrell attempted to have the War Department revoke the order and keep Patrick in the division, but his attempt was unsuccessful.[12]

On November 20, 1942, Lieutenant Colonel John W. Sheehy assumed command of the 357th Infantry Regiment vice Patrick. The latter's contributions to the 357th were summarized as follows:

> His dynamic personality, tactical knowledge, and conscientious effort had a great deal to do with the high standard of proficiency gained by the Regiment during its initial training. Colonel Patrick has never been forgotten by the original men who knew him.[13]

CHAPTER 12

ON ADMIRAL
HALSEY'S STAFF

Leaving Camp Barkeley, Patrick went to Washington, D.C., where he was ordered to report for duty on the staff of Vice Admiral William F. Halsey, Jr., commander, South Pacific Area (COMSOPAC). Halsey, like Patrick, was a graduate of both the Army War College and the Naval War College.[1]

For the conduct of operations in the South Pacific at the outset of the war, the Joint Chiefs of Staff had established two separate commands: the Southwest Pacific Area (SWPA), embracing the Philippine Islands, the South China Sea, the Gulf of Siam, the Netherlands East Indies (except Sumatra), the Solomon Islands, Australia, and the waters to the south, commanded by General Douglas MacArthur; and the South Pacific Area (SOPAC), including New Zealand, New Caledonia, and the New Hebrides, Santa Cruz, Fiji, Samoan, Tongan, Cook, and Society Islands, commanded initially by Vice Admiral Robert L. Ghormley, whom Halsey succeeded on October 18, 1942.[2]

The first operation in which SOPAC was to participate would be the seizure of Tulagi, Guadalcanal, and Florida in the Solomon Islands. Ghormley would exercise strategic control over the forces in this operation.[3]

On August 7, 1942, units of the 1st, 2d, and 5th Regiments, U.S. Marine Corps, carried out landings on the islands of Florida, Tulagi, Gavutu, and Guadalcanal, beginning the first American counteroffensive in the Pacific area. The Guadalcanal campaign would be long and bloody, fought on some of the most hostile terrain on earth; the Americans would not secure the island of Guadalcanal itself until February 9, 1943. By that time a total of approximately 60,000 marines and soldiers had been deployed on

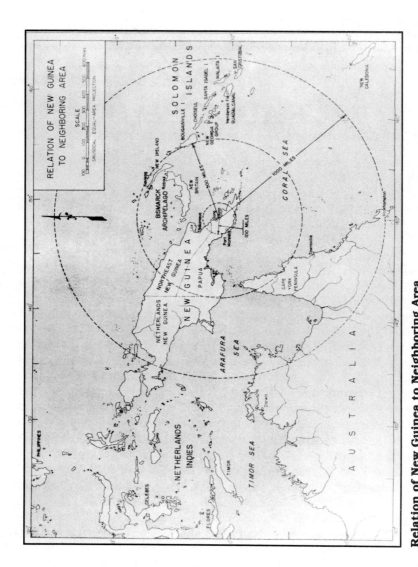

Relation of New Guinea to Neighboring Area
(Papuan Campaign: The Buna-Sanananda Operation, 16 November 1942-43 January, 1943, inside back cover)

Guadalcanal, of whom about 1,600 were killed in action and 4,245 were wounded. The Japanese suffered more than 14,800 killed or missing, with 9,000 dead of disease.[4]

As COMSOPAC, Ghormley had not established a ground command, and his headquarters, composed almost entirely of naval officers, did the planning for and retained control over all army and marine corps elements in the theater. Lieutenant General Millard F. Harmon, commander, U.S. Army Forces in SOPAC, felt that Ghormley's staff had not given enough emphasis to air power and did not sufficiently appreciate the importance of logistics in the Guadalcanal operation, a conclusion echoed to Marshall by General Henry H. Arnold, commander, U.S. Army Air Forces, in early October 1942. A few days later Marshall recommended to Admiral Ernest J. King, Chief of Naval Operations, that army officers be assigned to the staff of a naval officer exercising unity of command and that he, Marshall, select the officers for such assignment. King would likewise detail naval officers to army commands. Both men so informed the designated theater commanders and proceeded to select the officers for these assignments.

This move coincided with Halsey's becoming COMSOPAC. Halsey firmly insisted on the " 'one force' " principle, and began immediately to give Harmon and his staff more responsibility in the conduct of operations.[5]

In December 1942, Patrick joined the war plans section of Halsey's staff.[6] The nerve center of the Guadalcanal operation was at Nouméa, New Caledonia, some one thousand miles south–southeast of Guadalcanal. Halsey's chief of staff was Captain Miles Browning, USN, who directed fifteen seasoned staff officers and fifty navy enlisted men.[7] Patrick assured his family that he was "quite safe," although because of wartime censorship regulations he obviously could not reveal to them that he was in Nouméa. However, he complained that his job was "inactive to the point of boredom."[8]

As early as November 3, Halsey had recognized that the marines should be relieved because of their heavy losses, the vast majority from disease. On November 30, the Joint Chiefs of Staff ordered the 25th Infantry Division to move from Hawaii to Guadalcanal, to join two regiments of the army's Americal Division that had been deployed to Guadalcanal in October and mid–November to reinforce the marines, then organized as the 1st Marine Division. The Army troops were to be under the command of Major General Alexander M. Patch, USA, who would replace Major General Alexander A. Vandegrift, USMC, as the director of tactical operations on Guadalcanal. By the end of December, Halsey had withdrawn all of the marines from Guadalcanal, and the army had assumed responsibility for all tactical operations on the island.[9]

On March 7, Patrick wrote to Lieutenant General Walter Krueger, who in February had arrived in Brisbane, Australia, where he was commanding the newly–created Sixth Army. Patrick told Krueger that he had been "uneasy" about leaving the 357th Infantry Regiment, but "the anticipation of new and interesting things that might happen to me provided plenty of incentive to get going." He said that Terrell had expressed to him Krueger's concern that an assignment such as the one at Nouméa might cause him (Patrick) to become "hopelessly sidetracked away from the Army. I'm afraid your prediction has come true."

Patrick then went on to say that his job on Halsey's staff was "more or less nominal and a duplication of an existing arrangement of which the War Department was evidently unaware."[10] Although he admitted that he was enjoying himself there, Patrick felt that he was not contributing much toward winning the war.

He concluded by expressing his desire to "get back into the Army," and to serve under Krueger's command, where, although preferring command of a tactical unit, he would "take anything I can get." He then asked Krueger to request the War Department to "detail me over to your army."[11]

Krueger replied on June 7 that he would like very much to have him serve with Sixth Army, but told him that all of his past efforts to effect such a transfer had been in vain. In conclusion Krueger stated his hope that Patrick's "wish be fulfilled in the not too distant future."[12]

Patrick found out in May that his appointment to the rank of brigadier general had been sent to the Senate for confirmation, and that the news had come as a big surprise to him. However, while the news was "very pleasant to take, [it] sort of lacked the kick that I used to think I'd get if and when I was promoted to Brigadier General." He had been recommended for promotion to that grade in September 1942, while commanding the 357th Infantry Regiment, but was not selected by the promotion board. Nellie May told him that in February 1943, Terrell, his former division commander, had recommended that the War Department transfer Patrick back to the 90th Infantry Division to fill a vacancy for brigadier general, but the War Department had refused to do so.

Discontented with his duties on the COMSOPAC staff, Patrick determined

> to eventually get out of the job, get another one with troops and prove that I had promotion coming. To a certain extent the promotion left me cold. I had

made up my mind to get it the hard way and I was just a little disappointed at not getting a chance to get it that way.[13]

Patrick's often–expressed desire to leave the COMSOPAC staff became a reality the next month. The Sixth Army chief of staff, Brigadier General George Honnen, had become ill, necessitating his evacuation to the United States. Krueger selected Patrick, recently promoted to brigadier general, to succeed Honnen, effective June 21, 1943, just fourteen days after his letter to Patrick in which he had expressed his hope that Patrick's "wish to serve again with army troops may be fulfilled in the not too distant future." Patrick would join Sixth Army at its forward headquarters at Milne Bay, on the eastern tip of New Guinea.[14]

CHAPTER 13

CHIEF OF STAFF,
ALAMO FORCE

On January 26, 1943, the War Department directed Lieutenant General Walter Krueger, then commanding the Third Army at Fort Sam Houston, to activate the Sixth Army at the same location. To form the Sixth Army staff, Krueger transferred the key members of his Third Army staff, both officers and enlisted, to Sixth Army. Shortly thereafter, Krueger and his chief of staff, Brigadier General George Honnen, moved with the advance echelon of Sixth Army headquarters to Brisbane, Australia, arriving there on February 7, 1943. By February 16, the remainder of the advance echelon had arrived in Brisbane. The rear echelon, under command of the deputy chief of staff, Colonel George H. Decker, sailed from San Francisco on March 29, 1943, and arrived at Brisbane on April 17. The Sixth Army headquarters was established at Camp Columbia, about nine miles east of Brisbane.[1]

Initially making up Sixth Army were the 1st Marine Division, recently withdrawn from Guadalcanal to Melbourne; I Corps, comprised of the 32d Infantry Division, recently returned from action in New Guinea and located near Brisbane, and the 41st Infantry Division in the Dobodura area of New Guinea; the 503d Parachute Infantry Regiment near Cairns, Australia; the 158th Infantry Regiment near Port Moresby, New Guinea; the 2d Engineer Special Brigade at Rockhampton and Cairns, Australia; and antiaircraft and field artillery units in New Guinea and Australia. A few months later the 24th Infantry Division and the 1st Cavalry Division also became a part of Sixth Army.[2]

Krueger immediately initiated an intensive training program in jungle warfare, amphibious operations, and troop management, with emphasis on the health and welfare of his troops. He particularly emphasized preventive medicine, since malaria had been a serious problem on both Guadalcanal and New Guinea. Because of the tremendous distances over which the command was scattered, the inspection of the Sixth Army troops and the supervision of their training activities posed considerable difficulties for Krueger and his staff, and necessitated their spending a great deal of time traveling to their scattered units.[3]

The command structure in which Krueger found himself was very complex. In overall command of the Southwest Pacific Area (SWPA) was General Douglas MacArthur. Under MacArthur were four major commands: United States Army Forces, Far East (USAFFE), an administrative command to which all U.S. Army forces in the area were assigned; Allied Land Forces, commanded by General Sir Thomas A. Blamey, Australian Army; Allied Air Forces, commanded by Lieutenant General George C. Kenney, U.S. Army Air Force; and Allied Naval Forces, commanded by Vice Admiral Arthur S. Carpender, U.S. Navy. MacArthur retained the authority to assign his subordinate tactical ground, air, and naval commands to the operational control of the commanders of Allied Land Forces, Allied Air Forces, or Allied Naval Forces, or to his General Headquarters (GHQ) reserve.[4]

Further complicating this already awkward command structure was MacArthur's reluctance to place any American units under operational control of Blamey's Allied Land Forces during the planned actions in SWPA. To obviate any necessity for a transfer of American forces to the control of a non–American commander, MacArthur directed Krueger to create an independent tactical headquarters, originally designated as Escalator Force, but later known by the nonsecret designation, Alamo Force. Sixth Army as such would not conduct tactical operations; instead, these operations would be carried out by Alamo Force, composed of Sixth Army units and other units as needed. Since sufficient staff personnel were not available for a separate Alamo staff, Krueger found it necessary, as Alamo Force commander, to use the Sixth Army staff as his Alamo Force staff.[5]

Although MacArthur never divulged to Krueger his reasons for creating Alamo Force, the latter soon realized that it was a MacArthur ploy to avoid placing Sixth Army under operational control of the commanding general, Allied Land Forces, although that army formed part of those forces. Since American army units, under Alamo Force, would far outnumber other Allied forces in SWPA, this arrangement of command effectively reduced Blamey's status to that of little more than a task force commander.[6]

That command arrangement required the Sixth Army staff to operate in a dual capacity, thus increasing its workload. Further, although "Sixth Army provided the commander, the staff, and practically all the troops for Alamo Force, the arrangement inevitably deprived Sixth Army of the credit for operations which in reality it conducted in the guise of Alamo Force." That unwieldy command structure would persist in SWPA until September 1944, "and produce a great many perplexing difficulties."[7]

On May 6, 1943, GHQ issued the general plan that was designed to ensure the seizure or neutralization of Rabaul (Operation CARTWHEEL),[8] the great Japanese stronghold on the northeastern tip of New Britain. MacArthur envisioned a double envelopment, SOPAC forces advancing on the right through the Solomon Islands, and SWPA forces advancing in the center and on the left. Alamo Force was to seize and occupy Kiriwina and Woodlark islands in the Solomon Sea, north of the eastern tip of New Guinea, and then seize and occupy western New Britain. The operations were dubbed CHRONICLE and DEXTERITY, respectively.

Now operating from his advance command post at Milne Bay, which he had established in mid–June 1943, Krueger directed the 158th Regimental Combat Team(-) to seize and defend Kiriwina Island, and the 112th Cavalry Regimental Combat Team to carry out a like mission on Woodlark Island; both attacks would take place on June 30, 1943. The two units carried out these attacks successfully, meeting no Japanese ground opposition. Airfield construction on the islands began immediately, although torrential rains and a shortage of heavy engineering equipment retarded construction, especially on Kiriwina Island.[9]

Just prior to the launching of CHRONICLE, Krueger's chief of staff, Honnen, became ill, and required evacuation to the United States. Krueger contacted COMSOPAC, and requested of Halsey that Patrick be assigned to Sixth Army as Honnen's replacement. Halsey "wired the War Department and they said 'OK' so [Patrick] left at once," arriving at Brisbane in time to serve as chief of staff for Alamo Force's first operations.[10]

By August, Patrick was no longer in Australia, but had been "up north of there for about a month," presumably at Alamo Force headquarters at Milne Bay. He noted that it had rained constantly for ten days, causing everything to develop mildew. He was living in a native house that served as a combination office and living quarters. He was eating well and was in perfect health, but expressed concern that his family in Tell City was "having a little difficulty with rationing."[11]

MacArthur ordered on September 22 that Alamo Force be prepared to seize the Cape Gloucester area on the north coast of New Britain, neutralize Gasmata on the southern coast of the island, "establish control over such adjacent islands and parts of western New Britain as to insure uninterrupted operations by our air forces from Cape Gloucester," and be prepared to participate in the capture of Rabaul. Emergency airfields were to have been established in the vicinity of Lindenhafen Plantation near Gasmata, but when this area was found to be unsuitable for airfield development, GHQ canceled the Gasmata operation, and directed that a landing be made on Arawe Peninsula instead. The attack on Arawe, a peninsula projecting from the southwest tip of New Britain, was to be a diversion to draw the enemy's attention away from the main landings at Cape Gloucester.[12]

Because of the increasing congestion at Milne Bay, Krueger, on October 21, moved his Alamo Force headquarters to Goodenough Island, lying between the southeastern top of New Guinea and Kiriwina Island, from where he and his staff would coordinate DEXTERITY, which called for the assault on Arawe to take place on December 15, and for the assault at Cape Gloucester to follow on December 26. The 112th Cavalry Regimental Combat Team (Reinf), commanded by Brigadier General Julian W. Cunningham, would seize the Arawe Peninsula. The Cape Gloucester Task Force would be made up of units from the 1st Marine Division, the 12th Marine Defense Battalion, and supporting engineer, artillery, and medical and service units, under command of Major General William H. Rupertus, USMC. The 32d Infantry Division, less the 126th Regimental Combat Team, would serve as Alamo Force reserve.[13] As chief of staff, Patrick would be the coordinator of the Alamo Force staff as they prepared the plans for these operations. He would find it necessary to become deeply involved in solving personnel and administration problems, in preparing intelligence estimates, in writing operation plans, and in providing for and coordinating the massive logistical support required for the forces.

Patrick soon found his new position to be a "pretty big job," and during the coming months would tell his family of the long hours of work required to fulfill his duties as an army chief of staff. Sleep became a rare and precious commodity: he seldom got to bed before midnight, and arose early each morning; one day blended into another, as he soon found himself directing the staff in the planning of multiple operations simultaneously. The long and extended trips he took to coordinate with higher headquarters and to observe Sixth Army operations were especially fatiguing. He likened his job to that of running a four–ring circus. Still, despite the hardships, Patrick rejoiced that he was back with the army. In mid–October, he told them that he had not had a single day off since his hospitalization for a tropical fever in New Caledonia the previous February, while serving on Halsey's staff. He declared that "war isn't anything pleasant, [and] this war is especially unpleasant." Although his memories of his experiences in World War I "were all pleasant," he stated that this war was entirely different, and that he had not "had a good time," and knew of no one else who had.[14]

However, Patrick continued to express his sense of satisfaction with the job that he and others in SWPA were performing. Although lamenting that the troops in SWPA appeared to be playing "second fiddle" to the operations in Europe, he proudly pointed out that

> the operations of the Army and Navy in this area of the world will be second to none. The things that are being done out here—movement of troops and supplies to widely separated points in this vast area—establishing ports and docks for ships, covered storage for supplies airfields and roads—all in virgin jungle, mosquito infested territory, are going to make some interesting reading some time [sic].[15]

In the midst of his hectic schedule, Patrick learned that his son, Eddie, was planning to enlist in the U.S. Navy on his eighteenth birthday, July 8, 1944. He expressed concern about Eddie's neglecting his school studies as he concentrated on his upcoming enlistment. He said, however, that he and Nellie May had resigned themselves to Eddie's decision, noting that there was nothing either of them could do about it, and that he, his father, did not "want to make a sissy out of him." Patrick then went on to express his hope that Eddie would live "through it all, because he really is a nice boy."[16]

In late November, the Alamo Force headquarters on Goodenough Island enjoyed a brief respite from its intensive labors when actor Gary Cooper and actresses Una Merkel and Phyllis Brooks visited and entertained them and the troops in the area. Patrick commented that "on the whole they are very nice people," describing Brooks as "rather young and a bit giddy," Merkel as "very quiet and entirely sensible," and Cooper as acting "in real life exactly like he acts on the screen," chewing gum and discussing "most any subject with you just like he does in the pictures."[17]

Also during the time leading up to the execution of DEXTERITY, General George C. Marshall, Chief of Staff, U. S. Army, visited

Commanders of SWPA land, sea, and air forces, assembled at Alamo Force Headquarters, Goodenough Island, New Guinea, Dec. 12-16, 1943, for a discussion of operations against the Admiralties. Brig. Gen. Edwin D. Patrick is fourth from the right; Lt. Gen. Walter Krueger is second from the left.

(Courtesy of MacArthur Memorial, Norfolk, Va.)

Brig. Gen. Edwin D. Patrick, Chief of Staff, Sixth Army, with Brig. Gen. Julian W. Cunningham, Commander, 112th Cavalry RCT, and Lieut. Col. Philip Hooper, Arawe, New Britain, Jan. 16, 1944.

(U.S. Army photo)

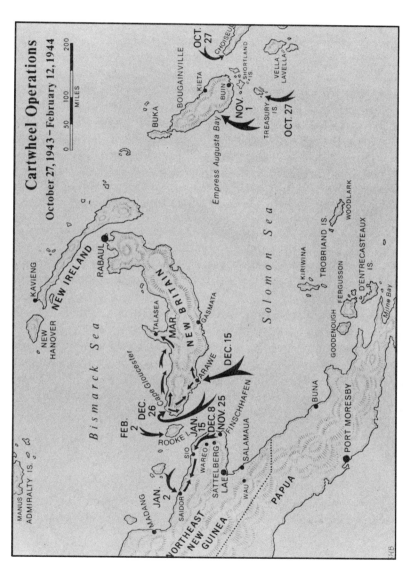

Cartwheel Operations, October 27, 1943 - February 12, 1944

(James, *The Years of MacArthur*, 338)

the Alamo Force headquarters. In a subsequent letter, Marshall told Nellie May that he had visited with her husband, and assured her that "he was in fine health and spirits, and ... enjoying his present assignment."[18]

The intensive planning of the Alamo Force staff, under Patrick's direction, culminated in the landings on Arawe Peninsula and Cape Gloucester on December 15 and December 26, 1943, respectively.

The Arawe task force met little opposition on landing, and soon secured its initial objectives. Against little ground resistance, but fairly heavy Japanese air attacks, Cunningham's troops continued their advance northeastward. Meeting the first heavy resistance on Christmas Day, Cunningham called for and received reinforcements, and was able to stabilize his lines. On January 16, 1944, Cunningham launched an attack, led by tanks from the 1st Marine Division, that completely cleared the area of the enemy. On February 10, the Arawe forces linked up with the marines who had landed at Cape Gloucester.

The Cape Gloucester operation entailed the landing of two regimental combat teams (basically reinforced regiments) of the 1st Marine Division at two beaches on the northeast coast of Cape Gloucester, with a simultaneous landing of a reinforced marine battalion on the west coast of the cape to cut off any Japanese attempting to escape southward. The two regimental combat teams were then to move to the northwest to capture airfields at the northern tip of the cape, at the same time expanding their beachhead to the southeast and south.

The marines made successful landings, after one week of preliminary air bombardment and heavy aerial and naval bombardment on D–day. Although impeded by increasing Japanese resistance and torrential rains, the marines seized the airfield objective on December 30. Meeting little resistance, the landing team that had assaulted the west coast of the cape linked up with the other marines in the airfield area on January 5.

Having broken the principal organized Japanese resistance, the marines continued to move southward and westward, linking up with the Arawe task force. This linkup virtually cleared Japanese forces from western New Britain.[19]

On December 17, in the midst of the execution of DEXTERITY, MacArthur directed Alamo Force to mount an additional mission, the seizing of Saidor on the northeast coast of New Guinea at the base of the Huon Peninsula. This operation was to take advantage of the success that the Australian forces had gained in their operations at Salamana, Lae, and Finschhafen on the New Guinea coast. The seizure of Saidor would block a key escape route for Japanese troops withdrawing from the Huon Peninsula in the face of the advancing Australians. The assault was to take place on January 2, 1944.

Patrick and his staff immediately began their planning for this new operation, and selected Brigadier General Clarence A. Martin's 126th Regimental Combat Team to carry out the assault. His assault force of some 7,500 troops successfully landed on January 2, and quickly seized the Saidor airfield, which at the time was unserviceable. The perimeter established by January 5 effectively blocked the coastal retreat route of the Japanese withdrawing from the Huon peninsula, forcing them to utilize the inland jungle trails, where unknown numbers perished of disease and starvation.[20]

DEXTERITY was, in Krueger's opinion, "a complete success." The Arawe and Cape Gloucester operations had cleared western New Britain of Japanese forces, placed Allied forces in a position to threaten Rabaul, provided additional airfields to support continuing operations, and gave the Allies control of the Vitiaz Strait leading from the Solomon Sea into the Bismarck Sea. The Saidor operation exploited these successes, protected the left flank of Alamo Force and completed the encirclement and destruction of the Japanese forces trapped on the Huon Peninsula. The development of the airfield at Saidor enabled the Allies to bring additional pressure to bear on the Japanese strongholds at Madang and Finschhafen.[21]

Krueger then went on to praise the effective planning by Patrick's Alamo Force staff, and their collaboration with representatives of Allied naval forces and the U.S. Fifth Air Force, insuring the close liaison among the three services and the naval and air support for the ground forces that contributed so greatly to the success of DEXTERITY.[22]

It appears to the author that Patrick's first operational planning as chief of staff of Alamo Force–Sixth Army should be regarded as a success. Alamo Force achieved all objectives established by GHQ, there were no major setbacks, and both Krueger and MacArthur were well satisfied with the planning and conduct of this complex three–pronged operation. Those long hours of study at the Command and General Staff School, the Army War College, and the Naval War College were at last beginning to translate into successes on the battlefield. Patrick modestly admitted to his mother and his sister, Clara, when commenting to them on the exploits of his army, that it had done "pretty well" However, he later lamented that "we deserve to get a little more publicity because we are doing practically the whole job here now, but it has to be passed around a little and we don't always get the credit."[23]

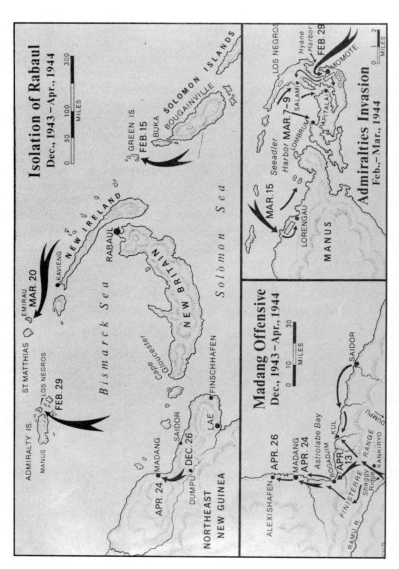

Isolation of Rabaul, Dec., 1943 - Apr., 1944, Madang Offensive, Dec., 1943 - Apr., 1944, and Admiralties Invasion, Feb., - Mar., 1944

(James, *The Years of MacArthur*, 378)

On December 24, 1943, Krueger, in order to exercise more effective control over the ongoing DEXTERITY operation, moved his headquarters from Goodenough Island to Cape Cretin, just south of Finschhafen, New Guinea. The Rear Echelon, Headquarters, Sixth Army, moved from Australia to Cape Cretin also.[24]

MacArthur next directed Krueger to have his Alamo Force seize Seeadler Harbor in the Admiralty Islands to establish a naval base there, and capture Lorengau and Momote airfields on the islands of Los Negros and Manus, respectively, within the Admiralties. MacArthur had chosen the Admiralties because their central location between Rabaul and the northern coast of New Guinea, excellent harbor off the north coast of Los Negros Island, and the two airfields on Manus and Los Negros Islands marked these islands as a natural air and naval base to support his planned upcoming operation along the northern coast of New Guinea.[25]

In 1943, MacArthur had named the Philippines as the final objective for his SWPA forces, planning to land in Mindanao in early 1945. To support the landing, MacArthur needed air bases from which land–based bombers could reach the Philippines, and settled on the northern coast of New Guinea as the location for these bases. He planned to bypass Japanese garrisons whenever possible, thereby reducing Allied casualties and increasing the speed of the drive along the coast. Lacking precise information about Japanese deployments along the coast, MacArthur's original plan called for an attack against strongly defended Hansa Bay on February 1, 1944, with successive attacks on Hollandia on June 1, Geelvink Bay on August 15, and the Vogelkop Peninsula on October 1. On December 1 his forces would then assault either Morotai or Halmahera, which lie approximately midway between the Vogelkop Peninsula and Mindanao.

However, in early February MacArthur received a message from his ULTRA intelligence unit, the Central Bureau, that dramatically altered his plans and timetable.[26] The message revealed that Lieutenant General Imamura Hitoshi, commander of the Eighth Area Army at Rabaul, intended to strengthen the forces in the Admiralties, New Ireland, and New Guinea; Lieutenant General Adachi Hatazo was strengthening his forces at Hansa Bay in anticipation of Allied landings there; a division was reconstituting at Wewak; and the defenses at Hollandia needed improvement. Armed with this information, Major General Charles A. Willoughby, MacArthur's G–2, recommended to MacArthur that he bypass Hansa Bay and attack Hollandia six months early. MacArthur quickly agreed. However, the assault on Hollandia necessitated the immediate seizure of the Admiralties.[27]

The operation, code–named BREWER, initially called for the 1st Cavalry Division to seize the islands by April 1, and Allied fliers had accordingly been softening up Los Negros and Manus. In late February, Allied fliers reported no signs of enemy activity on the islands, leading General George C. Kenney, commanding the Allied Air Forces, to recommend an immediate landing on Los Negros. MacArthur decided to risk a reconnaissance in force not later than February 29.[28]

However, Willoughby questioned Kenney's estimate of Japanese strength on Los Negros and Manus. In January ULTRA data had led him to estimate that some 3,250 Japanese troops were in the Admiralty Islands, and he felt that by late February the enemy strength was probably over four thousand. The report of advance scout patrols sent to Los Negros two days before the assault that the island " 'was lousy with Japs' " confirmed Willoughby's estimate. Although his radio traffic betrayed him, Colonel Ezaki Yoshio, overall commander in the Admiralties, had masterfully concealed his troops, leading to Kenney's mistaken estimate of enemy strength.[29]

Since February 13, Patrick and his staff had been planning, in cooperation with naval and air forces, to secure Seeadler Harbor, and had selected Major General Innis P. Swift's 1st Cavalry Division (Reinf) to carry out the mission on April 1, attacking from the north through the harbor. However, the sudden decision to attack Los Negros necessitated MacArthur to order the assault from the east, through Hayne Harbor. When notified on February 26 of the change in the landing site on Los Negros, Swift had virtually completed his operation plan. However, on February 27, Swift, after a remarkable display of planning expertise and flexibility by his staff, submitted his revised plan, calling for a reinforced squadron (battalion) of his division to make the landing from the east.

Ezaki too expected that the Americans would attack from the north, through Seeadler Harbor, feeling that Hayne Harbor on the east was too narrow for a large–scale landing. He therefore concentrated most of his troops in the north.

Swift's force landed on February 29, taking the enemy by surprise. The first wave met virtually no resistance, but the follow–on waves met heavier fire. However, after $4^1/_2$ hours the entire squadron was ashore, and soon seized the Momote airfield. Enemy counterattacks took place on March 1-2, but the troops held. Reinforcements followed on, and after intermittently heavy fighting, Swift's forces secured Los Negros on March 22.[30]

On March 2, naval vessels had attempted to enter Seeadler Harbor, but enemy fire prevented their doing so. However, after fire from supporting cruisers, the naval force entered and secured the harbor on March 8.

Swift, on March 15, dispatched a task force to seize the Lorengau airfield on adjacent Manus Island. Meeting only slight resistance, the cavalrymen captured the airfield on that day, and on April 1 had secured the island.[31]

The successful conclusion of BREWER vindicated ULTRA. Willoughby's estimate of 4,000 enemy troops in the Admiralties was remarkably close to the estimated 3,300 enemy casualties inflicted by the 1st Cavalry Division.[32]

With the Admiralty Islands now in their hands, the men of Alamo Force were in a "commanding position to complete the isolation of Kavieng [on New Ireland] and Rabaul." Again, the staff of Alamo Force and its subordinate commanders and their staffs had performed successfully. Worthy of mention is the rapidity with which the staffs were able to comply with the last–minute change in operation plans necessitated by the ULTRA data, and to mount successfully an entirely new operation just three days later. The fruits of these officers' earlier studies and of ULTRA were now being reaped on the battlefield. Costly assaults against the strongholds of Rabaul and Kavieng could be avoided, and operations could now be launched against the Japanese forces along the northern coast of New Guinea, with the rear and right flanks of the Allied forces now secure from enemy attack.[33]

In the meantime, Krueger's Alamo Force had increased in size. The 40th Infantry Division replaced the 1st Marine Division, which was returned to navy control; the 24th Infantry Division concentrated on Goodenough Island; and the 41st Infantry Division moved into the Cape Cretin area. The latter two divisions were to carry out the assault at Hollandia, a daring move made possible by ULTRA that would bypass and isolate major enemy strongholds at Hansa Bay and Wewak.[34]

On March 5, MacArthur alerted Krueger to be prepared to carry out the Hollandia operation, and two days later Alamo Force received orders directing it to seize Hollandia and Aitape, about 125 miles east–southeast of Hollandia. Willoughby, relying on ULTRA, estimated 16,297 enemy to be at Hollandia and Aitape, approximately 12,000 of these at Hollandia; in truth there were 16,000 men at Hollandia, but, as Willoughby correctly surmised, the units were overwhelmingly service, base defense, construction, and air service elements. Willoughby felt that the Japanese had no more than one combat battalion at Hollandia.[35]

At Cape Cretin, Patrick and his staff began planning on March 5 to seize the areas, establish control over the airfields there, assist the Allied Naval Forces in establishing naval facilities in the

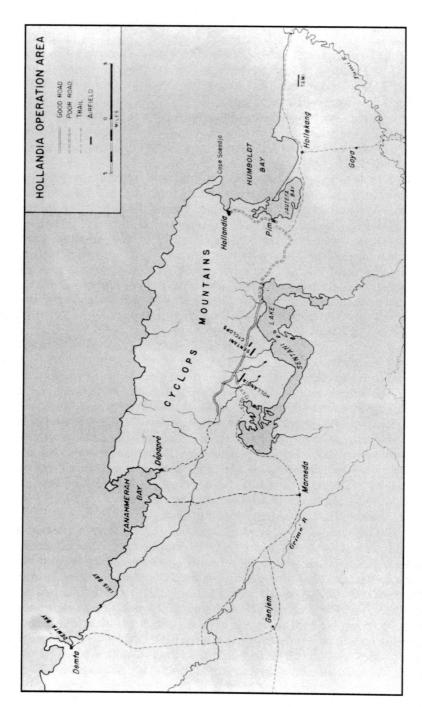

Hollandia Operation Area

(Smith, *Approach to the Philippines*, 17)

Humboldt Bay–Tanahmerah Bay area, and be prepared to continue offensive operations to the west.

The assault force for the Hollandia area was to be I Corps, commanded by Lieutenant General Robert A. Eichelberger, and composed of the 24th and 41st Infantry Divisions, the latter less its 163d Infantry Regiment. The 163d Infantry would form the nucleus of the 163d Regimental Combat Team (RCT), commanded by Brigadier General Jens A. Doe, and would seize and rehabilitate the airfields in the Aitape area. Both landings were to take place on April 22, 1944.

Humboldt Bay lies to the east of a broad but shallow peninsula containing the Cyclops Mountains, and provides an excellent anchorage. Some twenty–five miles west of Humboldt Bay is Tanahmerah Bay, which forms the western edge of the Cyclops Mountains peninsula, and which is a much inferior harbor. The 24th Division was to invade through Tanahmerah Bay, while the 41st Division would invade through Humboldt Bay, both divisions then driving toward the airfields lying south of the Cyclops Mountains. The operation received the code name RECKLESS. MacArthur approved Alamo Force's plan for the operation on April 10. In a radiogram to Krueger, MacArthur stated that he considered " 'Alamo Plan for Reckless excellent and a credit to all concerned. It should win without question.' "[36]

During the planning phase, the enemy radio traffic indicated that the Japanese had not moved any forces west of Wewak, and that the only strategic reserve was located at Sarmi, 150 miles west of Hollandia. Hoping to mislead the enemy of their plan to bypass Hansa Bay, the Allies staged air raids and reconnaissance flights in the Hansa–Madang area, and stationed torpedo boats off Hansa Bay. On April 20 and 21, the Japanese Eighth Area Army signaled that the American landings would most likely be at Wewak or the Ninigo Islands north of New Guinea, and that there were no clear indications of a landing at Hollandia.[37]

The landings on April 22 were a complete surprise to the enemy. The 24th Division made an unopposed landing at Tanahmerah Bay, and quickly advanced southeastward toward the airfields. Landing at Humboldt Bay, the 41st Division advanced rapidly inland, seizing Hollandia town and continuing its drive westward to the airfields. On April 27 the two divisions joined forces, completely securing the three airfields, on which the Americans found almost four hundred destroyed enemy planes, a tribute to the pre–D–day bombing by the Fifth Air Force. At Aitape, Doe's forces quickly overran the ineffective enemy opposition and seized the airfield.

Krueger described the RECKLESS operation as "a great success both strategically and tactically." The operation isolated the large Japanese forces to the east, particularly at Wewak, and provided airfields that enabled Allied air forces to project their power hundreds of miles westward to assist in the conquest of the entire northern coast of New Guinea. Once again, ULTRA and sound planning by Krueger's staff, the navy and air force staffs, and the staffs of their subordinate commands had paid off handsomely.[38]

MacArthur was present at the landings at Humboldt Bay and at Tanahmerah Bay, aboard the *Nashville*. He went ashore at both landing areas. After returning to the *Nashville*, MacArthur "celebrated with [Rear Admiral Daniel E.] Barbey, Eichelberger, and Krueger by ordering for all a favorite dessert of his, chocolate ice-cream sodas." The next morning the *Nashville* carried MacArthur to Aitape, where he once more went ashore to congratulate Doe and his men on their success.[39]

The tempo of Alamo Force operations was rapidly increasing. Patrick's staff was now preparing plans for "a number of impending [operations] while two and even three were actually in progress." Patrick and his staff worked out the Hollandia–Aitape plans at the height of the Admiralty Islands operations; the plans for the upcoming Wakde–Biak operations before the Hollandia–Aitape operations had started, and while they were in progress; and the plans for the Noemfoor Island and Sansapor operations while the operations at Aitape, Wakde, and Biak were in progress. Furthermore, Alamo Force had grown dramatically in size: as of May 24, 1944, the major combat units of Alamo Force included two corps headquarters, one cavalry (dismounted) and eight infantry divisions, one airborne division, and two regimental combat teams. It is no wonder that Patrick likened his job as Alamo Force chief of staff to that of running a "four–ring circus." Krueger acknowledged the very considerable difficulties faced by Patrick and his other staff officers when he wrote the following:

> The fact that we coped with this extremely complicated and burdensome system successfully bears eloquent testimony to the ability, skill, efficiency and devotion to duty of the members of my staff. Their effective planning and supervisory work entitles [sic] them to a large share of the credit for the success achieved by Sixth Army as such, and as Alamo Force.[40]

On April 10, MacArthur alerted Alamo Force to a possible extension of its Hollandia–Aitape operations to include the Wakde Islands–Sarmi area, slightly over one hundred miles west of Hollandia. MacArthur planned to use the area as an advanced air and naval base to prevent Japanese interference with the build-

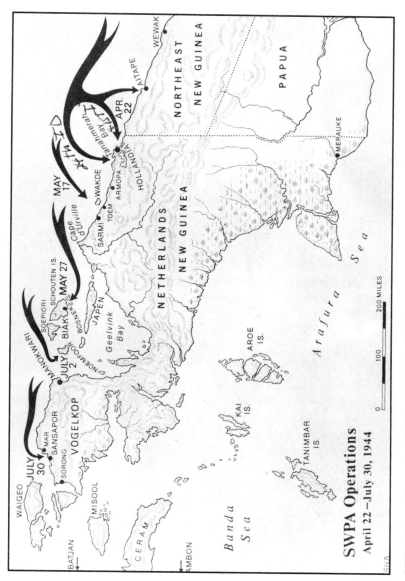

SWPA Operations, April 22 - July 30, 1944

(James, *The Years of MacArthur*, 446)

up of the Hollandia base. Krueger immediately directed his staff to begin planning for this operation, and to submit the proposed estimate of troops and the coordinated plan for the operation, with supporting naval and air plans, to MacArthur by April 16 and April 22, respectively.

On April 27, MacArthur directed Krueger to carry out the operation, as planned by his staff, on May 15. In this plan the 41st Infantry Division was to seize Wakde Island, the larger of the two Wakde islands,[41] and the adjacent coastal area in the vicinity of Sarmi village. However, on May 7, he informed Alamo Force that the Sarmi portion of the operation might be canceled, and an assault on Biak Island, some two hundred miles westward, might be substituted. With only sketchy information about Biak on hand, the Alamo Force staff began planning for the new operation. On May 10 MacArthur formally directed that the Wakde and Biak areas would be the next Alamo Force objectives.[42]

Doe's 163d Regimental Combat Team would make the landing in the Wakde area, with the objective of seizing a beachhead near the village of Arare for establishment of an airfield, and then seize three of the offshore islands, including Wakde. Doe's forces rapidly secured the beachhead, and on May 18 and 19 occupied the three offshore islands, meeting some stubborn Japanese defenders. Work on the airfield in the Wakde beachhead began promptly thereafter.[43]

On May 22, Krueger informed Doe that he had decided to enlarge the mission of the task force, code-named TORNADO Task Force. The task force was to advance westward across the Tor River toward Sarmi, some sixteen miles away. However, this move would not be made by the 163d Regimental Combat Team, which was to be sent back to the 41st Infantry Division to participate in the landing on Biak Island on May 27. The 158th Regimental Combat Team, which had arrived in the Wakde area from Cape Cretin on May 21, would replace the 163d Regimental Combat Team as TORNADO Task Force. Nor would Doe command the task force as it moved westward: TORNADO Task Force's new commander would be Doe's old friend from his days with the 14th Machine Gun Battalion in France and the 15th Infantry in Tientsin, Patrick.[44]

On May 11, 1944, Colonel George H. Decker replaced Patrick as the chief of staff of Sixth Army.[45] On May 25, Patrick relieved Doe as the commanding general of TORNADO Task Force in the Wakde beachhead area. Patrick was once again a commander of troops.[46]

During his tenure as chief of staff of Alamo Force, Patrick repeatedly emphasized to his family his satisfaction with his job, despite the long hours and the demanding requirements of the

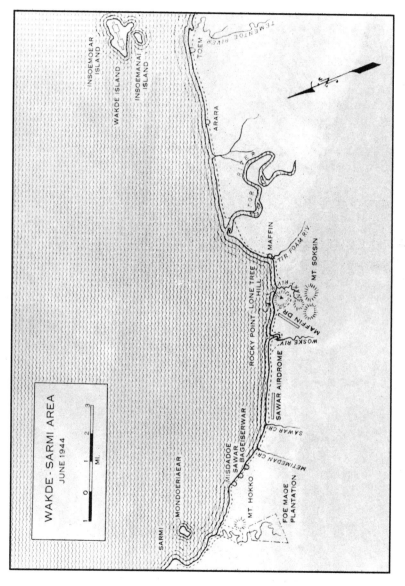

WAKDE-SARMI AREA

JUNE 1944

MI.
1 0 1 2 3

INSOEMOEAR ISLAND

WAKDE ISLAND

INSOEMANAI ISLAND

TOEM

TEMENTOE RIVER

ARARA

TOR RIVER

MAFFIN

TIR FOAM RIV.

MT SOKSIN

ROCKY POINT

LONE TREE HILL

MAFFIN DR.

WOSKE RIV.

SAWAR AIRDROME

SAWAR CR.

METIMEDAN CR.

MISDADOE

SAWAR

BAGE/SERWAR

FOE MAOE PLANTATION

MT HOKKO

MONDOERIAEAR

SARMI

Wakde-Sarmi Area, June 1944

(6th Infantry Division in World War II, 42)

position. He often took the time, despite the fatigue he must have felt as he wrote those letters late at night, to comment on the activities of his wife and sons; on his concern for the welfare and health of the members of his Tell City family; on the beauty of the flowers and trees he saw on a visit to Australia; on the house that Nellie May had recently purchased in Ruidoso, New Mexico, where they planned to spend their retirement years; on his hopes to be reunited with his family after the war; and on the Christmas presents that he had received. What emerges from those letters is a picture of a professional soldier carrying out the exacting demands of his job under incredibly trying circumstances, and of a devoted husband, father, son, and brother still able to find time to express his love and concern for his family, and to acknowledge their love and concern for him. Only once did Patrick express regret about his being overseas: on March 1 he wrote to his mother and sister that

> one of the features about this war that I never have liked is the necessity of my being away from home and far away from the boys at what is probably the most important period of their lives; when they need me most, if they need me at all.

Despite this regret, his devotion to duty and country clearly came through in an earlier letter, when he stated that although "it would be quite nice to get home by about this time next year ... I'm not as interested in getting home as I am to see this thing through out here to a successful conclusion and in that I'm quite hopeful."[47]

CHAPTER 14

TORNADO TASK FORCE: WAKDE–SARMI NEW GUINEA

Patrick informed his family that he had

> finally gotten a troop command. ... It isn't exactly the kind I wanted but I think my chances for something better will improve. At any rate, I'll have a chance to hear a few shots fired in anger before this war is over.[1]

When Patrick took over as its commander, TORNADO Task Force was composed of two infantry regimental combat teams, the 163d and the 158th. The 163d Regimental Combat Team, after securing the area about Arare and the three nearby offshore islands under Doe's command, now occupied an area extending along the coast from the Tementoe Creek on the east to a bridgehead approximately six hundred yards west of the Tor River, a distance of approximately eight miles. The perimeter extended inland for approximately one thousand yards. The 158th Regimental Combat Team arrived from Finschhafen on May 21, and established its bivouac in the Arare area, becoming a part of Patrick's task force.

Just three days prior to Patrick's becoming the commander of TORNADO Task Force, Krueger had ordered the task force to institute "a vigorous overland drive toward Sarmi, sixteen miles west of the Tor River"; he made this decision when Willoughby warned him about imminent counterattacks against his beachhead. Captured enemy documents indicated that two battalions of the Japanese 224th Infantry Regiment were near Sarmi, suggest-

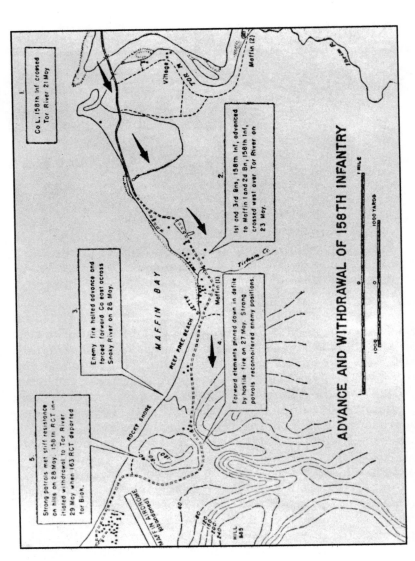

Advance and Withdrawal of 158th Infantry

(Krueger, *Down Under to Nippon*, 88)

ing that there would be only weak resistance. Krueger, therefore, decided to launch Patrick's forces on a spoiling attack westward against these supposedly weak Japanese forces. Patrick was equally sanguine about the Japanese opposition confronting TORNADO Task Force, stating in a letter to Krueger his belief that "there are possibly two thousand enemy troops in this area." No American intelligence officer was aware that the Japanese 223d Infantry had moved eastward and had crossed the Tor River south of the projected line of advance of Patrick's troops, and would eventually work its way behind the advancing infantrymen.[2]

On May 23, in conformance with Doe's decision to use the 158th to implement this expanded mission, elements of the 3d Battalion, 158th Infantry, began to relieve the 3d Battalion, 163d Infantry west of the Tor River, and then to continue westward to seize the area known to the Americans as "Maffin No. 1." However, the 3d Battalion ran into increasingly strong resistance as it advanced west of the Tor, necessitating the 158th Infantry Regiment's commander, Colonel J. Prugh Herndon, to order his 1st Battalion also to cross the Tor late in the afternoon of May 23. By the evening of that day the advance elements of the 3d Battalion had dug in some 400 yards east of Maffin No. 1.

The attack resumed on May 24, after mortar and artillery preparatory fires, and by that afternoon Company L had reached the outskirts of Maffin No. 1. Herndon then ordered his 1st Battalion to move forward to the left flank of the 3d Battalion. The units dug in for the night some two hundred yards east of the Tirfoam River.[3]

Patrick ordered the 158th Infantry to continue the attack to the west at 0900, May 25. With the 1st Battalion in the lead, Herndon's troops rapidly advanced and seized their initial objective, a bridge across the Tirfoam River. Herndon then pushed the 1st Battalion across the river and ordered the 2d Battalion to follow. Advancing against only sporadic resistance, the infantrymen reached a point just east of the Snaky River, where enemy machine gun and artillery fire halted the advance, and the troops dug in for the night.[4]

With the 1st Battalion north of the coastal road and the 2d Battalion on its left, Patrick ordered the attack to continue on the morning of May 26. The 1st Battalion objective was Lone Tree Hill, about 175 feet high, 1,200 yards north–to–south, and 1,100 yards east–to–west. On the north, the hill dropped steeply to a rocky shore on Maffin Bay. The hill, despite its name, was covered with dense rain forest and jungle undergrowth. At the base of its eastern slope was the short but twisting Snaky River. Just south of Lone Tree Hill was the hill mass Mt. Saksin, with two prominent noses projecting northward into the narrow defile separating Mt. Saksin and Lone Tree Hill. The more western of these two noses was Hill 225, the objective of the 2d Battalion.

The coastal road some 1,200 yards east of Snaky River pursued a southwesterly course, passing south of the river and continuing through the narrow defile between Lone Tree Hill and Mt. Saksin. Two small settlements lay along the road at either end of the defile.[5]

As the two–battalion attack against Lone Tree Hill and Hill 225 began on May 26, the troops met increasingly heavy fire from enemy automatic weapons, mortars, and artillery. At 1000 hours, the enemy resistance forced attacking forces to halt and reorganize just west of the Snaky River. The battalions sent out patrols toward the two objectives. Company A succeeded in moving approximately two hundred to three hundred yards up the north slope of Lone Tree Hill, where its members found the enemy well entrenched within caves and crevices, forcing the troops to withdraw.

On the 27th, the battalions largely limited their activities to patrolling, which revealed that the enemy's main defenses were in the area of Hill 225 and within the ravines leading from that hill into the defile. Lone Tree Hill, except along its northeastern slope, did not appear to be occupied. Still basing his estimate of the strength of the enemy forces facing him on Willoughby's inaccurate intelligence, Patrick ordered the attack against Lone Tree Hill and Hill 225 to resume the next day.[6]

Two rifle companies of the 1st Battalion were to advance across Lone Tree Hill, while the other company would accompany a rifle company of 2d Battalion through the defile. The remaining 2d Battalion rifle companies would move across Hill 225 to the western end of the defile.

Although the 1st Battalion reached the crest of Lone Tree Hill, Lieutenant Colonel Paul Shoemaker, the 1st Battalion commander, requested and received permission to withdraw in the late afternoon, when water and ammunition became critically low. The two rifle companies in the defile and the 2d Battalion troops on Hill 225 ran into heavy enemy resistance, and the troops could not advance beyond a line east of the village that lay at the eastern entrance to the defile. Fearing that his forward positions were rapidly becoming untenable because of the strength of the Japanese forces and because of his difficulty in supplying his two forward battalions west of the Snaky River, Herndon radioed Patrick that he intended to withdraw to and consolidate his position along the

Snaky River. Patrick approved Herndon's plan, and told him the next morning to cease offensive efforts.[7]

Patrick had decided that further movement westward with his available forces would be hazardous, since he now had a fifteen-mile long line of coastal perimeters to defend, extending from the vicinity of Arare–Toem to Lone Tree Hill. Further movement would await a combat team from the 6th Infantry Division that he had requested.

Patrick's decision to delay was reinforced by Krueger's order on the night of May 28–29 to embark the 163d Infantry (less one battalion), now defending the task force support area in Arare–Toem, to rejoin the 41st Division at Biak. Krueger had made this decision based on faulty intelligence reports that the enemy could put up only weak resistance within the task force area. Patrick, fearing that the remaining battalion would not be adequate to defend the Arare–Toem area, ordered the 1st Battalion, 158th Infantry, back to that area. He then ordered the remainder of the 158th Infantry to defend the line along the Snaky River until the arrival of the regimental combat team from the 6th Division on or about June 4.[8]

Patrick's decision to stabilize and defend the position along the Snaky River was also part of a daring plan that he had formulated. Estimating correctly that the enemy would defend on the Lone Tree Hill–Hill 225 line, Patrick proposed a shore–to–shore amphibious operation that would place troops on the west shore of Sarmi Point, in the rear of the main enemy defenses at Lone Tree Hill–Hill 225. Scouts sent to reconnoiter Sarmi Point confirmed that it was virtually undefended. Patrick planned to land the 1st Infantry Regiment(-) of the 6th Infantry Division on the point on June 8, and have these infantrymen drive eastward, taking the Japanese defenders on Lone Tree Hill–Hill 225 in the rear, while the 158th Infantry applied pressure against their front. However, the navy destroyers that were to provide the fire support for the landing did not arrive, and the operation was postponed until June 12. When Major General Franklin C. Sibert took command of TORNADO Task Force on June 12, he postponed the operation indefinitely, since he did not favor mounting such an operation.

About noon of May 29, while organizing his position, Herndon received reports that enemy forces were infiltrating around his left flank and his rear. Feeling that his position along Snaky River was becoming untenable, Herndon telephoned Patrick at 1515, and told him "that [since] his front line was surrounded, that he was being driven back and that his position was untenable," he planned to withdraw at once to the Tirfoam. Patrick at first declined to give his consent, considering the late hour and the fact that such a withdrawal would necessitate Patrick's changing the disposition of other units. However, he acceded to Herndon's request, and the withdrawal began.[9]

Patrick immediately went to Herndon's forward areas to ascertain for himself if the withdrawal was a necessity. He "questioned several officers and many enlisted men," and "established the fact that the only pressure he [Herndon] had had was earlier in the morning when 'F' Company had extricated itself from an alleged ambush," in which three men were wounded. Patrick could not ascertain from those with whom he had talked that there had been any other casualties, and determined that "the enemy had not exerted any pressure against the front of the regiment." By this time, however, the withdrawal was almost 50 percent complete. Although the withdrawal to the Tirfoam was executed without any interference from the enemy and without casualties, Patrick felt Herndon had not executed it well, and at that point relieved Herndon of command of the 158th Infantry, replacing him with Colonel Earle O. Sandlin, a Regular Army officer who had recently arrived in the theater, and had been acting as Patrick's chief of staff.[10]

Patrick's relief of Herndon sparked immediate and ongoing controversy. Patrick felt completely justified in relieving Herndon, stating that he had been compelled "to push him from the beginning and as his casualties were counted he became increasingly pessimistic and hesitant in his prosecution of the advance." In addition, Patrick believed that Herndon's "administration of his regiment was faulty." Patrick went on to state that although Herndon had been "entirely sincere" and that he had "many good qualities," he had "no confidence in [Herndon's] ability to command the 158th Infantry in combat. He appeared bewildered from the beginning," he was "worried and pessimistic," and "his staff reflected his attitude."[11]

Patrick was undoubtedly under pressure from Krueger to keep the operation moving, as Krueger was under pressure from MacArthur to advance his Sixth Army along the northern coast of New Guinea to expedite MacArthur's return to the Philippines. MacArthur had recently ordered the relief of Major General E. Forrest Harding when he became impatient with the performance of Harding's 32d Infantry Division earlier in the New Guinea campaign, and had told General Robert L. Eichelberger " 'to take Buna, or not come back alive.' "[12]

In defense of Herndon, one must acknowledge that GHQ, Alamo Force, and Headquarters, TORNADO Task Force, had all seriously underestimated the strength of the Japanese forces that the 158th Regimental Combat Team faced, their intelligence personnel having failed to detect the presence of the 223d Infantry in the west, and the 224th Infantry, which had worked its way back from Hollandia to a position just east of Toem. Feeling that only weak Japanese forces confronted Patrick, Krueger further weakened the American force by withdrawing two battalions from Toem to join the forces fighting on Biak Island. Patrick then increased the odds against Herndon's regiment by sending one of its battalions to Toem.

As early as May 26, Herndon felt that the estimates of enemy strength he had received were woefully inaccurate, and that, based on the resistance his troops were meeting, the enemy was present in much greater strength. However, Krueger and Patrick appear to have ignored his protestations, and continued to base their orders to Herndon on the assumption that he faced only weak Japanese opposition.[13]

Many of the members of the 158th Infantry, a federalized unit from the Arizona National Guard, did not respond favorably when they heard of Herndon's relief. He had commanded the 158th Infantry since 1932, and, although known throughout the regiment as a stern disciplinarian, he had, during his long tenure with the 158th, developed many close friendships. Numerous subordinates would in the future come to regard Herndon's relief as "a great pity."[14]

However, some of his officers did express doubts about Herndon's ongoing competence as a combat commander. Lieutenant Colonel Boysie Day, Herndon's S–3, was, by the time of the withdrawal from Lone Tree Hill, "reluctantly beginning to wonder whether Herndon was the best man to lead them into battle." Lieutenant Colonel George Colvin, one of Herndon's battalion commanders, "thought his judgment sometimes was bad, especially in terms of personnel," citing an incident where Herndon had overturned Colvin's recommendation to relieve an officer who feigned illness in order to avoid combat.[15]

Patrick's relief of Herndon will probably continue to be shrouded in controversy. Patrick's decision to do so was based in part, however, on his firsthand observation of conditions in the area, and on his conversations with members of the 158th Infantry at the time of the withdrawal, all of which seemed to him to indicate that the Japanese were not exerting sufficient pressure against Herndon's position to require the withdrawal of the regiment.

Patrick's comments to Krueger also indicate that this was not a precipitous decision. Herndon's actions on May 29 merely seemed to confirm Patrick's doubts as to Herndon's qualifications to continue to command his regiment in combat.[16]

Following Herndon's relief and the departure of two battalions of the 163d Infantry for Biak, Patrick now found his task force spread out over almost twelve miles of coastline. In the east there was the remaining battalion of the 163d Infantry covering the flank at Toem. In the west the 2d and 3d Battalions of the 158th Infantry held perimeters west of the Tor River. Task force headquarters at Arare and the nearby supply and ammunition dumps were guarded by the 1st Battalion, 158th Infantry. Antiaircraft and field artillery units held other perimeters along the coast.

The Japanese forces that had been moving eastward from the Sarmi area along inland routes to participate in a double envelopment with the 224th Infantry would soon threaten Patrick's forces in the Arare–Toem area. On May 27–28, they carried out a preliminary attack against the 163d Infantry's 1st Battalion near Toem, leading Patrick to request that Krueger postpone the 163d Regimental Combat Team's departure for Biak until the arrival of the regimental combat team from the 6th Infantry Division; Krueger disapproved this request. Despite that initial attack, Patrick did not appear overly concerned about any significant Japanese forces on his south flank, sending out only a few patrols to probe the area.[17]

On the night of May 30, the Japanese attacked an antiaircraft battery near Arare. Later, the enemy launched a "furious, suicidal attack" against Company B, 158th Infantry, which was guarding food and ammunition dumps in the Arare–Toem area. The company's strength at that time was approximately ninety men. The Japanese, who knew the name of Company B's commander, Captain Hal Braun, broke out of the jungle screaming, "Braun, Braun—tonight you die." With their "backs to the ocean and surrounded by enemy we had no choice but to beat their butts." Using rifles, hand grenades, pistols, knives, and bayonets, Braun's infantrymen beat off the assault, at a cost of twelve killed and ten wounded. Fifty–two Japanese bodies were counted in front of the infantry and artillery positions the next day.[18]

On the morning of May 31, expecting more attacks, Patrick set to work to strengthen his western defensive positions, and to reduce the number of separate perimeters along the beach. Notified that the sole remaining battalion of the 163d Infantry was to depart for Biak, Patrick ordered the elements of the 158th Infantry west of the Tor River to withdraw to its east bank, there to draw up a defensive perimeter between the Tor River and Tementoe Creek, retaining only a battalion bridgehead west of the Tor. No further offensive actions were to take place until after the arrival of the regimental combat team from the 6th Division. After the first of June, raids on the perimeters ceased, although the battalion west of the Tor "had numerous encounters with the Jap and inflicted a daily toll of casualties on him."[19]

The 1st Infantry Regiment, 6th Division, arrived during the night of June 4–5. The 1st Battalion, 1st Infantry, relieved the 1st Battalion, 158th Infantry, in the beachhead perimeter on June 6, the latter then joining the 2d Battalion, 158th Infantry, west of the Tor River.[20]

On June 8, the 1st and 2d Battalions, 158th Infantry, jumped off on an attack westward, and, against sporadic but sometimes heavy resistance, reached the east bank of the Tirfoam River the afternoon of June 9.

Undoubtedly the 158th Infantry could have crossed the Tirfoam River, but that day Krueger changed the unit's mission: he had decided to employ the 158th Regimental Combat Team in an assault on Noemfoor Island, three hundred miles northwest of Sarmi, and had ordered that the combat team take part in no further offensive actions. On June 14, the 20th Infantry, 6th Division, relieved the 158th Infantry at the Tirfoam, and on June 22 Krueger relieved the entire regimental combat team of all combat responsibility in the Wakde–Sarmi area, to begin preparing for the Noemfoor Island operation. On June 12, Major General Franklin C. Sibert, commanding general of the 6th Infantry Division, assumed command of TORNADO Task Force.[21]

During its operations in the Wakde–Sarmi area, the 158th Regimental Combat Team lost 70 men killed, 257 wounded, and 4 missing. The unit estimated that it had killed 920 Japanese.[22]

In assessing the operations of Patrick's TORNADO Task Force in the Sarmi operation, a reasonable conclusion appears to be that the difficulties faced by the 158th Infantry were a direct product of the failure of Allied intelligence. Both GHQ in Australia and Alamo Force headquarters at Cape Cretin seriously underestimated the strength of the Japanese forces defending the approach to Sarmi. Although Patrick's task force initially included two regimental combat teams, he felt it necessary to retain one as a security force along his eastern flank and to provide security for his ammunition and supply dumps in the Arare area, leaving only the 158th Regimental Combat Team to conduct operations against the numerically superior Japanese forces entrenched in well fortified and concealed positions in the Lone Tree Hill–Hill 225 area. When Krueger decided to move the 163d Regimental Combat Team to Biak prior to arrival of the 1st Infantry at Toem, Patrick decided to reduce even further his forces facing the Japanese on his west flank by redeploying one battalion of the 158th Infantry to take over the security mission of the 163d Infantry in the Arare–Toem area. This, for all practical purposes, meant that he would be unable to mount any further offensive operations west of the Tor River until the 1st Infantry arrived. The Japanese thereby gained valuable time to strengthen even more their positions on Lone Tree Hill and Hill 225.

With numerous perimeters to defend along the twelve miles of coastline occupied by units of the task force, TORNADO Task Force presented an attractive target for defeat in detail by the Japanese. Fortunately for Patrick and his troops, Lieutenant General Tagami Hachiro, the commander of the Japanese forces at Wakde–Sarmi, was unable from his headquarters on Mt. Saksin to coordinate optimally his two forces converging on the perimeters east of the Tor, resulting in uncoordinated piecemeal attacks that the Americans were able to beat back.

One of the most serious failures of TORNADO Task Force during this operation was its failure to patrol regularly and deeply into the areas south and east of its perimeters. Had Patrick insisted that such patrolling operations be conducted, he most likely would have been aware that large enemy forces were moving west toward the Toem area, and were infiltrating eastward in the jungles south of the task force positions along the coast. This signal failure of Patrick to order regular patrolling could well have resulted in the task force's being defeated in detail, if Tagami had better coordinated his attacks.

Brig. Gen. Edwin D. Patrick at Memorial Day Service, 1944, USF No. 1 Cemetery, Toem, New Guinea.
(U.S. Army photo)

One must credit Patrick for his early recognition that his forces would probably not be able to force the Lone Tree Hill–Hill 225 line by frontal assault. His decision to outflank the position by a shore–

to–shore movement to Sarmi Point illustrated that he was a bold and ingenious commander. Unfortunately, the naval fire support necessary for the success of this mission failed to materialize as scheduled, forcing Patrick to cancel the operation. There is every reason to believe that the landing in the enemy's rear would have been successful, and quite probably would have resulted in the destruction of Tagami's forces in the Lone Tree Hill–Hill 225 area.

Overall, the operation must be considered as only partly successful. Because of insufficient combat troops and operating against a numerically superior and well–entrenched enemy, Patrick's task force did not achieve its objective of destroying "enemy forces between the Tor River and Sarmi Point." In fact, Patrick's forces were not able to maintain a significant beachhead west of the Tor.

The 158th Infantry did gain valuable combat experience, however, and its troops performed admirably in a hostile environment against an experienced enemy that far outnumbered them, their actions causing a significant number of casualties among Tagami's forces. TORNADO Task Force had also maintained and improved the Arare–Toem beachhead secured earlier by the 163d Regimental Combat Team. Still, the operation against the Lone Tree Hill–Hill 225 position was probably doomed to failure from its outset, because there were "just too many Damn Japs up there."[23]

Patrick himself appeared to be satisfied with the results of his first outing as a combat commander in World War II, as was his superior, Krueger. Patrick told his family that he "already had my outfit up against the Jap and we did quite well, liquidated over a thousand in a comparatively short time." Krueger expressed to Patrick his "sincere appreciation of duty well done," and told him that "the energy, skill and fortitude displayed by all ranks during the operations in the Topheavy [Toem-Wakde] area have been of the highest order."[24]

CHAPTER 15

OPERATION TABLETENNIS: NOEMFOOR ISLAND

On June 5, 1944, MacArthur alerted Krueger that the seizure of Noemfoor Island in Geelvink Bay "might be necessary in order to consolidate our success at Biak." Krueger directed his staff to begin planning of that operation immediately. On June 14, MacArthur directed Krueger "to prepare and submit plans for the immediate seizure of Noemfoor Island, and for establishing air and light naval facilities there and to recommend the earliest date for D–day."[1]

Noemfoor Island lies on the northern edge of Geelvink Bay, about halfway between Biak Island and the east coast of the Vogelkop Peninsula of New Guinea. It is about fifteen miles long north–to–south, and twelve miles wide, and is covered by rain forest. Its northern part is generally low and flat, but the southern part of the island is rugged; the highest elevation is 670 feet. The only trails are at the periphery of the island, and the central areas of the island were practically uninhabited in 1944. The island is surrounded by a wide reef.[2]

In 1943, using some three thousand "imported" Indonesian laborers, the Japanese began development of the island, and by mid–1944 had completed three airfields: Kamiri and Kornasoren on the north shore, and Namber on the southwestern side of the island. Those airfields were the reason for MacArthur's selecting Noemfoor as his next objective on his march to the Philippines.[3]

Allied intelligence sources estimated that there were approximately 1,750 Japanese troops on Noemfoor. There were three companies from the 219th Infantry and one company from the 222d Infantry. There was also a provisional battalion of miscellaneous airfield construction, transport, and auxiliary formations. Aerial photographs revealed five coastal defense positions. The intelligence sources indicated that the Japanese considered Noemfoor only a delaying position, and would make no effort to reinforce it.[4]

Although MacArthur had originally wanted to use a regimental combat team from the 6th Infantry Division for the operation, Krueger asked that the 158th Regimental Combat Team, under Patrick, be substituted, since he planned to use the 6th Division in the upcoming invasion of the Vogelkop Peninsula. MacArthur concurred.[5]

On June 16, Krueger directed Patrick and key members of his staff to go to Finschhafen to attend a planning conference at Alamo Force Headquarters. Allied air and naval force representatives were also in attendance. By the close of the one–day conference, the attendees had outlined the general plan for the operation.

CYCLONE Task Force, the major component of which would be the 158th Regimental Combat Team, was to assault Noemfoor Island, code-named TABLETENNIS, on July 2. MacArthur indicated to Marshall that the possession of Noemfoor's airfields "will give added breadth and depth to our air deployment and will further penetrate and dislocate enemys [sic] main supply and defense axis."[6]

The task force would consist of 8,069 combat and 5,495 service troops. The 158th Regimental Combat Team would land at 0730 on July 2 near the Kamiri airfield, and rapidly seize and occupy that area. The regimental combat team was then to occupy .and defend the entire island, rehabilitate the airfields, and establish necessary port and base and minor naval facilities.[7]

Krueger chose the Kamiri area on the northwest coast of Noemfoor as the site for the landing. As Alamo Force Reserve for the operation, Krueger chose the 503d Parachute Infantry Regiment, which he directed to prepare for immediate aerial movement to Noemfoor if required. He also alerted the 34th Infantry Regiment, 24th Infantry Division, on Biak to prepare for movement by water on twenty–four hours' notice.[8]

Because of the reef that surrounded the island, the operation plan called for amphibious tractors (LVTs) and trucks (DUKWs) to land the two assault reinforced battalions on the beach simultaneously. The LVTs would proceed immediately, without disembarking the troops, to the edge of the objective, Kamiri airfield.[9]

Patrick and his staff returned to task force headquarters at Toem on June 23, and began readying the troops for the operation. On June 29, the task force held a landing rehearsal east of the Tementoe River. Rear Admiral William M. Fechteler, the commander of Task Force 76, "pronounced it most successful."[10]

Meanwhile, ULTRA had reported on June 27/28 that the Japanese Second Area Army expected another Allied landing soon. Because of the need to seize Noemfoor's airfields before the Japanese could reinforce the island's garrison, Krueger decided to attack the strongest Japanese defenses near Kamiri Airfield, because such an attack would put the assaulting troops almost directly on their immediate objective, the airfield. He planned to have this area "softened up" by a more intense pre–invasion air and naval bombardment than in earlier operations.[11]

The main body of the task force departed from the Toem area on June 30, and arrived off the Kamiri beach at 0630, July 2. Shortly after 0700, the pre–assault bombardment began; officers experienced in the use of naval gunfire described it as "the most effective they had ever seen." At 0730, the first wave of LVTs left their LSTs (landing ship, tank), and crossed the line of departure promptly at H–hour, 0800. Landing without opposition, the LVTs proceeded across Kamiri airfield into a fringe of coconut palms at the foot of a coral ridge overlooking the airfield. The troops unloaded, and quickly seized the ridge. Subsequent waves of troops in LVTs and DUKWs reinforced the position. By 1050, all field artillery pieces were in position.[12]

The troops did not meet any opposition until they reached a point about five hundred yards from the east end of the airfield, where they encountered about thirty "completely demoralized" Japanese and quickly disposed of them with machine gun and rifle fire. By nightfall on D–day, the beachhead extended to the north bank of the Kamiri River, where the 158th established a defensive perimeter. Repair work on Kamiri airfield began immediately after its seizure.[13]

A dazed Japanese prisoner told his interrogators that because of recent reinforcements there were now between 3,500 and 4,000 enemy troops on the island. Remembering the understated enemy strength that intelligence estimates provided to him at Sarmi, and knowing from ULTRA the enemy's concerns over an Allied landing, Patrick, at 1100 on D–day, asked Krueger to send the 503d Parachute Infantry to Noemfoor. Krueger replied that the 1st Battalion, 503d Parachute Infantry, would land on Kamiri airfield at 1000 hours, D+1 (3 July), with the remaining two battalions following at the same hour on July 4 and 5.[14]

The transports were to fly over the airfield in flights of two each, the first plane at an altitude of four hundred feet, and the second plane echeloned to the right rear at 450 feet. About 0600, July 3, Patrick asked to have the planes fly over the airfield in

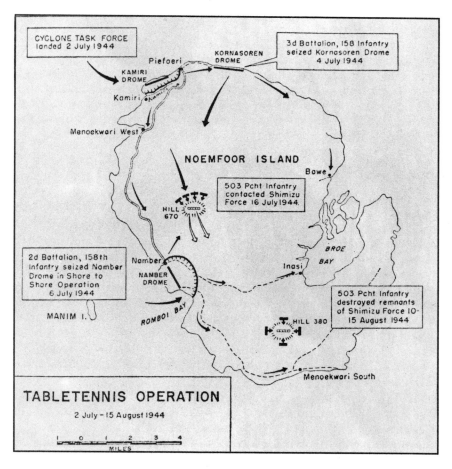

TABLETENNIS Operation, 2 July-15 August 1944
(Krueger, *Down Under to Nippon*, 107)

single file to avoid dropping the paratroopers on obstacles along
the sides of the narrow airfield. For unknown reasons Headquarters, Fifth Air Force did not receive this message until sometime
between 0740 and 0915. By that time all of the aircraft carrying
the paratroopers had departed from Cyclops Airfield at Hollandia
and were well on their way to Noemfoor. There is no record of any
attempt to contact the aircraft in flight to change their flight pat-
tern for the drop.[15]

When the planes, in flights of two, arrived over Kamiri, the
first two planes dropped their troops at about 175 feet; the other
eight planes dropped their paratroopers at altitudes below 400
feet. These low–altitude drops caused many casualties, and the
landing of some paratroopers among obstacles lining the airstrip
compounded those problems. There were 72 casualties among the
739 men who made the drop, an unacceptably high casualty rate
of almost ten percent.

As Krueger received word of the casualties, he ordered that
the planes scheduled to drop the 3d Battalion fly in a single file on
July 4, and he also told Patrick to insure that the airfield was free
of all obstacles.

At 0955, July 4, the 3d Battalion began dropping on the airfield. Although there were no obstacles obstructing the landing,
there were fifty–six casualties, due to the hard impact made by the
parachutists as they landed on a runway that engineers had hardened since the previous day by considerable grading, rolling, and
packing. Because of the high casualties suffered in both drops,
Patrick requested Krueger to cancel the third drop; Krueger complied, and sent the remainder of the paratroopers to Noemfoor by
water. The airborne reinforcements, despite the poorly executed
drop, did however enable Patrick to accelerate his occupation of
the island.[16]

On the same day the 1st Battalion, 158th Infantry, crossed
the Kamiri River near its mouth, and advanced to a Japanese garden, near Hill 201, where they encountered the first serious opposition. On the following morning at 0500, approximately three
companies of the enemy attacked the battalion's position. The attack continued until after daylight, when the Japanese withdrew
to the southeast, leaving 201 Japanese dead behind. Only two
Americans were wounded, and none were killed.

Also on July 4, the 158th's 3d Battalion advanced to and
occupied the Kornasoren Airfield, meeting no resistance. The following day the battalion conducted patrolling in their sector.

In a shore–to–shore movement on July 6, the 158th's 2d Battalion landed at 0925 on the north side of Roemboi Bay against no
resistance, and by 0945 had occupied Namber Airfield.

From July 6 to July 10, all units, including the paratroopers, conducted extensive patrolling, but encountered only scattered enemy groups. On July 10, therefore, Patrick concluded that "in all probability no organized sizeable [sic] force remained on the island."[17]

To hunt down and destroy the remaining small enemy groups, Patrick assigned the 158th Infantry responsibility for clearing the northern half of Noemfoor, while the 503d Parachute Infantry would take responsibility for the southern half of the island, where, it turned out, the bulk of the remaining Japanese forces were located.

After a series of small–unit actions, the paratroopers had forced the enemy into the area around Hill 670, where, on July 16, the 1st Battalion launched an attack and seized the hill, killing 116 Japanese. The 503d continued its pursuit of the Japanese in a generally southeastward direction, but made no further contact.

By July 21, Patrick thought that a significant Japanese force had concealed itself in the center of the island southeast or east of Hill 670, and ordered extensive patrolling by both the 158th and the 503d in this area. However, the Americans made only scattered contacts.

On August 8, a prisoner of war indicated that the Japanese forces might be in the area of Inasi, in the eastern part of Noemfoor. Moving to that area, the 503d engaged a body of the enemy, estimated at two hundred, near Hill 380. During the period August 10–17, the paratroopers, assisted by artillery and air strikes, attacked this force. When the enemy disengaged, he left behind 342 dead and 43 prisoners.

The 503d continued to chase the elusive Japanese commander and his troops, but were never able to bring them to ground. When the operation officially closed on August 31, 1944, "Colonel Shimizu [Suesada] and his small body guard [sic] were still at large."[18]

At the close of the operation, CYCLONE Task Force had killed 1,729 Japanese and had captured 186 prisoners. American casualties totaled 45 Americans killed, and 121 wounded.

The Americans soon learned of Japanese atrocities perpetrated on the Javanese and Formosans who had been brought to Noemfoor. Of the approximately 900 Formosans on the island, more than 550 were suffering from malnutrition to the point of starvation, beriberi, tropical ulcers, malaria, dysentery and other diseases.

The Javanese suffered even more. Some three thousand, including women and teen-age boys, had been "imported" to Noemfoor to work as laborers. With no food, clothing, or bedding, they constructed the airfields and roads by hand. Driven by hunger, these laborers sometimes stole rations from the Japanese. When apprehended, they suffered beheading or were hung by their hands or feet until dead. The Americans recovered only 403 of the 3,000 Javanese, and "the physical condition of practically all of these was indescribable."[19]

Although Samuel E. Morison, the noted naval historian, has described the Noemfoor operation as "probably the smoothest of all Southwest Pacific operations," the two ill-fated parachute assaults on July 3 and 4 detract sharply from what otherwise would have been an almost perfectly executed operation.[20]

Patrick apparently requested the airborne reinforcements based on information from a single "dazed" enemy prisoner taken on the first day. Although one can sympathize with Patrick's understandable lack of confidence in the Allied intelligence estimates of enemy strength on Noemfoor based on his experience at Wakde–Sarmi, he apparently made no further effort to confirm that enemy strength facing him was indeed greater than the estimates he received prior to the assault. Krueger likewise is open to serious criticism. Apparently without hesitation, he complied with Patrick's request for the airborne reinforcements, even though he knew that the report of his Alamo Scouts, who had extensively patrolled the island for two days just before the assault, had confirmed the earlier intelligence estimates of enemy strength on Noemfoor. Based on this report, he should at the very least have asked Patrick to provide additional confirmation of enemy reinforcements before committing such a valuable resource as airborne troops.

One must question Patrick's performance on other grounds also. When he requested the airborne reinforcements, he, as ground commander, should have immediately ordered that the drop zone be kept free of obstacles, and personally verified that fact on the evening prior to the

Lt. Gen. Walter Krueger awarding Maj. Gen. Edwin D. Patrick the Legion of Merit, September 25, 1944, Hollandia, New Guinea.

(U.S. Army Photo)

drop, rather than belatedly finding on the morning of the drop that obstacles were present. Furthermore, knowing that the second contingent of paratroopers would follow on the next day, he should have deferred the hardening of the runway/drop zone until after the drop, or, if his engineers had to ready the runway immediately, request that the remaining reinforcements be brought by water. It is of interest that the casualties from the jumps, 128, exceeded the 121 wounded during combat operations.

The Noemfoor airbases would play an important role in support of the invasion of the Vogelkop Peninsula and Morotai Island. Bombers from Noemfoor conducted the first large–scale attacks on Japanese sources of petroleum products at Balikpapan, Borneo. Brigadier General Samuel D. Sturgis, Jr., chief engineer, Sixth Army, pointed out the critical importance of such airfields, stating that "the principal element to success or failure of amphibious operations has been air supremacy. This meant the construction of airdromes in newly won territory in the shortest possible time." He then went on to say that Patrick "was outstanding in his keen appreciation of this terribly important situation," and at Noemfoor "he practically directed as much, if not more, of his personal attention to the construction of the airdromes ... as he did to clean up the Japs," breaking all records in the construction of this strip "in the virtually impossible time demanded by GHQ." Sturgis then referred to a "personal letter" from MacArthur that he had seen, in which MacArthur stated that he thought that Patrick was "one of the few commanders" who discerned the importance of rapid construction of airfields in the advance areas.[21]

On July 4, 1944, MacArthur congratulated Krueger:

For General Krueger from General MacArthur, My heartiest congratulations to you, your fine staff, to General Patrick and to all ground troops engaged for the splendid execution of the Noemfoor Operation. It upheld the best soldiers [sic] tradition.[22]

On July 5, Krueger told Patrick:

My hearty congratulations to you and all members of your command for a splendid performance at Noemfoor. The enthusiasm, fighting spirit and aggressiveness displayed by all ranks were noteworthy and desere [sic] the highest praise. My appreciation for a job well done.[23]

Patrick was undoubtedly proud of the achievements of his troops in their rapid conquest of Noemfoor Island with very few

American casualties, as echoed in the messages of commendation from MacArthur and Krueger. He also paid tribute to his adversary, Shimizu, writing that his "elusive movements were brilliantly executed and he succeeded in denying any knowledge to his opponent of the size of his force."[24]

MacArthur awarded a commendation to Patrick for his conduct of the operation, and he also received the second award (Oak Leaf Cluster) of the Legion of Merit for his services as commander of the two task forces; his first award of that decoration was for his performance as chief of staff, Sixth Army.[25]

In August 1944, Krueger recommended new officer assignments to various major units under his command, and MacArthur's headquarters promptly approved these recommendations. Kreuger's recommendations for "promotions in the line were limited to officers who had demonstrated their fitness by actual command of troops for three months or more in combat." Among those officers whom Krueger had recommended for promotion "for outstanding combat performance" was Patrick, who would assume command of the 6th Infantry Division, now in the Cape Sansapor area of New Guinea.[26]

CHAPTER 16

WITH THE "SIGHTSEEING SIXTH" FROM SANSAPOR TO DINGALEN BAY

On June 30, 1944, MacArthur directed Alamo Force to seize, occupy, and defend the Cape Sansapor area of the Vogelkop Peninsula of Netherlands New Guinea. The purpose of this operation, to be code–named GLOBETROTTER, was to establish airbase and minor naval facilities in that area to support subsequent operations northwest toward the Philippines.[1]

Krueger selected the 6th Infantry Division, still in active combat in the Maffin Bay area as TORNADO Task Force, to seize and protect the Cape Sansapor area for the development of the air bases and naval facilities. The division, minus one regimental combat team that would serve as Alamo Force Reserve, was to land on a beach just northeast of the village of Mar at the mouth of the Wewe River on July 30. On D+1, the division would mount a shore–to–shore movement to seize and occupy Cape Sansapor, some nine miles to the southwest. The division was also ordered to seize and occupy two offshore islands, Middleburg and Amsterdam.[2]

ULTRA had informed MacArthur that there were two Japanese strongholds on the Vogelkop Peninsula: at Manokwari 120 miles east of Sansapor, where there were about 15,000 troops, and at Sorong about 60 miles west of Sansapor, where there were about 12,500 troops. There were no significant numbers of Japanese at Sansapor. ULTRA further reported that the enemy expected the Americans to land at either Sorong–Halmahera, or on Mindinao at Davao. Armed with this information, MacArthur ordered the assault forces to land at Sansapor.[3]

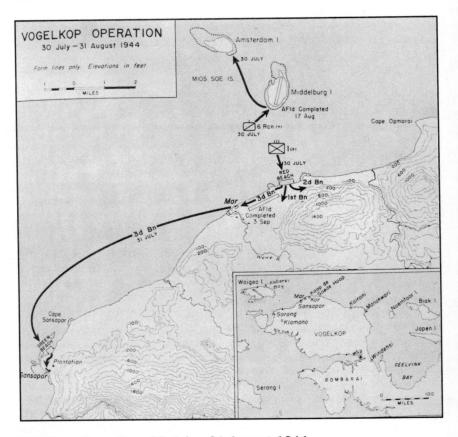

Vogelkop Operation, 30 July—31 August 1944
(Smith, *Approach to the Philippines*, 431)

At 0700, July 30, two battalions of the 1st Infantry landed
abreast southwest of Cape Opmarai against no opposition and
moved inland to the hills. About forty–five minutes later, other
elements of the division secured Amsterdam and Middleburg Islands, and on July 31 the 1st Infantry's third battalion landed
unopposed at Cape Sansapor and rapidly secured the area. By
landing at Sansapor, MacArthur had divided the Japanese forces
on the Vogelkop Peninsula, rendering the two troop concentra-
tions incapable of seriously threatening the Americans on the
peninsula.

Throughout August, the division conducted extensive patrolling, encountering some Japanese troops withdrawing to Sorong.
By August 17, a 5,400 foot runway was operational on Middleburg
Island, and the airfield near Mar became operational on September 3. Krueger terminated GLOBETROTTER on August 31.[4]

On August 24, Major General Franklin C. Sibert relinquished command of the 6th Infantry Division to become commanding general of X Corps. Brigadier General Charles E. Hurdis, the division artillery commander, assumed temporary command of the division until its newly promoted commander, Major General Edwin D. Patrick arrived in early September; Patrick received his promotion on September 5, 1944.[5]

One wonders if, as he assumed command of the 6th Infantry Division, Patrick might have heard or read of the "NBC Army Hour" broadcast of September 18, 1944, during which Krueger spoke on the occasion marking the Infantry School's commissioning of fifty thousand enlisted men as second lieutenants since the program began:

> Your men will follow where you lead, if you have their confidence and respect. Look to their welfare always, share their hardships, be fair in all things, and they will never let you down. No matter how small any task assigned to you may be, do it well; there is no greater pleasure than the satisfaction of a job well done. Your reward will be the good will and approbation of your comrades. Set your standards high; place duty above all else, and remember always that only he who has learned to obey is fit to exercise command.[6]

This code of the infantry officer, which Krueger so eloquently expressed, was indeed to become the standard that would guide Patrick's actions during his six and one–half months as commander of the "Sightseeing Sixth."

Under their new commander the "Sightseers" began an intensive training program in preparation for their next operation, rumors suggesting that it might take place at Morotai, Palau, Borneo, or Leyte. The 6th Division soldiers soon learned, however, that they would be landing on the island of Luzon.

During the final two months of 1944, the pace of training intensified. Patrick placed particular emphasis on small unit tactics, with platoon and squad leaders controlling their troops' fire and maneuver by a system of arm and hand signals, known as "Able–Baker–Charlie or "ABC" tactics. In addition to daily drills in the "ABC's," the troops engaged in weekly problems that took them into the nearby jungles and up the rugged hills behind the garrison area. This intensive training in very rugged territory would soon reap rich dividends in the difficult terrain the division would encounter on Luzon. The division personnel also took part in familiarization studies to acquaint them with Luzon, its terrain, its people and their customs, and its languages.[7]

On December 24, the division conducted a rehearsal ship-to-shore landing at the request of Rear Admiral William M. Fechteler, the commander of Task Group 78.5, which was the amphibious force that would transport the "Sightseers" to Luzon, and land them on "Blue Beach" at Lingayen Gulf.[8]

Fechteler was concerned about the inexperience of some of his assault landing craft crews, particularly those that were to man the LVTs (landing vehicle, tracked) and the LCVPs (landing craft, vehicle and personnel) that would carry the assault troops to the beaches. He therefore asked Patrick for permission to conduct the rehearsal with the actual assault troops embarked in the landing craft. Lieutenant Colonel Bruce Palmer, chief of staff of the 6th Division, felt this would pose an unnecessary risk to the infantrymen, and so advised Patrick. Patrick, however, disagreed, and authorized the rehearsal as Fechteler desired.[9]

The fully-loaded LVTs sailed at night, traveled about one hundred miles, crossing the equator, and returned for a dawn landing at Sansapor. The surf was "particularly wicked and numerous LVTs broached." Five LVTs sank, trapping their occupants. Twenty-five men drowned, and considerable equipment was lost. Palmer was quite upset about the incident, as was Patrick, who in private had "some harsh words" with Fechteler.[10]

Patrick, however, was apparently not a man to hold a grudge. Several days later, on December 28, Patrick invited Fechteler and his staff ashore for a "Farewell to New Guinea" party. By the time the party was over and it was time for Fechteler to return to his ship, "both Fechteler and Patrick were feeling no pain." Patrick and Palmer accompanied Fechteler back to his ship aboard a DUKW (amphibian, 2½ ton, 6x6 truck) . When they arrived, the gangplank leading up to the deck was moving up and down some six to eight feet in the heavy swells. Fechteler successfully made it aboard, but Patrick slipped and "went into the drink." Concerned that the general might be crushed between the two ships, Palmer and the others aboard the DUKW quickly fished Patrick out of the ocean without further mishap. Despite his chief of staff's concern for his safety, Patrick "thought it was pretty funny."[11]

Although very occupied with the preparation of his division for combat on Luzon, Patrick found time to go fishing from his boat every Sunday and when he would visit his division outposts by boat. He indicated, however, that the fishing off New Guinea was "not as good as back home and the fish aren't nearly as good to eat." He also kept his family in Tell City up to date on the activities of his sons: Ricky with the army in Iceland, Eddie now in the navy in San Diego, and Tom in school in New Mexico.

Preparing to leave New Guinea, Patrick, in a letter dated November 11, recalled the World War I armistice twenty–six years before, contrasting the heat of that day in 1944 with the frigid conditions he had experienced on November 11, 1918. In closing he said that he was going to tune in "Tokyo Rose's program ... the only one I can get clearly." Despite the propaganda, "she plays some good American phonograph records."[12]

On December 29, 1944, the 6th Infantry Division boarded its ships, and the following afternoon mounted out of the Sansapor area, beginning the voyage to Luzon. Patrick traveled aboard Fechteler's flagship, the *Fremont*, an APA (attack transport).[13]

While aboard the *Fremont*, Patrick enjoyed a "fine New Year's dinner" that day: turkey with all the trimmings. Contrasting the style of living enjoyed by navy personnel with that of soldiers, Patrick opined that "the Army lives in abject poverty [and that it was] a treat to travel with the Navy." He reassured his family that he was not worried about the upcoming operation, and was "rather looking forward to it." He believed that his division was a good one and I'm sure it will give a good account of itself."[14]

All elements of the amphibious attack force rendezvoused in Leyte Gulf during the period January 1–5, 1945. On the night of January 4–5, the VII Amphibious Force, carrying I Corps troops, of which the 6th Division was a part, left Leyte Gulf, as part of a convoy over forty miles long.[15]

The voyage north was quite uneventful until January 7, when a small group of Japanese kamikaze aircraft attacked that part of the convoy containing Fechteler's task group. Naval antiaircraft fire destroyed two of the planes, but a third managed to crash into a LST (landing ship, tank), causing only slight damage to the superstructure. The following day an enemy plane crashed into the transport *Calloway*, killing several men, most of whom were naval personnel.[16]

In the early morning hours of January 9 the convoy steamed into Lingayen Gulf, amid flashes of gunfire from the ships that had been shelling the assault beaches for two days. As day began to break, the men of the 6th Division saw spread out before them the armada that was to carry out the largest amphibious assault in the Pacific theater to date.

The operation plan called for the landing of elements of two corps on the assault beaches along the south and southeast shores of Lingayen Gulf. The 40th and 37th Infantry Divisions, of the XIV Corps, would each land two regimental combat teams on the west-

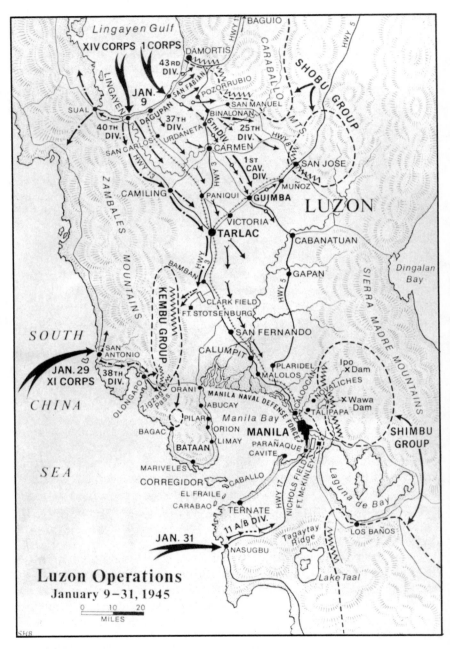

Luzon Operations, January 9—31, 1945

(James, *The Years of MacArthur,* 624)

ern most beaches, code–named from east to west, "Crimson," "Yel-low," "Green," and "Orange." The 40th Division would be on the corps right flank. East of the XIV Corps, the I Corps assault divisions, the 6th on the right and the 43d on the left, would land on beaches "Blue 1" and "Blue 2" in the 6th Division's sector, and on "White 1," "White 2," and "White 3" in the 43d Division's sector. In contrast to the proximity of the XIV Corps beaches, those of I Corps were widely separated.[17]

At 0700 hours, January 9, the pre–assault naval and air bombardment began, continuing for the next two hours. At about the same time the men of the 6th Division began to load into the LVTs, LCVs, and LCMs that would carry them to the beach. All landing craft were loaded and launched by 0830, H–1. Just after daybreak Palmer left the *Fremont* in a LCVP to observe the marshaling of the division's assault waves, and to check the time that the LVTs crossed the line of departure, from which they would begin their "run–in" to the beaches. Because of a strong ebb tide, there was "some confusion" in getting the assault waves organized. Although the leading waves of the 1st Infantry and 20th Infantry landed simultaneously, they were about ten minutes late.[18]

Meeting virtually no opposition on the beaches, the assault elements of the 1st and 20th Infantry moved rapidly inland in their LVTs. They quickly seized one of the S–day[19] objectives, the Dagupan Bridge across the Pantal River, and by dusk had secured a line along the Mangaldan–Dagupan highway, some $3^1/_2$ miles inland.[20]

Patrick had observed the landings from the *Fremont*, and about noon came ashore to join Palmer and other staff officers at the 6th Division command post. A short time later, Major General Innis P. Swift, Commanding General, I Corps, arrived at the command post, where he reviewed the situation with Patrick and his staff. Shortly after Swift departed to visit his other division, the 43d, Patrick left his command post to locate the commanders of the 1st and 20th Infantry, not returning to the command post until late that afternoon. Patrick thus established a style of command that would characterize his actions as a division commander until his death less than two months later: He believed that a commander must visit the forward areas frequently if he were to have an accurate assessment of the situation; effective command and control could best be exercised from the division forward areas, rather than from the CP.[21]

As Patrick was visiting his forward elements, additional troops, artillery, ammunition, rations, and other supplies poured into the beachhead. By early afternoon some three hundred Filipinos had been recruited to assist in off-loading supplies.[22]

Maj. Gen. Innis P. Swift, Commander, I Corps, with Maj. Gen. Edwin D. Patrick at 6th Infantry Division CP, January 9, 1945, Luzon
(Courtesy of Thomas B. Patrick)

Gen. Douglas MacArthur (right) and Lt. Gen. Richard Sutherland (left) with Maj. Gen. Edwin D. Patrick at 6th Infantry Division CP, January 9, 1945, Luzon
(Courtesy of MacArthur Memorial, Norfolk, VA.)

Lieut. Gen. Walter Krueger with Maj. Gen. Edwin D. Patrick at 6th Infantry Division CP, January 1945, Luzon
(Courtesy of Thomas B. Patrick)

On January 10, the 1st and 20th Infantry infantrymen consolidated their positions, while division engineers worked feverishly on a bridge across the Binloc River to provide a route that would ensure supply of the division's forward elements. Hampered by a cave–in and the lack of bridging materials, the engineers finally resorted to an earthen fill to span the stream, and by noon on the 12th had completed the task. Supplies and supporting artillery were soon moving rapidly to the forward infantry elements.[23]

On January 10, Swift had ordered Patrick's 63d Infantry to land in the 43d Division's sector to support that division in its attack to the east and northeast of the division assault beaches. Because of the strong enemy resistance, the 43d Division was meeting in the Damortis–Rosario area, the 63d Infantry would remain with that division until the end of January. During that time Patrick would have only two regiments to accomplish the missions assigned to his division by I Corps.[24]

Although enemy resistance continued to be light in the 6th Division sector, the division had not advanced as rapidly as the 37th Division on its right, mainly because the I Corps sector was considerably larger in area than that assigned to the XIV Corps, necessitating a slower overall advance of Patrick's troops as they

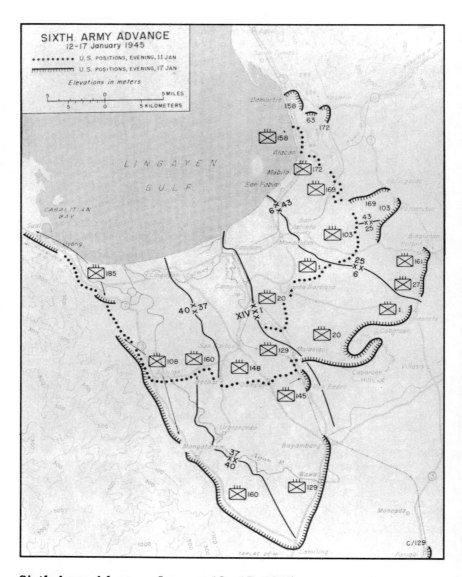

Sixth Army Advance, January 12—17, 1945

(Smith, *Triumph in the Philippines*, 116)

cleared their sector of the enemy. Fearing that a sizable gap would soon appear between the I Corps right flank and the left flank of the more rapidly advancing XIV Corps, Krueger decided on January 11 to commit the 158th Regimental Combat Team, a portion of his Sixth Army Reserve, in the I Corps area to maintain the speed of the advance.[25]

Thus far Patrick's troops had met only light resistance, and by nightfall of the 11th were disposed generally along the line Mapandan–Santa Barbara–Balingueo. Undoubtedly the division could have moved forward to the Army Beachhead Line and the Agno River against the light enemy opposition, but Swift held the division back to avoid creating a dangerous gap between the 6th Division and his remaining I Corps forces to the east and north. He therefore directed Patrick to move his division south only to a line extending northeast from Malasiqui, on the I–XIV Corps boundary about twelve miles inland, and from there across almost ten miles of open farm land to the 6th–43d division boundary near Manaoag. On January 12 and 13, the "Sightseers" displaced forward to this new line against negligible opposition. Patrols soon established that there were significant enemy forces in the vicinity of Urdenata and in Villasis, a town five miles south of Urdenata on the north bank of the Agno River.[26]

When Krueger committed the 25th Division to replace 43d Division units on the 6th Division's left flank on January 17, Patrick was able to order an advance toward Urdenata and the Cabaruan Hills. Up to this point his division, less the 63d Regiment, had suffered no more than twenty men killed and ninety wounded.[27]

On January 17, the XIV Corps had established a salient extending south to the village of Camiling, some twelve to fifteen miles south of the most forward elements of the 6th Division on the corps left flank. Krueger intended to hold XIV Corps along the line of the Agno River until Swift's I Corps could overcome the enemy resistance from Damortis to Urdenata, and begin moving south in conjunction with Lieutenant General Oscar W. Griswold's XIV Corps, with no fear of an enemy attack on Sixth Army's left flank and base areas. Krueger reasoned that this threat could not be effectively eliminated until the end of January. MacArthur, however, felt that the threat to Krueger's left was not as great as the latter supposed, and urged him to move more quickly southward into the Central Plains–Manila Bay region. In addition to his desire to seize Manila at an early date, MacArthur felt that seizure of Clark Field was imperative if the Fifth Air Force were to support the ground action on Luzon effectively.[28]

MacArthur ordered that XIV Corps advance toward Manila, with the right flank I Corps forces echeloned to the XIV Corps rear, protecting XIV Corps and simultaneously containing Japanese forces that might threaten the XIV Corps' eastern flank. On January 18, Krueger issued orders that would provide for the execution of MacArthur's directive. I Corps was to secure that segment of Route 3 running north from Pozorrubio to its junction with Route 11, and the segment of Route 31 running west of that junction to Damortis. The 6th Division was to advance along a line just east of Route 3 to a point east of the former XIV Corps outpost line, and establish an outpost line running from Victoria northeastward eight miles to the town of Giumba. Patrick would have to begin this mission without his 63d Infantry Regiment, still busily fighting with the 43d Division to secure the Damortis–Rosario road.[29]

By January 17, when Patrick's men began moving south, they knew from patrol reports that there was a pocket of Japanese resistance in the Cabaruan Hills, a four-mile-square area of low hills covered with bamboo, some scrub growth, and a few palms, and some open fields. These hills dominated the "Sightseers" approach to Route 3 and the Agno River south and southeast of the present division line.

Patrick planned to attack the hills with the 20th Infantry, which on the 17th moved toward the hills.[30] The 2d Battalion, which was to make the main attack, moved southeast from the barrio of Lunec across open rice paddies into the hills. By the evening of the 18th, the battalion occupied lines about 2,500 yards southeast of the town of Cabaruan. The main enemy force appeared to lie in a group of knolls and ridges 1,000 to 1,500 yards to the front of the battalion position. Since the troops had met lighter than expected resistance, Patrick estimated that the hills could be secured by the evening of the 19th, when the division could resume its southerly movement.

Patrick's optimism appeared to be confirmed by the success his troops had on the 19th. He therefore ordered two battalions out of the hills, leaving only a reinforced battalion to finish mopping up. This battalion probed forward on January 20–21, and jumped off the next day on what it expected to be the final attack to clear the hills.

However, the attack soon ran into trouble, in part because the preparatory air strike was four hours late, subjecting the infantrymen to " 'a nerve racking wait,' " and did not include the napalm Patrick had requested. The infantrymen moved out at 1230, and advanced slowly but steadily for about two hours, at which time they were stopped by a "tremendous burst of rifle, machine gun, and light artillery fire." The troops were forced to fall back, after suffering ten men killed and thirty–five wounded.

Colonel Washington M. Ives, Jr., the regimental commander, requested reinforcements, and Patrick dispatched a battalion from the 1st Infantry to Ives so that the division's advance to the south and east would not be delayed by the resistance in the Cabaruan Hills.

On January, the newly–arrived battalion resumed the attack, and by nightfall had closed with the main enemy defenses. Once again optimistic about a rapid conclusion to the battle for the hills, Patrick ordered the remaining battalion of the 20th Infantry out of the hills, confident that the 2d Battalion of the 1st Infantry could complete the task. The January 25–26 attacks by this battalion shattered Patrick's optimism, when the attacks gained only 450 yards against determined enemy resistance. Patrick then ordered another battalion from the 1st Infantry into the hills, and a two–battalion attack on the 28th finally destroyed all enemy resistance in the hills by 1600 hours.

The battle for the Cabaruan Hills cost the 6th Division 81 dead and 198 wounded. The Japanese lost 1,432 killed, and the Americans captured 7 prisoners. Although the Japanese forces in the hills fought to their deaths, their resistance produced no significant slowing of the 6th Division's advance, as the bulk of the division swept around and beyond the hills.

As the 20th Infantry began its attack on the Cabaruan Hills on January 17, the 1st Infantry started its advance toward the village of Urdenata, moving on it from the west and northwest. The regiment engaged a small enemy detachment in the village, and, after a brisk fire fight lasting one–half hour, secured the village, killing one hundred Japanese at a cost of five men killed and fifteen wounded.

Relieved at Urdenata by elements of the 25th Division, the 1st Infantry on January 19, moved quickly down Route 3 to Villasis. The regiment occupied Villasis with no opposition, and crossed the Agno River in LVTs to secure Carmen, on the river's south bank, and Rosales, three miles east of Carmen. On the 20th, the 1st Infantry continued its advance eastward along Route 8 to Balungao, which lay on the division objective line established by I Corps.

As the 2d Battalion, 1st Infantry, was completing the clearing of the Cabaruan Hills, the 20th Infantry moved south and southeast to Cuyapo, the southern anchor of the division objective line, which stretched from Bactad through Balungao to Cuyapo. Patrick's division had now secured its portion of the I Corps objective line, and was poised to go on to the corps reconnaissance line, extending from Victoria, fourteen miles south of Cuyapo, to Giumba, some ten miles southeast of Cuyapo.

Patrick's former chief of staff, then-Colonel Bruce Palmer, Jr., states that in the battle for the Cabaruan Hills he began to see traits in his division commander that would manifest themselves repeatedly during the Luzon campaign: impatience, impulsiveness, a tendency to drive his troops and their leaders "hard," a belief in exerting "strong personal leadership" from forward areas, and a strongly–held belief that the mission must always come first.[31]

Patrick's impatience and possible impulsiveness showed in his frustration at not being able to clear the enemy from the Cabaruan Hills as quickly as he had anticipated. Ignoring warnings from both the commander of the 20th Infantry and the commander of the 1st Infantry that this would be "a very tough nut to crack," and pressed by higher headquarters to make faster progress, Patrick left only one battalion to "mop up," sending the rest of the 20th Infantry on its way south. Ultimately, two battalions of the 1st Infantry would be required to complete the destruction of the enemy forces in the Cabaruan Hills.[32]

During the battle for the Cabaruan Hills Patrick was frequently in the regimental forward areas. On one occasion he and Second Lieutenant Joseph A. Castagnetto, his aide–de–camp, were lying in a ditch watching an air strike that Patrick had ordered. As the planes dropped their loads of napalm, Castagnetto heard "zing, zing, zing," and commented to Patrick that "there must be bees around here." But Castagnetto quickly realized that they were under sniper fire, and "knocked" the general out of the line of fire. Patrick asked, "Castagnetto, what the hell are you doing?", to which his aide replied that he would not allow Patrick to be killed during his tour of duty as the general's aide. Castagnetto also admonished Patrick not to have the two stars on his helmet facing toward the enemy, since they provided an inviting target.[33]

By January 31, XIV Corps units had seized Clark Field and had secured a line in the mountains to the west of the airfield. In addition, XI Corps had landed on the west coast of Luzon in the San Antonio–San Narciso area in Zambales Province, and had moved inland to Olongapo at the head of Subic Bay, opening the bay to Allied shipping. Krueger now ordered XIV Corps to mount a two–division attack to seize Manila. To cover the east flank of the advancing XIV Corps, Krueger ordered I Corps to launch a two–pronged attack to secure San Jose and a line that ran from Bongabon northwest to Rizal.[34]

On the 28th, 6th Division troops were in Victoria and Giumba, and on the next day they moved up to relieve a 37th Division out-

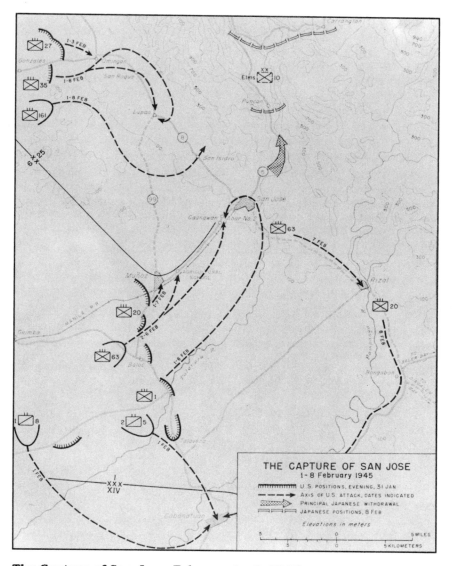

THE CAPTURE OF SAN JOSE
1-8 February 1945

U.S. POSITIONS, EVENING, 31 JAN
AXIS OF U.S. ATTACK, DATES INDICATED
PRINCIPAL JAPANESE WITHDRAWAL
JAPANESE POSITIONS, 8 FEB

Elevations in meters

5 MILES
5 KILOMETERS

The Capture of San Jose, February 1—8, 1945
(Smith, *Triumph in the Philippines*, 191)

post at Licab, five miles east of Victoria. Against no opposition, the "Sightseers" moved rapidly eastward and on January 30 secured the barrio of Baloc on Route 5. By cutting Route 5 at Baloc, the 6th Division had severed the main line of communications between the Japanese forces in northern Luzon, the *Shobu* Group, and those in southern Luzon, the *Shimbu* Group.[35]

Muñoz, a small town five miles north of Baloc on Route 5, marked the northern end of the 6th Division position on the Licab–Lupao line that Krueger had ordered I Corps to occupy. The initial division reconnaissance had suggested that the town was unoccupied. However, when a rifle company of the 20th Infantry attempted to enter the town they met heavy resistance, and withdrew.

Krueger, on the basis of I Corps reconnaissance, believed that a Japanese tank division and a large portion of an enemy infantry division were in the San Jose–Muñoz–Lupao area. Accordingly, on January 30, he ordered I Corps to seize San Jose and secure the line San Jose–Rizal–Cabanatuan.

Swift's plan ordered the 6th Division to attack northeast up Route 5 through Muñoz, while the 25th Division would drive southeast through Lupao on Route 8.

On February 1, after an artillery preparation, the 20th Infantry's third battalion attacked through the relatively open terrain west of Muñoz, hoping to seize a portion of Route 99 along the western edge of the town. Heavy tank and artillery fire, however, stalled the attack short of Route 99. The 1st Battalion, coming up on the right reached only the southeast corner of the town. A continued attack on February 2 resulted in only slight gains.[36]

Already dissatisfied with the performance of the 20th Infantry in the Cabaruan Hills, and losing his patience with what he felt to be its "inordinately slow progress at Muñoz," Patrick relieved Ives, the 20th Infantry's commander, "an action he later came to regret."[37]

The 3d of February saw no further progress in the attack on Muñoz, even though the 2d Battalion, 20th Infantry, moved in on the northwest. Patrick now realized that Muñoz "was going to be a costly, hard, and time–consuming nut to crack." The 25th Division had also run into a similar situation at Umingan, on the approach to Lupao.

Although not anticipating the delay at Muñoz, Patrick had fortuitously directed the 1st Infantry to reconnoiter east of Muñoz along the Talavera River, with the hope of finding an overland approach to the San Jose–Rizal road, where it could assemble and attack San Jose from the southeast, as the 20th Infantry drove northeast along Route 5. Patrick also had the 63d Infantry, once more back with his division, move east of Muñoz to Route 5 north of the town, ready to move on San Jose "in concert with the 1st Infantry."

On the 2d, the 3d Battalion, 1st Infantry, had secured the San Jose–Rizal road at the bridge over the Talavera River. The 1st's second battalion bypassed Rizal to the west and took position on the San Jose–Rizal road near Bicos. On that afternoon the 63d Infantry reached the agricultural school on the road between Muñoz and San Jose, and, leaving Company L to clear the school of the enemy, moved to within two miles of San Jose by nightfall. At 2000, on February 3, Patrick ordered the 1st Infantry, from their positions 1,000 yards south and 1,500 yards east of San Jose, to join in a two–pronged attack with the 63d Infantry on the south against San Jose the next day.

The 63d Infantry was held up the next morning by Japanese forces south of San Jose, and took no part in its capture. The 1st Infantry entered the town against practically no opposition, at a cost of two killed and twenty–five wounded: one of the killed and seven of the wounded resulted from an unscheduled strafing run across the regimental front by Fifth Air Force medium bombers.

The 20th Infantry, meanwhile, had kept up its attack against the stubborn defenders of Muñoz. By the 4th, the attack against Muñoz had become "a siege." By the evening of the 6th, the 20th Infantry had destroyed approximately thirty–five enemy tanks, but the Japanese still possessed an additional twenty to twenty–five. The enemy forces continued to hold half the town, and still were at more than half their original strength. Thus far the 20th had lost 40 men killed and 175 wounded.

Patrick realized that if he were to take the town soon, and with reasonable casualties, he would have to change his tactics. He therefore planned a massive air and artillery bombardment, climaxing with a napalm saturation of the enemy positions, for February 7. Behind a rolling artillery barrage, the 20th Infantry, joined by the redeployed 63d Infantry, would launch the final assault. But in the early hours of February 7, the main body of the Japanese force defending Muñoz attempted to escape northward along the road to San Jose, apparently not realizing that the road was in American hands. As they attempted to run a gantlet lined by American infantry troops and artillery battalions, the Japanese force was destroyed. Shortly after daylight that morning the 20th Infantry entered Muñoz almost unopposed, and by noon had cleared the town. The taking of Muñoz had cost Patrick 90 men killed and nearly 250 wounded.

On the same day the 63d Infantry seized Rizal against light opposition. The next day the 20th Infantry secured Bongabon and cleared the road leading from Rizal through Bongabon to Cabanatuan.

Swift then ordered Patrick to reconnoiter to the east coast of Luzon. On February 11, a 20th Infantry–6th Reconnaissance Troop patrol reached Dingalen Bay. The following day a patrol of 63d Infantry and 6th Reconnaissance Troop soldiers reached Baler Bay. Finding no enemy at either location, the "Sightseers" turned over security of the bays' shores and the roads leading back from them to Filipino guerrillas, and returned to the division.

Once again Patrick's impatience manifested itself in the action at Muñoz, where he relieved Ives. Palmer, however, offers some mitigating factors, stating that "both I Corps and Sixth Army HQ grossly underestimated the enemy strength at Muñoz and pressed Patrick very hard for quick results." Patrick, therefore, "issued an ultimatum to the C.O. 20th Infantry to take Muñoz in 24 hours or be relieved." However, Patrick later expressed regret about Ives' relief, although "the damage had been done."[38]

With his regiment making no significant gains in two days of attacks, Patrick, as the commander on the ground, should have initiated appropriate reconnaissance activities to attempt a reassessment of the enemy strength at Muñoz. Such reconnaissance might have revealed that the enemy was in fact stronger than he had been led to believe, and induced Patrick to call for the combined aerial and artillery attack, including napalm, earlier than February 7.

The battle for Muñoz aside, Patrick's otherwise masterful handling of his division during this operation exemplified his sound grasp of tactical principles, and his knowledge and proper application of the principles of war. Not losing sight of the Sixth Army and I Corps objectives, i.e., the seizure of San Jose and the destruction of enemy forces within the San Jose–Rizal–Cabanatuan triangle, Patrick had moved his 1st Infantry eastward, hoping to use it in an attack against San Jose from the east in concert with the attack of the 20th Infantry from the west. He also ordered his 63d Infantry to bypass Muñoz to the east and secure the road leading from Muñoz to San Jose, and be prepared to attack Muñoz from the north to assist the 1st Infantry in its attack. That deployment of the 63d Infantry also placed it in a perfect position to destroy the Muñoz force as it attempted to escape to the north on the 7th. Patrick then rapidly moved a portion of the 63d Infantry eastward to seize Rizal, and ordered troops of the 20th Infantry also to move eastward to secure the Rizal–Cabanatuan road at

Bongabon. These moves not only closed the triangle thought to contain major Japanese forces, but placed Patrick's troops in position to perform their additional mission of reconnaissance to Luzon's east coast. Patrick thus did not lose sight of the missions assigned to his division, and by skillful and rapid maneuver of his forces massed them at points to accomplish those missions and to seize assigned objectives. Throughout the operation Patrick maintained the offensive, never breaking contact with the enemy, nor allowing himself to be forced to go on the defensive.

As the 6th Division was completing its operations in the San Jose area, the 37th and 1st Cavalry Divisions of XIV Corps were poised to enter Manila.[39] After the divisions had cleared that part of Manila north of the Pasig River and had secured Manila's close-in water supply facilities, Griswold ordered the 37th Division to cross the Pasig on February 7, and assigned to it a sector that included most of Manila south of the river. The 1st Cavalry Division crossed the river during the night of February 9–10, and advanced to place itself on the left of the 37th Division. At the same time that these divisions were entering Manila from the north, the 11th Airborne Division had arrived at the southern outskirts of the city after an advance from Nasugbu Bay, where the division had made an amphibious landing on January 31.

Griswold was prepared by the 18th to begin the final assault to clear Intramuros (the Walled City) and the Manila port area. The assault began on February 23, and two days later, after bitter fighting, the Americans had crushed the enemy resistance in Intramuros and in most of the rest of Manila. However, it was not until March 4 that Krueger declared Manila completely liberated.[40]

After the fall of Manila, Krueger put into operation his plan to clear Manila Bay by seizing the Bataan peninsula, Corregidor island at the entrance to Manila Bay, and the south coast of the bay in the Ternate area. Krueger planned to send a reinforced regimental combat team down the east coast of the Bataan peninsula, while another reinforced regimental combat team seized the Mariveles area at the southern tip of the peninsula by a shore–to–shore movement. Krueger directed that Corregidor be taken by a combined airborne and shore–to–shore assault.[41]

Krueger had originally planned to use XI Corps to clear the Bataan peninsula. This corps had landed on the west coast of Luzon in Zambales Province on January 31, with the mission of driving across the base of the Bataan peninsula and linking up with XIV Corps on the eastern coast of Manila Bay. Krueger had estimated that this link–up would occur by mid–February, and that XI Corps troops could then be used to implement his plan for clearing the peninsula. On February 1, however, the 38th Division ran into heavy enemy resistance in an area known as Zigzag Pass, and was not able to clear this area until the 15th. Krueger now realized that not all XI Corps troops would be available to take part in the clearing operation along the eastern coast of the peninsula, now scheduled to begin on February 15. Krueger, therefore, directed Patrick to send his 1st Infantry Regiment to XI Corps to assist it in carrying out the advance southward along Bataan's eastern coast.[42]

On February 1, the 1st Infantry, now operating under command of Brigadier General William Spence, commander of the 38th Division's artillery, began its advance from Orani. By nightfall the force had reached Pilar, and on the next day moved on to Orion, where that night the regiment beat off an attack by an estimated three hundred Japanese. During the period February 17–20, the 1st Infantry, augmented by forces from the 38th Division, moved across the peninsula to Bagac, encountering only a few Japanese stragglers. On the 21st, south of Bagac, the 1st Infantry made contact with elements of the 151st Infantry, advancing northward along the west coast from Mariveles, where the regiment had landed on February 16. The 38th Division's 149th Infantry relieved the 1st Infantry in the Bagac area on February 20, freeing the 1st to rejoin its parent division on the 25th.[43]

CHAPTER 17

ASSAULTING THE SHIMBU LINE

By March 5, 1945, Krueger's Sixth Army had split the enemy forces on Luzon into three main groups: those in the mountains east and northeast of Manila and in southern Luzon (*Shimbu* Group), those in western Luzon (*Kembu* Group), and those in northern Luzon (*Shobu* Group). From the beginning of the Luzon campaign Krueger had realized that he would have insufficient forces to conduct operations against those three groups simultaneously. He did believe, however, that he would be able to undertake some operations against each group, since he expected to be able to retain all of the troops, except some elements of the 24th Division, deployed on Luzon as of early February.

However, during early February MacArthur decided that Krueger should devote his principal efforts to clearing the Manila–Manila Bay area, and that attacks against the *Shobu* and *Shimbu* Groups should assume secondary importance to that task. In order to clear the Visayan Passages to provide a shorter shipping route to Luzon, MacArthur also directed Krueger to divert forces to clear southern Luzon and the Bicol Peninsula. MacArthur further limited Krueger's ability to bring adequate forces to bear against the *Shimbu* and *Shobu* forces by reassigning to the newly created Eighth Army, charged with clearing the southern Philippines, one division and two regimental combat teams already on Luzon and another division slated to arrive on Luzon. In addition, the 37th Division was to be held in Manila as a garrison force for at least two months after the capture of that city. Thus, instead of the eleven divisions and four regimental combat teams he had planned to use to complete the Luzon campaign, Krueger now found himself with nine divisions, one of which was to remain in Manila for an undetermined time, and two regimental combat teams.

Despite MacArthur's insistence that Sixth Army clear southern Luzon, Krueger felt that if he were to insure the safety of the Manila–Manila Bay area, he must initiate at least a limited offensive against the *Shimbu* Group in the mountains east and northeast of Manila. In addition to posing a physical threat to Manila, this force controlled the main sources of Manila's water supply.

Krueger decided to attack the *Shimbu* Group with XIV Corps, and to increase its combat strength he "reluctantly" redeployed Patrick's 6th Division from I Corps, slated to conduct operations against the *Shobu* Group in the north, to Griswold's XIV Corps.[1]

Twenty–five miles northeast of Manila lay Ipo Dam on the Angat River, which supplied about one–third of Manila's water. Fifteen miles northeast of Manila and south of Ipo Dam, the smaller Wawa Dam was located on the Marakina River, which Sixth Army and XIV Corps erroneously believed was a part of the Manila water system. In fact, this water source had been abandoned in 1938, when Ipo Dam and the Novaliches Reservoir had been completed. In this area Lieutenant General Yokoyama Shizuo, *Shimbu* Group commander, had deployed about thirty thousand troops in "excellent defensive terrain and well–prepared positions." Defending the Ipo Dam was the nine thousand–man Kawashima Force. South of this force was the twelve thousand–man Kobayashi Force, responsible for a line south to a point midway between Wawa Dam and Antipolo. The nine thousand–man Noguchi Force defended south from this point to the north–central shore of Laguna de Bay. Sixth Army had incorrectly estimated that only twenty thousand Japanese troops confronted XIV Corps.[2]

Griswold directed Patrick to have his division seize Ipo and Wawa Dams, while the 2d Cavalry Brigade to his south would secure the Antipolo–Tagig area. Patrick ordered his 20th Infantry to strike directly east toward Wawa Dam. The 112th Cavalry Regimental Combat Team, attached to the 6th Division, would protect the XIV Corps line of communications south along Route 5, and patrol on the 6th Division's left flank toward Ipo Dam. The 63d Infantry was to patrol toward Ipo Dam with its left flank forces, and, in concert with the 20th Infantry on its right, attack Wawa Dam. The 2d Cavalry Brigade would seize Antipolo and secure the Antipolo–Tagig segment of the corps objective line. The line of departure would be the west bank of the Marakina River, where the troops would be concealed behind a high ridge that formed the west bank.[3]

Looking across the Marakina River, Patrick's troops could clearly see the formidable terrain they were to attack. Rising from the Marakina Valley some four miles east of the river was the Sierra Madre, a range of mountains that rose in height progressively

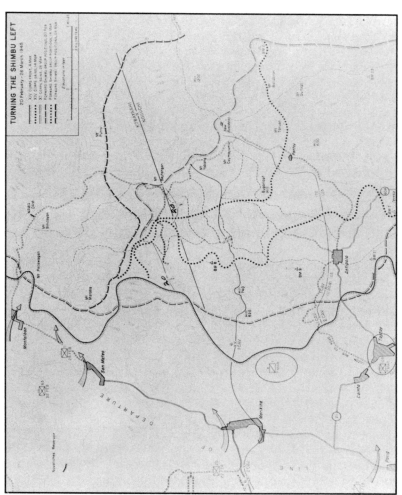

Turning the Shimbu Left, February 20—March 26 1945.
(Smith, *Triumph in the Philippines*, Map VIII)

to peaks of up to 1,500 feet. The western slopes were steep and grassy, but at higher elevations forest interspersed with dense jungle undergrowth covered the hills. The infantrymen knew that each of these formidable ridges and peaks was bristling with well–emplaced Japanese troops. The Japanese had positioned themselves in caves within the limestone hills and had improved these natural defensive positions by digging numerous interconnected subterranean strongholds. The entrances were protected by manned bunkers, and machine guns covered all avenues of approach. The enemy artillery pieces were also concealed in caves, out of which they would be moved to fire, and to which they would withdraw before effective American counterbattery fire could be mounted.[4]

On February 22, the 20th Infantry began to cross the Marakina River at Marakina town, while the 63d Infantry crossed to the north at Montalban and San Mateo.[5] By the evening of the 23d, the men of the 20th Infantry were in the steep grassy hills a mile northeast of Marakina, while the 63d Infantry troops were pushing into the high ground east of San Mateo. Thus far the Japanese had offered no resistance.

With the 20th Infantry making the main effort, Patrick directed his division against both 1,500 foot Mount Pacawagan and 1,400 foot Mount Mataba. However, the regiment gained little ground against the Japanese resistance. When the 1st Infantry returned from Bataan on February 25, Patrick directed it to attack between the 20th and 63d regiments, seizing the southern third of Mount Pacawagan and the northern two–thirds of Mount Mataba and the intervening ground, and then strike toward Wawa Dam with the 63d Infantry, which had the responsibility of seizing the northern two–thirds of Mount Pacawagan. The 20th Infantry, after securing the southern portion of Mount Mataba, and extending its front southward from the mountain some two miles, was to strike east toward Mount Baytangan and the corps objective line.

By March 4, however, the 1st Infantry had not yet cleared its portion of Mount Pacawagan or of Mount Mataba, and the 63d Infantry had gained only a tenuous foothold on its portion of Mount Pacawagan. The 20th Infantry, unable to seize its sector of Mount Mataba, had shifted its attack south of the mountain, and had advanced almost two miles to the southwestern and western approaches to Mount Mataba. By nightfall of the 4th, the 20th Infantry commander, Lieutenant Colonel Harold G. Maison, was prepared to send his troops over the ridges leading to the crest of the mountain. From February 22 through March 4, Patrick's division had lost approximately 85 men killed and 255 wounded, while accounting for approximately 1,100 Japanese dead.

By March 4 Griswold had decided to concentrate his attack on a narrower front, believing that his forces were too thinly spread to mount effective attacks along the entire fifteen–mile corps front. He decided to make his main effort against the southern (Noguchi) force and the left of the Kobayashi force to its north. Since the southern end of the Japanese line was weakly held, Griswold hoped to outflank the Noguchi force to its south and debouch into the Bosoboso Valley in its rear, where his troops could then attack the Noguchi and Kobayashi forces from the rear. Griswold believed that such a maneuver could succeed, since he estimated, erroneously, that Yokoyama had no reserves to reinforce his western forces or to mount a counterattack.

Griswold planned to make his main effort against a line extending about six miles northward from Antipolo. The 6th Division and the 1st Cavalry Division to its south would make the attack; the division boundary line would be the Nanca River valley.

Believing that Yokoyama had no reserves, Griswold planned to attack with virtually his entire force, retaining only one infantry battalion from the 6th Division as his corps reserve. Hampering the effectiveness of this attack, however, would be the fact that both divisions were severely under strength. The 6th Division had 2,630 fewer men than it had when it entered Luzon, and the 1st Cavalry Division was some 2,500 men under strength. Neither division had received any replacements, other than returned casualties, since arriving on Luzon. The only reserve available to Patrick was his battalion that was also serving as corps reserve. Griswold directed the attack to begin on March 8.

Deciding that he would need two regiments on his right, where the main effort of the 6th Division's attack would take place, Patrick redeployed his 1st Infantry, commanded by Colonel James E. Rees, from its former northern location with the 63d Infantry, to a position to the right of the 20th Infantry. The 1st Infantry was to drive eastward on a two–mile wide front, with its right flank along the Nanca River, to seize most of the corps objective that lay within the 6th Division sector, at the same time uncovering the approaches to Mount Baytangan. The 63d Infantry, commanded by Colonel Everett M. Yon, gave up its toehold on Mount Pacawagan and established a defensive line that extended north from San Mateo to hills about two miles northwest of Montalban. In preparation for the attack, the 20th Infantry abandoned its positions on the southern and southwestern slopes of Mount Mataba.

On March 10, the 1st Infantry secured the western end of the ridge approaches leading to Mount Baytangan. By the evening of the next day the regiment had captured Benchmark 8 Hill, and had penetrated deeply between the left flank of Kobayashi Force and the right flank of Noguchi Force, and had secured about one–third of the northern half of the XIV Corps objective area.

Desiring to exploit the success of the 1st Infantry, Patrick ordered the 20th Infantry to drive northward on the 12th toward Wawa Dam, while the 1st Infantry continued its attack to the east. Meanwhile, the 1st Cavalry Division was making steady progress against the southern portion of the Noguchi Force.

Concerned about the penetration of the 6th Division and about the 1st Cavalry Division's success against the Noguchi Force, Yokoyama directed the Noguchi Force to pull back to prepared defensive positions on a line running south from just west of the 1st Infantry's penetration, through Sugarloaf Hill, and then south-east to Benchmark 23 Hill. The Kobayashi force was to hold in its present positions.

Yokoyama also scheduled a counterattack, to be launched on March 12, utilizing a three–pronged attack. One force was to move south from Wawa Dam to Mount Mataba, from where it would strike south and southeast against the 6th Division salient. Another was to attack westward to recapture Benchmark 8 Hill. The third force, from the Kawashima Force to the north, was to attack from the Ipo Dam area and move against the 6th Division rear area west of the Marakina River.

The high degree of coordination required for such a complex operation, the difficult terrain, and Yokoyama's severely impaired communications with his forces would of themselves have almost foreordained the counterattacks to failure. However, the failure of the operation was virtually guaranteed by Yokoyama's decision to launch the counterattacks on the very day, March 12, that Patrick had chosen to launch his new offensive northward to Wawa Dam and eastward toward Mount Baytangan.

The artillery fires and aerial attacks that preceded Patrick's new offensive knocked out or forced into hiding much of the Japanese artillery that was to support the counterattacks, and destroyed many of the trails over which the Japanese forces were to move. Those preparatory fires and aerial attacks also disrupted the enemy's communications and destroyed his command posts, fur-ther hampering Yokoyama's control and coordination of his forces. As a result, "the *Shimbu* Group counterattack was broken up vir-tually before it got under way," and when Yokoyama saw that the attacks were failing, he called them off on March 15. In the at-tempted counterattacks the Noguchi Force had lost two battal-ions, and Yokoyama's *Shimbu* Force Reserve had also been severely weakened. Yokoyama now realized that any future offensive op-erations were out of the question, and that he could henceforth only "trade lives for time."

Maj. John D. Humphrey with Maj. Gen. Edwin D. Patrick at 1st Infantry OP, March 13, 1945.

(6th Infantry Division in World War II, 110)

By the evening of March 14, the 43d Division, which had completed its relief of the 1st Cavalry Division earlier that day, had advanced against light resistance for a gain of up to 1¹/₂ miles in its center, a greater advance than the 1st Cavalry Division had made in the previous ten days.

Patrick's May 12 attack had met with success. The 20th Infantry had advanced a mile northward by the 14th, clearing a portion of a grassy ridge less than a mile southeast of Mount Mataba. The 1st Infantry did not begin its attack until the 14th, and by mid–afternoon, advancing against stiff resistance, had moved across the corps objective area to a peak 1¹/₄ miles southwest of Mount Baytangan.

On that same day, however, the 6th Division suffered two severe blows: the mortal wounding of its dashing division commander and the death of the commander of the 1st Infantry.

Krueger had decided to shift the American operations against the *Shimbu* Group to the responsibility of XI Corps, commanded by Lieutenant General Charles P. Hall. XIV Corps, thereby freed of responsibility for operations east and northeast of Manila, could now devote all of its efforts to clearing the enemy from southern Luzon and opening Balayan and Batangas Bays, as MacArthur had directed.[6]

In preparation for XI Corps' taking over command of the forces operating against the *Shimbu* Line, Hall and Griswold went to the observation post (OP) of the 1st Infantry on the afternoon of March 13, to observe the disposition of the division, and to study the situation. Major John D. Humphrey, the 1st Infantry S–3, briefed them on the situation, after which they insisted upon visiting the OP of the 1st Battalion, over the objections of Humphrey and Colonel James E. Rees, the regimental commander. "While in the forward area they paraded around with large binoculars over their shoulders and 3 stars on their respective helmets," all the while under observation by the enemy.[7]

The following morning Patrick and his aide, Captain James Young, Jr., arrived about 0845 at the 1st Battalion OP, some six miles east–northeast of Marakina, where Rees and Humphrey met them. Patrick wanted to observe the "kick–off" of the 1st Infantry's attack eastward, scheduled to begin at 0900.

Patrick, Rees, and Lieutenant Colonel Francis Corbin, the commander of the 1st Battalion, were sitting in the northernmost two of four slit trenches on the ridge occupied by the 1st Battalion observation post. Corbin occupied the first trench. Rees was in the second trench and was facing south, looking at a map spread out on the ground between himself and Patrick, who was sitting in the next trench, facing Rees. At about 0900, a ten–to fifteen–round

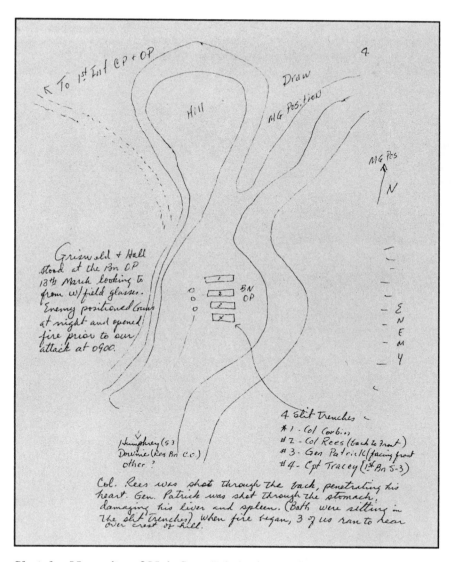

Sketch—Map, site of Maj. Gen. Edwin D. Patrick's wounding, March 14, 1945

(Courtesy of Col. (Ret.) John D. Humphrey.)

Maj. Gen. Edwin D. Patrick's funeral procession, March 16, 1945, U.S. Army Forces Far East Cemetery No. 1, Manila.
(6th Infantry Division in World War II, 175)

Maj. Gen. Edwin D. Patrick's interment, March 16, 1945, U.S. Army Forces Far East Cemetery No. 1, Manila.
(6th Infantry Division in World War II, 7)

burst of machine gun fire from a draw about seventy–five to one hundred yards north of the OP sprayed the ridge. Rees fell dead as a bullet struck his back, penetrating his heart. A round struck Patrick on the left side of his abdomen, just below the twelfth rib.[8]

Chaplain Walther A. Huchthausen, who had been in the slit trench with Corbin, immediately crawled to Patrick, and "comforted him as best [he] could." A stretcher bearer then came up, and the chaplain assisted in getting the general onto the stretcher. "At a dead run and crouched low" they carried Patrick down the hill, where an ambulance was waiting.[9]

At 1020 the general arrived at the aid station, about one–half mile to the rear of the OP. By 1040, Patrick was on his way to the 29th Evacuation Hospital, some eight miles to the rear. He received more plasma and opiates there, and was then evacuated to the 54th Evacuation Hospital, set up in the Quezon Institute, on the outskirts of Manila.[10]

At about 1630, Lieutenant Colonel Fernando I. Wilson, Chief of Surgery of the 54th Evacuation Hospital, and Lieutenant Colonel James T. Priestley II, a surgical consultant, formerly of the Mayo Clinic, who had been flown to the hospital on orders of either Krueger or MacArthur, operated on Patrick. They found that the bullet had entered the left side of his abdomen just below the twelfth rib, "coursed laterally and upward across the entire upper portion of the abdomen to a point of exit on the right side, [in the] mid–axillary line, at the level of the 10th rib." The colon and stomach were perforated and lacerated, and the liver was "severely damaged." The bullet traversed the liver, "traumatizing a great portion of the right lobe." A portion of liver tissue protruded from the wound of exit.

The surgeons closed the stomach and colon perforations and lacerations, and removed the detached portion of liver tissue. The wound was loosely packed, and the general was returned to his bed, in fair condition.[11] After asking his aide for water at about 2030, Patrick spent a rather restless night, suffering considerable pain.[12]

At 1030 the next day, Patrick asked Young "about the Division and who was in Command." When told that Brigadier General Charles E. Hurdis, Division Artillery commander, had succeeded him, Patrick told Young " 'to tell Mike to keep pushing the 1st., east and the 20th., north and that he would be back soon.' " Shortly after 1200, Patrick asked that the oxygen mask be removed and that he have some water.[13]

His condition deteriorated progressively during the day, and about 1600 he went into shock and lapsed into a coma. Patrick died at 1725, Thursday, March 15, 1945, at the age of fifty–one.[14]

Patrick's funeral was held on March 16 at U.S. Army Forces Far East Cemetery No. 1, in the northern suburbs of Manila. He received full military honors. Generals Krueger, Swift, Griswold, and Hall, and two personal representatives from MacArthur's staff were in attendance. Pallbearers were men from the 6th Division headquarters. Patrick was buried among the men he had led in the 6th Infantry Division, and among those other men who had died liberating Luzon from Japanese domination.[15]

As news of Patrick's death spread, many messages of condolence arrived at the homes of his widow and his mother:

Secretary of War, Henry L. Stimson, writing at the request of President Franklin D. Roosevelt, told Nellie May that her loss was "a loss shared by all of us," and expressed his hope that "time and the victory of our cause will finally lighten the burden of your grief."[16]

General George C. Marshall consoled Nellie May by assuring her that "as division commander [General Patrick] was literally leading his troops at the time he was fatally wounded," and expressed his hope that she might "have the faith to bear [her] great loss."[17]

General Douglas MacArthur wrote Mrs. Patrick that her husband's "death in action came as a great shock to all of us...who knew how much of the division's magnificent fighting power came from his inspiration and courage."[18]

General Krueger attempted to comfort Patrick's widow with "the knowledge that Pat died as he lived, faithful to his friends, his duty and his country."[19]

Major General Charles P. Hall, commanding general of XI Corps, assured Mrs. Patrick of the love and respect that "those above him and under him" held for her husband, and expressed the hope that "Pat's career will always be a source of just pride to you and to your three fine sons."[20]

Sturgis, who, as Engineer, Sixth Army, had worked with Patrick when he was serving as Sixth Army's chief of staff, told his widow of Pat's "driving spirit," his "broad and profound vision to discern what the real problems were and to solve them in advance," his "intelligence..., his moral guts..., his tremendous drive and energy..., [and] his great big heart and his wonderful sense of humor." Sturgis went on to tell her of the memories that he had of her husband:

> a great friend; a man who lived with zest, whose presence was always a joy to his fellow men and evoked a warmth like wine in the blood; and a great and courageous soldier. ... [May] God rest his magnificent soul.[21]

Mr. Sam Tron, a former sergeant in 6th Division headquarters, told Mrs. Patrick of his great respect for the general. He told her of Patrick's constant concern for the "front–line infantrymen to whom he was in reality fully devoted." Tron also told of Patrick's fondness for classical music, particularly an aria from *La Boheme* that he frequently whistled when "engrossed at night in a tactical problem while drinking his black coffee." He closed his letter with the hope that Mrs. Patrick and the general's family and mother would understand "how one man feels about the General's inspiration for a better world tomorrow."[22]

Charles E. Zanzalari, who had served as a corporal in Patrick's machine gun company in World War I, wrote to the general's son, Tom, to assure him that "anyone who ever knew your dad or who served under him can think of the very best. ... A man's man through and through."[23]

George Ress, one of Patrick's boyhood friends, recalled for the general's mother that "Pat" was "just a little smarter than the rest of us," and that he was "the best liked and in our kid ways,—respected, of all the group." He assured her that his own life had been "richer for having known him and to have had the privilege of being one of his chums."[24]

On March 17, U.S. Army Forces Far East awarded Major General Edwin D. Patrick the Distinguished Service Cross posthumously for "extraordinary heroism in action near Bayan–Bayanan, Luzon, Philippine Islands on 14 March 1945."[25]

At Fort Bliss, Texas, on June 15, 1945, Mrs. Edwin D. Patrick received the Distinguished Service Medal awarded posthumously to her husband for "exceptionally meritorious service to the Government in a position of great responsibility in the Southwest Pacific from September 1944 to March 1945."[26]

In 1948, at the request of Patrick's mother, then ninety–five years old, the army disinterred his body from the cemetery near Manila and returned it to Tell City, where it arrived on June 29. Funeral services were held the following day at the Zoercher Funeral Home, owned by his brother–in–law, Mr. Louis Zoercher. Reverend Hilbert H. Peters, pastor of the First Evangelical and Reformed Church, Tell City, conducted the services. The body was then reinterred in the family burial plot in Greenwood Cemetery, Tell City.[27]

CHAPTER 18

EDWIN D. PATRICK AS DIVISION COMMANDER: AN ASSESSMENT

Most biographers of World War II allied commanders have chronicled the careers of the great captains of the war: Marshall, Eisenhower, MacArthur, Bradley, Montgomery, Patton. A few have produced abbreviated biographies of some of those senior subordinates of the great captains,[1] Berlin has compiled a "composite biography" of U.S. Army corps commanders of World War II,[2] and there is one brief critical study of twenty–three U.S. Army division commanders of World War II.[3] There is a relative paucity, however, of biographies, autobiographies, or studies of those men who commanded and led the soldiers whose mission was to "close with and destroy the enemy": the infantry, armor, and airborne division commanders.[4]

When I decided to embark on the writing of a critical biography of Major General Edwin D. Patrick, I did so in the hope that his career would prove to have been unique when compared to the careers of his fellow World War II combat division commanders, and that this very uniqueness would of itself be of sufficient magnitude to justify the expenditure of the time and financial resources to seek out the materials to complete a meaningful study of Patrick's life and military career. And, indeed, my research soon indicated that Patrick was in many ways a unique division commander. I also soon recognized, however, that his career shared many similarities to the careers of his contemporaries who led our combat divisions, and that Patrick's life and career could well serve as a paradigm of those of the other U.S. Army officers who commanded these divisions, on the whole quite successfully.[5] In this final chapter I hope to bring together both those qualities unique to Patrick, and those qualities and characteristics he shared with most of his fellow division commanders.

The inter–war Regular Army officer corps, averaging a little more than twelve thousand men and from which would rise all but a handful of the World War II division commanders,[6] was no longer dominated by men from the Southern states, as it had been before World War I. Indeed, the largest single group of officers, 33.4 percent, was from the midwest,[7] as was Patrick.

Of those officers who served during the inter–war years, only 37.4 percent had received their commissions as graduates of the United States Military Academy. Patrick was among the considerable majority whose commissions were received through other routes, e.g., by direct appointment from civilian life, the National Guard, or Officers' Reserve Corps; by appointment from the Regular Army enlisted ranks; and from among the officers who had received temporary commissions during World War I.[8] Although the percentage of West Point graduates who led divisions in World War II combat was somewhat higher than the percentage of academy graduates among all commissioned officers in the inter-war army, 51 percent of those division commanders, including Patrick, were not graduates of the United States Military Academy.[9]

In looking at the inter–war careers of these officers, one is struck by the fact that the vast majority of them had successfully completed the entire spectrum of the army's progressive formal schooling, designed to prepare officers for successively higher command and staff positions. This should not be surprising, since one would expect that only those officers with the highest potential would be chosen for the most prestigious of the army's schools, from the graduates of which would come most of the army's senior commanders.

Virtually all inter–war army officers were enrolled in and completed the basic and advanced schools of their respective branches, where instruction focused on the tactics and command of battalions through reinforced brigades.[10] From that level of schooling onward, however, the selection process became increasingly discriminating.

Of the graduates of the advanced branch courses, some were chosen to attend the Command and General Staff School at Fort Leavenworth, graduation from which was a virtual necessity if an officer hoped to serve beyond regimental level, and to serve in the General Staff Corps.[11] Patrick was among the 95 percent of division commanders who completed this rigorous course of study.[12]

Approximately 10 percent of the graduates of the Command and General Staff School went on to attend a senior service college, usually the Army War College; approximately 50 percent of those graduates eventually became general officers.[13] Patrick was among the 70 percent of combat division commanders who graduated from one of the senior service colleges, and was one of only four who attended both the Army War College and the Naval War College.[14]

Another characteristic of the careers of the World War II combat division commanders was their service as members of the General Staff Corps during a portion of their service: 75 percent of them, including Patrick, served in the General Staff Corps.[15]

Of further interest is that the median age at which those men assumed command of their divisions was fifty, the age at which Patrick became commanding general of the 6th Infantry Division at Sansapor, New Guinea.[16]

I feel that the preceding data support my conclusion that Patrick's career was in many respects quite similar to those of his fellow division commanders, and that his career can serve as a legitimate model for a study attempting to uncover those factors that distinguished the careers of those inter–war officers who rose to command combat divisions of the American army during World War II from the careers of their less distinguished contemporaries.

Certainly one of the most important of those factors was an officer's ability to navigate successfully the army's progressive system of formal military education. For in the "lean" years between the two world wars, with little opportunity to command or serve as staff officers in units above battalion–size, those officers would look to the schools, particularly the Command and General Staff School and the Army War College, to provide the foundation of military knowledge on which they would build as they assumed command of the divisions, corps, armies, army groups, and theaters of future wars. I concur in Kirkpatrick's conclusion that those schools "literally 'saved' the army by assuring the quality of the officer corps."[17]

Another factor that I think accounted for the success of American generalship in World War II was the small size of the inter–war Regular Army officer corps. For in those years, both in duty assignments and in the army's schools, the officers developed close personal, social, and professional relationships. Knowing the backgrounds, strengths, and weaknesses of each other, they were able to utilize their fellow officers and their talents to fullest advantage.

Furthermore, senior officers in the small Regular Army of those years were more readily able to identify promising junior officers. Through their personal counseling of those young officers, and because of their influence in duty assignments and in the selection process for the army's formal schools, those senior officers were in positions to insure that promising junior officers would attain the professional background that would enable them to rise to positions of high responsibility in time of war.[18]

Even though the inter-war army had few units of battalion-size and larger, severely limiting an officer's ability to apply the lessons of command and staff procedures learned at the schools, the army compensated by assigning the most promising of those officers to serve on the faculties of the schools or with regiments assigned to the schools. There they learned to deal with large-scale administrative and organizational problems while serving as "school secretaries, executive officers, quartermasters, and the like." Kirkpatrick states that "a reasonable generalization about the careers of officers commissioned from 1909 through 1935" was assignment one or more times as an instructor at the army schools.[19]

Certainly the most famous of those schools was the Infantry School during the years 1927–1932, when George C. Marshall served as the school's assistant commandant. The school was indeed "the cradle of many of WW II's greatest field commanders," among them Collins, Bradley, Stilwell, and Van Fleet.[20]

Although some have denigrated the quality of American army generalship in World War II,[21]

> the great majority performed capably, waging war in a style that accorded well with the American temperament. If not intuitive tacticians, such American commanders almost universally shared a superb managerial ability that was largely unmatched among the Allied officers. Inexperienced, unblooded, and relatively junior in the years immediately before the war, they became generals who could organize, train, and wield divisions in battle— units few had ever seen before.[22]

Patrick appears to fit the above description of the typical World War II American general quite well. And his success, if one accepts Kirkpatrick's conclusions, can, in part at least, be reasonably attributed to his inter-war path of career development, one shared by most of his fellow combat division commanders:

1. Successful completion of the Command and General Staff School and the Army War College.
2. Assignment to the General Staff Corps.
3. Two assignments to the faculty of the Infantry School, one during the tenure of George C. Marshall.
4. Professional relationships and friendships with other officers, of both equal and higher rank: Bolté, Castner, Doe, Eisenhower, Harding, Krueger, Marshall, Ridgway, Stilwell.[23]

But Patrick as a task force commander and as a division commander displayed other qualities that are not so clearly seen to be a direct product of his military schooling and duty assignments. To understand the development of those aspects of Patrick's character we must examine his personal life, for in his heritage, his upbringing, his education, and his friendships we can define some of those characteristics that distinguished Patrick as an outstanding combat commander.[24]

Patrick grew up as the youngest child in a large but close–knit family that placed great emphasis on religious faith, duty to country, education, hard work, and independence (see "Chapter 2: The Formative Years"). Patrick's niece believes that her uncle had a strong "feeling of patriotism," as a result of his grandfather's service in the Revolutionary War and his father's service in the Civil War. Mrs. Werner stated that "perhaps Ed had a feeling of patriotism, of wanting to be a part of making the history of this country."

Mrs. Werner credits Patrick's mother for instilling into her children the qualities that would distinguish her son's conduct throughout his military career: "a great sense of responsibility, of integrity, of the importance of truthfulness, of honesty, and [of] loyalty to family." His mother also put a great value on education, undoubtedly producing in Patrick the thirst for education that he displayed not only in his public school days, graduating as salutatorian of his high school class, but in his going on to college, where he paid his tuition from money he earned or borrowed, promptly repaying the latter.[25]

From this background, what character qualities did Patrick bring to his military career that would mark him as an outstanding combat division commander?

As one studies the interviews of his former chief of staff and his former aide–de–camp, and letters from fellow officers and enlisted men, one is struck, first of all, by the frequent observation that Patrick cared very much for the welfare of his enlisted men. Palmer stated that Patrick "understood troops and men and soldiers and what motivated them, and he treated them like human beings. I think he was very much liked by the troops."[26]

His aide, former–Second Lieutenant Joseph A. Castagnetto, commented that Patrick was "very compassionate and warm," and that he felt that all of the men in his division "were like his sons." Castagnetto recalled that on one occasion when Patrick's troops were pulled off the line and returned to rest camps, the general tried "to get the water carriers full of beer" to send to them, although by the time the beer arrived it was hot and "all the gas was out of it."[27]

Colonel John D. Humphrey, while serving as assistant G–3, 6th Division, noted that Patrick "was greatly concerned with the welfare of the entire command, especially enlisted men. In staff meetings he was always careful to question the G–4 concerning supplies and other staff regarding morale and welfare issues."[28]

In early February 1945, Castagnetto accompanied Patrick on a visit to the recently released American survivors of the Bataan Death March, who had been in a prison near Cabanatuan. The freed Americans were in Giumba, recently secured by the 6th Division. Castagnetto relates that the prisoners "looked like pictures of the Holocaust." As the general walked in, "some tried to get up and salute him," but Patrick told them, " 'No, no, no, sit down.' " Soon, tears appeared in Patrick's eyes as he continued to view the emaciated soldiers, and he told Castagnetto, " 'Come on, let's go'; he couldn't take it anymore to see the condition that they were in."[29]

Patrick was a very visible commander, rarely in his command post, almost always in the forward areas of his regiments, exerting strong personal leadership, and heeding General Ulysses S. Grant's admonition to General Don Carlos Buell at the battle of Shiloh in April 1862: "The distant rear of an army engaged in battle is not the best place from which to judge correctly what is going on in front." Wearing "a special green uniform, a jump suit," Patrick could be seen "a mile away," and soon earned from the troops the sobriquet, "Green Hornet." The two stars on his helmet also helped make him very visible to his men and, tragically, to the enemy. That Patrick's almost constant presence in the forward areas of his division was a distinctly rare practice among division commanders appears attested by the fact that he was one of only three division commanders killed in World War II combat.[30]

Also testifying to Patrick's frequent presence in the forward areas was Sergeant Rudolph Schaal of the 6th Division, who commented, on learning of Patrick's death, " 'Gen. Patrick was always up in the front lines with his men, assisting and advising them and helping as much as he could.' " He went on to say that, " 'It helped us a lot when the going was tough to know that the general himself was in there with us.' "[31]

Palmer described him as "a man of great courage, ... a very courageous man, very bold man. ... Bold to the point where he was a little *too* bold."[32] Palmer cited an incident in the Cabaruan Hills where Patrick, when one of his battalions was being held up by the well–entrenched enemy, suggested using flame throwers to reduce the position. When the flame throwers were brought up, Patrick "wanted to go in there with the flame throwers," and it was only with considerable difficulty that he was prevented from doing so.[33] Palmer states that in his ranking of division commanders whom he has known throughout his military career, Patrick "ranks very high," and "in battle was well above many div[ision] cmdrs that I have known. ... [O]n balance a very fine gentleman and scholar."[34]

Although Patrick was "a courageous man and a fine combat leader," he was "impatient, at times impulsive." Humphrey agreed with Palmer that Patrick was "a very bold and aggressive combat commander," but that he sometimes acted too quickly, "without full and complete information." Both men cited the relief of Ives as regimental commander at Muñoz as the most blatant example of Patrick's sometimes impulsive action.[35]

As one listens to the Palmer and Castagnetto interviews, and reads the oral history interview of Palmer and the Palmer, Simmons, and Humphrey letters, Patrick emerges as a vigorous, tireless, constantly moving, and very courageous commander, intensely concerned with carrying out his assigned mission successfully, always looking out for the welfare of his men, even at risk to his own safety. "A very courageous combat leader, ... he always got out to see for himself how things were going with his troops, even in the best and worst of situations." When I asked Palmer if he agreed with my assessment of Patrick as having been one of World War II's outstanding U.S. Army combat division commanders, he replied, "I confirm your high evaluation of Gen. Patrick." Certainly one must give heavy weight to the evaluations of Patrick by such experienced combat officers as Bruce Palmer, John D. Humphrey, and Floyd H. Simmons.[36]

I feel, however, that one must also look to the combat rifleman in order to make a completely valid assessment of a general's skills in combat leadership, for it is the rifleman who ultimately bears the burden of the battle, and whose very life depends upon the skill and knowledge of his division commander.

Reverend Roy Clark, a former infantryman in Patrick's 1st Infantry Regiment, stated that "we sure loved this man. He was one of the Great Ones In worl [sic] war 2." Only one hundred feet from Patrick when he was wounded, Reverend Clark related that Patrick's last words before his evacuation to the rear were, "Take it easy men I am just another Soldier."[37]

Sergeant Rudolph Schaal recalled that Patrick, when his officers encouraged him to go to the rear, would laugh at them, and say that " 'a general's place was with his troops. ... He fought like a soldier and he died like one.' "[38]

> No other figure in the American pantheon of heroes
> is more honored than the military commander at

the head of his troops. The cause may be futile, the tactics may be faulty, but the leader who gallantly risks his own life while asking his men to do the same deserves whatever praise he may receive. Johann deKalb at Camden, George Custer at the Little Big Horn, Stonewall Jackson at Chancellorsville [and Edwin D. Patrick on the Shimbu Line], each demonstrated a willingness to lead by example and made the supreme sacrifice to achieve the results desired.[39]

But possibly Lieutenant Colonel Bernard J. Macauley, MC, Division Surgeon, 6th Infantry Division, expressed most eloquently the highest accolade that any combat division commander could hope to earn:

General Patrick was highly esteemed and respected by every soldier in the Division for his outstanding courage. His first and last thought was always the welfare of his men. In the front line of battle as much as was possible for one of his high rank and responsibility, he shared the common soldier's fate beside his men, and there he died.[40]

EPILOGUE

On a morning in late May 1990, I turned south from Interstate 64 onto Indiana Route 37, the final leg of a journey that I had begun almost exactly forty years earlier on a pier at Oakland Army Terminal, California. As my wife and I motored across the rolling hills toward Tell City, the boyhood home of Edwin D. Patrick, I wondered how often Patrick had traveled through these hills, and how often his mind had turned back to Tell City during the long days of combat in the Southwest Pacific Area.

Although we spent only a few days in Tell City, I had the opportunity to meet two of the general's nieces, share their memories of their uncle, read the carefully preserved letters that Patrick had written to his family during his long military career, and examine photographs, newspaper articles, and other memorabilia from his life.

We visited the home in which he had grown up, the school from which he had graduated (although no longer used as a school), the church where he was confirmed at age twelve, and his Masonic Temple. We also toured the nearby Indiana and Kentucky countryside where he had roamed with his childhood friends, crossing the Ohio River, where he swam and fished.

I went to the new National Guard armory that replaced the one where then–Second Lieutenant Patrick began his distinguished military career. There I viewed the memorial that the present Tell City Indiana Army National Guard rifle company has placed in the armory entrance to honor one of the most illustrious former members of the Indiana Army National Guard.

Finally, my wife and I accompanied Patrick's nieces and their husbands to Greenwood Cemetery, on the northern edge of Tell City, Patrick's final resting place. As I stood there, reflecting on Patrick's life, I became even more firmly convinced that this gallant and courageous soldier's career was indeed worthy of a formal biography. I sincerely hope that my effort to write such a biography has been at least partly successful.

APPENDIX A

ORGANIZATION AND EMPLOYMENT OF DIVISIONAL MACHINE GUN UNITS IN THE AEF

The infantry division in the American Expeditionary Force contained 260 machine guns, 36 of which were used as antiaircraft weapons within the division field artillery brigade. The remaining 224 guns were distributed among a machine gun company organic to each infantry regiment and three machine gun battalions.

Assigned to each of the two infantry brigades within the division was one machine gun battalion, commanded by a major, and composed of four machine gun companies; these companies were identical in organization to the regimental machine gun companies. Each battalion had an assigned strength of 28 officers and 748 enlisted men and was authorized 64 heavy machine guns, divided equally among the companies.

The machine gun company, commanded by a captain, had an assigned strength of 6 commissioned officers and 172 enlisted men and carried sixteen guns, four of which were spares. Within the company there were three platoons and a headquarters section. A first lieutenant led the first platoon, while second lieutenants led platoons two and three. Each platoon, with four guns, was made up of two sections, each having two guns, and led by a sergeant. Within each section there were two gun squads, each with one gun and nine men, led by corporals. The gun squad had one combat cart, pulled by a mule, to transport its gun and ammunition as close to the firing positions as enemy fire allowed. From there the crews moved the guns and ammunition forward by hand.

The third machine gun battalion, commanded by a major, was a division unit. The battalion had a strength of 16 commissioned officers and 377 enlisted men, and was motorized. However, it had only two companies, identical to the other machine gun companies in personnel and weapons. Each gun squad used a special motor car to transport its personnel, weapon, and equip-

155

ment. The battalion was generally in division reserve, ready to carry out missions as the division commander ordered.[1]

The machine gun units in the 5th Division entered combat with the 1914 model of the French–made Hotchkiss machine gun. The gun and mount weighed 88 pounds, fired 8mm. Lebel Mle 1886 rounds from a 30–round metal strip and had a rate of fire of 600 rounds per minute. It was gas–operated and air–cooled, and had a maximum effective range of 3,800 meters. The Hotchkiss served in both ground combat support and antiaircraft roles.[2]

In training and in combat each of the four machine gun companies within the infantry brigade was attached to one of the brigade's six infantry battalions; attached to each of the other two infantry battalions within the regiments was that regiment's organic machine gun company. In the 5th Division those attachments remained effective throughout the entire training period or campaign. In the attack, the attached machine gun companies accompanied their battalions by bounds, maintaining close liaison with the infantry battalion commanders. Machine gun companies that were attached to infantry battalions designated as division or brigade reserve for a particular mission, were usually placed under the direct command of their respective brigade commanders, to fill in gaps of fire and to protect the brigade flanks.[3]

Since the usual plan of maneuver of an infantry battalion called for three of its four rifle companies to be used as the attacking force, with the fourth company serving as a reserve, the machine gun company commander would usually place one of his three machine gun platoons in support of each maneuver rifle company.[4]

Machine guns were used for both indirect and direct fire missions. When in the former role, the guns were placed to cooperate with the field artillery units in neutralizing suspected enemy observation posts and machine guns during the attack, and to sweep the approaches for possible enemy counterattacks after the capture of the final objective.[5]

The guns were most effectively used in overhead fire missions to support the infantry attacks. In this role the guns were placed three hundred to a thousand meters to the rear of the front line. When they employed their guns in that fashion, the machine gun officers often ran into opposition from the rifle company commanders, who preferred to have the guns farther forward, fearing that their infantrymen would be at risk of stray low rounds as they advanced under the overhead machine gun fire. However, over time the infantrymen came to accept this arrangement as they saw the reliability of the machine guns proved again and again in combat.

Furthermore, they soon discovered that the machine guns were high priority targets for enemy fire, and that it was advantageous to have the guns at some distance from the infantry positions.

Since enemy machine guns posed the greatest threat to the attacking troops, the machine gun crews made every effort to locate the enemy guns and to concentrate their fire upon them. As the attack moved forward and the overhead fire became less effective, some of the gun squads would carry their guns and ammunition forward either into or onto the flanks of the advancing infantry. A proportion of the guns were held back as a reserve under command of the machine gun officer.[6]

Machine gun tactical doctrine dictated that in the defense the Hotchkiss guns should only rarely be located within a hundred yards of the front line, and that at least two–thirds of the guns should be echeloned back through the whole defensive position, located so that adjacent guns would be mutually supporting. From such positions all guns could fire in defense of the front line, and in the event of an enemy breakthrough, the rear guns could continue to defend, even if the enemy overran the forward guns.[7]

APPENDIX B

SILVER STAR CITATION

Patrick, Edwin D., Capt. 14th M G Bn.   5899 [Written in]

Hqrs. Ninth Inf. Brig., 31st Dec 1918.
G.O. No. 11 (a.n.) [Written in]

..........................cited in orders for distinguished conduct in action:

"On Nov. 4th 1918, near Clery–le–Petit, France when his company was crossing the Meuse River, a soldier in his company was seriously wounded. With absolute disregard for his personal safety Captain Patrick left his place of security, advanced to the wounded soldier and personally administered first aid, thereby exposing himself to intense enemy machine gun and shell fire which was being delivered from the opposite bank of the Meuse. His heroism self–sacrifice and devotion to duty was an inspiration to the men whom he commanded."

By Command of Brigadier General Castner:
Ray K. Chalfant
LJC   Major and Adjutant.
10–12–33Jak [Written in]

~~Miscellaneous Citations~~   ~~Miscellaneous Citations~~
Silver Star Medal Authorized WWC [Written in]
SILVER STAR CITATION

[Note: This is a verbatim copy of the citation on file at the U.S. Army Reserve Personnel Center, St. Louis, Mo., a copy of which is in the author's possession. The initials "Jak" and "WWC" in the copy are difficult to discern; the above rendering shows the author's interpretation of these initials.]

APPENDIX C

LEGION OF MERIT
(OAK LEAF CLUSTER) CITATION

Major General EDWIN D. PATRICK, (0-4903), (then Brigadier General), United States Army. For exceptionally meritorious conduct in the performance of outstanding services in Dutch New Guinea from 25 May to 31 August 1944. Assuming command of a task force, in the Wakde–Sarmi area, General Patrick quickly expanded and completed operational facilities, and with sustained vigor and exceptional skill continued the offensive against the enemy. One month later, in the assault against Noemfoor Island, despite difficult beaches and a scattered and determined enemy garrison, he quickly secured and reconstructed the airfields and eliminated the enemy with minimum casualties to our troops. General Patrick by his bold and exemplary leadership, notable organizational ability, and sound judgment, contributed greatly to securing Allied ascendency in the Dutch New Guinea area.

Home address: Mrs. Edwin D. Patrick (wife)
P. O. Box 595
Ruidoso, New Mexico[1]

APPENDIX D

DISTINGUISHED SERVICE CROSS CITATION
HEADQUARTERS
UNITED STATES ARMY FORCES IN THE FAR EAST

GENERAL ORDERS)   A.P.O. 501
          :   17 March 1945
NO....................53)

Section

DISTINGUISHED–SERVICE CROSS—Posthumous awards..I
PHILIPPINE SERVICE RIBBONS.................................. II

I. DISTINGUISHED-SERVICE CROSS (POSTHUMOUS AWARDS). By direction of the President, under the provisions of the Act of Congress approved 9 July 1918 (Bulletin 43, WD, 1918), the Distinguished–Service Cross is posthumously awarded by the Commanding General, United States Army Forces in the Far East, to the following–named officers:

Major General EDWIN D. PATRICK, (04903), United States Army. For extraordinary heroism in action near Bayan–Bayanan, Luzon, Philippine Islands on 14 March 1945. General Patrick's division was engaged in an attack in which heavy fighting, supported by artillery, mortar and machine-gun fire, had driven a salient into the enemy line. Observation of the enemy areas was limited by the extremely rugged and mountainous terrain of the Sierra Madre foothills. Existing map and aerial photographs did not present a true picture of the terrain. In order to make proper estimates and plans for continuance of the attack, General Patrick moved to a forward battalion observation post but a short distance from the enemy. This post was under constant direct artillery fire. While conferring with one of his commanders General Patrick was struck by a single burst of enemy machine–gun fire which mortally wounded him. General Patrick's active personal leadership and outstanding devotion to duty were responsible for the high state of efficiency and superior morale of his division. His unwavering courage and appearance among the forward elements of his command in complete disregard for his own safety contributed materially to the success of the combat operations, and exemplify the highest traditions of the military service. Home address: Ruidoso, New Mexico.[1]

APPENDIX E

DISTINGUISHED SERVICE MEDAL CITATION (POSTHUMOUS)

Major General Edwin D. Patrick, rendered exceptionally meritorious service to the Government in a position of great responsibility in the Southwest Pacific from September 1944 to March 1945. Assuming command of the 6th Infantry Division at Cape Sansapor, New Guinea, General Patrick rapidly completed the occupation and consolidation of this vital stepping stone to the Philippines. On being alerted for the Luzon operation, he brought the division to a high peak of combat efficiency, perfected coordinated plans for its movement and led it ashore in a successful assault landing. For more than two months he fought and maneuvered his division in a continuous and aggressive offensive in the face of determined enemy resistance. His conduct of these operations was uniformly characterized by sound judgment, vigorous personal leadership, and skillful utilization of the combined arms. In his determination to carry the battle to the enemy he courageously and repeatedly disregarded his own safety, and was personally directing an attack when mortally wounded by enemy machine gun fire. General Patrick exemplified the finest type of American leadership. His determination, aggressiveness, and high degree of professional skill contributed outstandingly to the success of operations in the Southwest Pacific.[1]

APPENDIX F

COMBAT DIVISION COMMANDERS DATA[a]

Commander, Division, Dates of Command	DOB	Commission SRC,YR,BR,ED	C&GS	SSC	GSC
MG Ward, Orlando 1 AD (3/42–4/43) 20 AD (9/44–8/45)	11/4/91	USMA '14 CAV, FA	'26 DG	AWC '36	Yes
MG Harmon, Ernest N. 1 AD (4/43–7/44) 2 AD (9/44–1/45)	2/26/94	USMA '17 CAV	'33	AWC '34	Yes
MG Prichard, Vernon E. 1 AD (7/44–9/45)	1/25/92	USMA '15 INF	'31	AWC '40	Yes
MG Gaffey, Hugh J. 2 AD (5/43–4/44) 4 AD (12/44–3/45)	11/18/95	ORC '17 FA NRC	'36	No	Yes
MG Brooks, Edward H. 2 AD (4/44–9/44)	4/25/93	Vt. NG '15 CAV CG	'34	AWC '37	Yes
MG White, Isaac D. 2 AD (1/45–5/45)	3/6/01	Norwich '23 CAV	'39	No	No
MG Watson, Leroy H. 3 AD (8/42–8/44)	11/3/93	USMA '15 INF	'30	AWC '34	Yes
MG Rose, Maurice[b] 3 AD (8/44–3/45)	11/26/99	ORC '17 INF NRC	'37	No	Yes
BG Hickey, Doyle O. 3 AD (3/45–6/45)	7/27/91	ORC '17 FA CG	'36	No	No

COMBAT DIVISION COMMANDERS DATA (Continued)

Commander, Division, Dates of Command	DOB	Commission SRC,YR,BR,ED	C&GS	SSC	GSC
MG Wood, John S. 4 AD (5/42–12/44)	1/11/88	USMA '12 CAC,ORD,FA	'24 DG	*ESG* '31	Yes
MG Hoge, William M. 4 AD (3/45–6/45)	1/3/94	USMA '16 CE	'28	No	No
MG Oliver, Lunsford 5 AD (3/43–7/45)	3/17/89	USMA '13 CE	'28	AWC '38	No
MG Grow, Robert W. 6 AD (5/43–7/45)	2/14/95	Minn. NG '16 FA,CAV CG	'29	AWC '36	Yes
MG Silvester, Lindsey[c] 7 AD (3/42–11/44)	9/30/89	'11 INF CG	'24	AWC '30	No
MG Hasbrouck, Robert 7 AD (11/44–9/45)	2/2/96	USMA '17 CAC,FA	'34	AWC '37	Yes
MG Devine, John M. 8 AD (10/44–8/45)	6/18/95	USMA '17 FA	'38	No	Yes
MG Leonard, John W. 9 AD (10/42–10/45)	1/25/90	USMA '15 INF	'28	No	Yes
MG Morris, William, Jr. 10 AD (7/44–5/45)	3/22/90	USMA '11 INF	'25	AWC '30	Yes
MG Kilburn, Charles S. 11 AD (3/44–3/45)	1/2/95	USMA '17 CAV	'35	AWC '37	No
MG Dager, Holmes E. 11 AD (3/45–8/45)	6/24/93	N.J. NG '12 INF NRC	'31	AWC '36	Yes
MG Allen, Roderick[c] 12 AD (8/44–7/45)	1/29/94	'16 CAV CG	'28	AWC '35	Yes
MG Wogan, John B. 13 AD (10/42–4/45)	1/1/90	USMA '15 CAC	'30	AWC '33	Yes
MG Millikin, John 13 AD (4/45–11/45)	1/7/88	USMA '10 CAV	'26 DG	AWC '31	Yes

COMBAT DIVISION COMMANDERS DATA (Continued)

Commander, Division, Dates of Command	DOB	Commission SRC,YR,BR,ED	C&GS	SSC	GSC
MG Smith, Albert C. 14 AD (7/44–8/45)	6/5/94	USMA '17 CAV	'36	No	Yes
BG Pierce, John L. 16 AD (9/44–10/45)	4/29/95	'17 INF NRC	'38	No	Yes
MG Swift, Innis P. 1 CAV DIV (4/41–8/44)	2/7/82	USMA '00 CAV	'23	AWC '30	No
MG Mudge, Verne D. 1 CAV DIV (8/44–2/45)	9/5/98	USMA '20 CAV	'35	AWC '40	Yes
BG Hoffman, Hugh 1 CAV DIV (2/45–7/45)	11/27/96	USMA '18 CAV	'41	No	No
MG Allen, Terry 1 ID (6/42–7/43) 104 ID (10/43–11/45)	4/1/88	'12 CAV CG	'26	AWC '35	No
MG Huebner, Clarence[d] 1 ID (7/43–12/44)	11/24/88	'16 INF NRC	'25 DG	AWC '29	Yes
MG Andrus, Clift 1 ID (12/44–46)	10/12/90	'12 FA NRC	'30	AWC '34	Yes
MG Robertson, Walter 2 ID (5/42–6/45)	6/15/88	USMA '12 INF	'26 HG	AWC '30	Yes
MG Anderson, J. W. 3 ID (3/42–4/43)	6/7/90	USNA '12 FA	'25 DG	AWC '30 NWC '38	Yes
MG Truscott, Lucian 3 ID (4/43–2/44)	6/9/95	ORC '17 CAV AC[r]	'36	No	Yes
MG O'Daniel, John W. 3 ID (2/44–8/45)	2/15/94	Del. NG '16 INF NRC	'39	No	No
MG Barton, Raymond 4 ID (7/42–12/44)	8/22/89	USMA '12 INF	'24	AWC '33	Yes

COMBAT DIVISION COMMANDERS DATA (Continued)

Commander, Division, Dates of Command	DOB	Commission SRC,YR,BR,ED	C&GS	SSC	GSC
MG Blakeley, Harold 4 ID (12/44–11/45)	12/29/93	ORC '17 FA NRC	'36	AWC '39	No
MG Irwin, Stafford L. 5 ID (6/43–4/45)	3/23/93	USMA '15 CAV	'27 DG	AWC '37	No
MG Brown, Albert E. 5 ID (4/45–45) 7 ID (10/42–5/43)*ᵉ*	6/13/89	USMA '12 INF	'25	AWC '30 NWC '31	Yes
MG Sibert, Franklin C. 6 ID (10/42–8/44)	1/3/91	USMA '12 INF	'25 DG	AWC '29	Yes
MG Patrick, Edwin D.*ᵇ* 6 ID (8/44–3/45)	1/11/94	Ind. NG '15 INF AC	'34	AWC '37 NWC '38	Yes
MG Hurdis, Charles E. 6 ID (3/45–46)	10/6/93	USMA '17 FA	'33	AWC '34	Yes
MG Landrum, Eugene 7 ID (5/43–9/43)*ᶠ* 90 ID (7/44–8/44)	2/6/91	'16 INF NRC	'33	AWC '36	Yes
MG Corlett, Charles H. 7 ID (9/43–2/44)*ᵍ*	7/31/89	USMA '13 INF	'23	AWC '25	Yes
MG Arnold, Archibald 7 ID (2/44–46)	2/24/89	USMA '12 FA	'30	AWC '35	Yes
MG Stroh, Donald A. 8 ID (7/44–12/44) 106 ID (2/45–10/45)	11/3/92	USMCR '17 CAV CG	'33	AWC '37	Yes
MG Weaver, William 8 ID (12/44–2/45)	11/24/88	USMA '12 INF	'25	No	Yes
MG Moore, Bryant E. 8 ID (2/45–11/45)	6/6/94	USMA '17 INF	'39	No	No
MG Eddy, Manton S. 9 ID (8/42–8/44)	5/16/92	'16 INF NRC	'34	No	Yes

COMBAT DIVISION COMMANDERS DATA (Continued)

Commander, Division, Dates of Command	DOB	Commission SRC,YR,BR,ED	C&GS	SSC	GSC
MG Craig, Louis A. 9 ID (8/44–5/45)	7/29/91	USMA '13 CAV,CAC,FA	'31	AWC '39	No
MG Hays, George P. 10 MTN DIV (11/44–11/45)	9/27/92	'17 FA CG	'34	AWC '40	Yes
MG Swing, Joseph M. 11 ABN DIV (2/43–46)	2/18/94	USMA '15 FA	'27 HG	AWC '35	Yes
MG Miley, William M. 17 ABN DIV (4/43–8/45)	12/26/97	USMA '18 INF	'38	No	No
MG Irving, Frederick 24 ID (8/42–11/44)	9/3/94	USMA '17 INF	'38	No	No
MG Woodruff, Roscoe 24 ID (11/44–11/45)	2/9/91	USMA '15 INF	'27 HG	AWC '32	Yes
MG Collins, J. Lawton 25 ID (5/42–1/44)	5/1/96	USMA '17 INF	'33	AWC '38	Yes
MG Mullins, Charles L. 25 ID (1/44–46)	9/7/92	USMA '17 INF	'34	AWC '39	No
MG Paul, Willard S. 26 ID (8/43–6/45)	2/28/94	'17 INF CG	'35	AWC '37	Yes
MG Smith, Ralph C. 27 ID (11/42–6/44)	11/27/93	'16 INF CG	'28	AWC '35 ESG '37	Yes
MG Griner, George W. 27 ID (6/44–12/45)	9/28/95	ORC '17 INF CG	'33	AWC '39	Yes
MG Brown, Lloyd D. 28 ID (1/43–8/44)	7/28/92	'17 INF CG	'30	No	No
BG Wharton, James E.[h] 28 ID (8/44)	12/2/94	ORC '17 INF CG	'33	AWC '37	Yes

COMBAT DIVISION COMMANDERS DATA (Continued)

Commander, Division, Dates of Command	DOB	Commission SRC,YR,BR,ED	C&GS	SSC	GSC
MG Cota, Norman D. 28 ID (8/44–12/45)	5/30/93	USMA '17 INF	'31	AWC '36	Yes
MG Gerhart, Charles H. 29 ID (7/43–1/46)	6/6/95	USMA '17 CAV	'33	No	Yes
MG Hobbs, Leland S. 30 ID (9/42–9/45)	2/24/92	USMA '15 INF	'34	AWC '35	Yes
MG Persons, John C. 31 ID (11/40–9/44)	No biographical data found.				
MG Martin, Clarence 31 ID (9/44–12/45)	9/13/96	VMI '17 INF	'37	AWC '40	Yes
MG Harding, Edwin F.[s] 32 ID (3/42–2/43)	9/18/96	USMA '09 INF	'37	No	No
MG Gill, William H. 32 ID (2/43–2/46)	8/7/86	Va. NG '12 INF CG	'25 HG	AWC '30	Yes
MG Clarkson, Percy[c] 33 ID (10/43–11/45)	12/9/93	'16 INF CG	'28	AWC '34	Yes
MG Ryder, Charles W. 34 ID (5/42–7/44)	1/16/92	USMA '16 INF	'26 DG	AWC '34	Yes
MG Bolté, Charles L. 34 ID (7/44–11/45)	5/8/95	ORC '16 INF AC	'32	AWC '37	Yes
MG Baade, Paul W. 35 ID (1/43–12/45)	4/16/89	USMA '11 INF	'24 HG	AWC '29	Yes
MG Walker, Fred L.[c] 36 ID (9/41–7/44)	6/11/87	'11 INF CG	'27 HG	AWC '33	Yes
MG Dahlquist, John E. 36 ID (7/44–11/45)	3/12/96	ORC '17 INF NRC	'31	AWC '36	Yes
MG Beightler, Robert[f] 37 ID (10/40–11/45)	3/21/92	Ohio NG '14 INF AC	'26	AWC '30	No

COMBAT DIVISION COMMANDERS DATA (Continued)

Commander, Division, Dates of Command	DOB	Commission SRC,YR,BR,ED	C&GS	SSC	GSC
MG Jones, Henry L. C.ᶜ 38 ID (4/42–2/45)	8/20/87	'11 CAV,FA CG	'24 HG	AWC '31	Yes
MG Chase, William C. 38 ID (2/45–8/45)	3/9/95	'16 CAV CG	'31	AWC '35	Yes
MG Brush, Rappʲ 40 ID (4/42–7/45)	11/7/89	'11 INF AC	'23 DG	AWC '26	Yes
MG Fuller, Horace H. 41 ID (7/41–6/44)	8/10/86	USMA '09 CAV,FA	'23 DG	AWC '28	Yes
MG Doe, Jens A. 41 ID (6/44–12/45)	6/20/91	USMA '14 INF	'26	AWC '33	No
MG Collins, Harry J. 42 ID (7/43–5/46)	12/7/95	ORC '17 INF NRC	'34	AWC '35	Yes
MG Hester, John H. 43 ID (8/41–8/43)	9/11/86	USMA '08 INF	'23	AWC '27	Yes
MG Wing, Leonard F.ⁱ 43 ID (8/43–11/45)	12/11/93	Vt. NG '17 INF CG	No	No	No
MG Spragins, Robertᵏ 44 ID (8/44–1/45)	11/12/90	USMA '13 INF	'27 DG	No	Yes
MG Dean, William F. 44 ID (1/45–11/45)	8/1/99	'23 INF CG	'36	AWC '40	Yes
MG Middleton, Troyˡ 45 ID (10/42–12/43)	10/12/89	'12 INF CG	'24 HG	AWC '29	Yes
MG Eagles, William W. 45 ID (12/43–12/44)	1/12/95	USMA '17 INF	'36	No	Yes
MG Frederick, Robert 45 ID (12/44–9/45)	3/14/07	USMA '28 CAC	'39	No	Yes

COMBAT DIVISION COMMANDERS DATA (Continued)

Commander, Division, Dates of Command	DOB	Commission SRC,YR,BR,ED	C&GS	SSC	GSC
MG Hibbs, Louis E. 63 ID (6/43–8/45)	10/3/93	USMA '11 FA	'27	AWC '34	No
MG Reinhart, Stanley 65 ID (8/43–8/45)	9/15/93	USMA '16 FA	'32	AWC '36	Yes
MG Kramer, Herman 66 ID (4/43–8/45)	11/27/92	Nebr. NG '16 INF CG	'33	No	Yes
MG Reinhardt, Emil F. 69 ID (9/44–8/45)	10/27/88	USMA '10 INF	'23	AWC '31	No
MG Barnett, Allison J. 70 ID (7/44–7/45)	4/2/92	Ky. NG '17 INF NRC	'33	No	No
MG Wyman, Willard 71 ID (11/44–8/45)	3/21/98	USMA '18 CAC,CAV	'37	No	Yes
MG Prickett, Fay B. 75 ID (8/43–1/45)	4/29/93	USMA '16 CAV,FA	'30	AWC '33	Yes
MG Porter, Ray E. 75 ID (1/45–6/45)	7/29/91	ORC '17 INF NRC	'35	AWC '37	Yes
MG Schmidt, William 76 ID (12/42–8/45)	10/14/89	USMA '13 INF	'28	AWC '31	Yes
MG Bruce, Andrew D.ᶜ 77 ID (5/43–3/46)	9/14/94	'17 INF CG	'33	AWC '36 NWC '37	Yes
MG Parker, Edwin P. 78 ID (8/42–9/45)	7/27/91	'13 FA NRC	'25 DG	AWC '37	No
MG Wyche, Ira T. 79 ID (6/42–5/45)	10/16/87	USMA '11 INF	'25 DG	AWC '34	Yes
MG McBride, Horace 80 ID (3/43–10/45)	6/28/94	USMA '16 FA	'28	AWC '36	Yes

COMBAT DIVISION COMMANDERS DATA (Continued)

Commander, Division, Dates of Command	DOB	Commission SRC,YR,BR,ED	C&GS	SSC	GSC
MG Mueller, Paul J. 81 ID (8/42–1/46)	11/16/92	USMA '15 INF	'23 DG	AWC '28	Yes
MG Ridgway, Matthew 82 ABN DIV (6/42–8/44)	3/3/95	USMA '17 INF	'35	AWC '37	Yes
MG Gavin, James M. 82 ABN DIV (8/44–46)	3/22/07	USMA '29 INF	'42	No	No
MG Macon, Robert C. 83 ID (1/44–3/46)	7/12/90	'16 INF CG	'31	AWC '34	Yes
MG Bolling, Alexander 84 ID (6/44–1/46)	8/28/95	ORC '17 INF NRC	'35	AWC '38	Yes
MG Coulter, John B. 85 ID (2/43–8/45)	4/27/91	'12 CAV NRC	'27 DG	AWC '33	Yes
MG Melasky, Harris 86 ID (1/43–1/46)	4/11/93	USMA '17 INF	'35	AWC '37	Yes
MG Culin, Frank L., Jr. 87 ID (4/44–8/45)	3/31/92	'16 INF CG	'30	AWC '40	No
MG Sloan, John E. 88 ID (7/42–9/44)	1/31/89	USNA '11 CAC	'26 DG	AWC '32	No
MG Kendall, Paul W. 88 ID (9/44–6/45)	7/17/98	USMA '18 INF	'36	No	Yes
MG Finley, Thomas D. 89 ID (2/43–12/45)	6/2/95	USMA '16 CE,INF	'33	AWC '35	Yes
MG MacKelvie, Jay[d] 90 ID (1/44–7/44)	9/23/90	'17 CAV,FA NRC	'32	AWC '36	Yes
MG Landrum, Eugene 90 ID (7/44-8/44)	(For biographical data see "7 ID" supra)				
MG McLain, Raymond[h] 90 ID (8/44–10/44)	4/4/90	Okla. NG '14 INF NRC	'38	No	No

COMBAT DIVISION COMMANDERS DATA (Continued)

Commander, Division, Dates of Command	DOB	Commission SRC,YR,BR,ED	C&GS	SSC	GSC
MG Van Fleet, James 90 ID (10/44–2/45)	3/19/92	USMA '15 INF	No	No	No
MG Rooks, Lowell W.[l] 90 ID (2/45–3/45)	4/11/93	'17 INF NRC	'35	AWC '37	Yes
MG Earnest, Herbert 90 ID (3/45–12/45)	11/11/95	ORC '17 CAV NRC	'34	No	Yes
MG Livesay, William[d] 91 ID (7/43–12/45)	3/2/95	'16 INF NRC	'26	AWC '33	Yes
MG Almond, Edward 92 ID (10/42–8/45)	12/2/92	VMI '16 INF	'30	AWC '34	Yes
MG Lehman, Raymond[m] 93 ID (5/43–8/44)	10/26/95	ORC '17 INF NRC	'34	No	Yes
MG Johnson, Harry H.[d] 93 ID (8/44–2/46)	4/11/95	'17 CAV NRC	No	No	No
MG Malony, Harry J. 94 ID (9/42–5/45)	8/24/89	USMA '12 INF,FA	'26	AWC '36	Yes
MG Twaddle, Harry L. 95 ID (7/42–10/45)	6/2/88	'12 INF CG	'23	AWC '25	Yes
MG Bradley, James 96 ID (8/42–2/46)	5/18/91	USMA '14 INF	'27 HG	AWC '32	Yes
MG Halsey, Milton B. 97 ID (1/44–9/45)	3/6/94	USMA '17 INF	'33	No	Yes
MG Lauer, Walter E. 99 ID (7/43–8/45)	6/29/93	ORC '17 INF NRC	'38	No	Yes
MG Burress, Withers 100 ID (11/42–9/45)	11/24/94	VMI '16 INF	'31	AWC '35	Yes

COMBAT DIVISION COMMANDERS DATA (Continued)

Commander, Division, Dates of Command	DOB	Commission SRC,YR,BR,ED	C&GS	SSC	GSC
MG Taylor, Maxwell 101 ABN DIV (3/44–9/45)	8/26/01	USMA '22 CE,FA	'35	AWC '40	Yes
BG McAuliffe, Anthony 101 ABN DIV (12/44) 103 ID (1/45–8/45)	7/2/98	USMA '18 FA	'37	AWC '40	Yes
MG Keating, Frank A. 102 ID (1/44–3/46)	2/4/95[n]	N.J. NG '17 INF NRC	'39	No	Yes
MG Haffner, Charles[t] 103 ID (11/42–1/45)	3/15/95	'18 FA CG	No	No	No
MG Jones, Alan W.[o] 106 ID (3/43–12/44)	10/6/94	'17 INF NRC	'36	AWC '38	Yes
BG Perrin, Herbert T. 106 ID (12/44–2/45)	9/8/93	'17 INF CG	'33	No	Yes
MG Patch, Alexander[p] Americal Div. (5/42–1/43)	11/23/89	USMA '13 INF	'25 DG	AWC '32	No
BG Sebree, Edmund B. Americal Div. (1/43–5/43)	1/7/98	USMA '18 INF	'37	No	Yes
MG Hodge, John R. Americal Div. (5/43–4/44)	6/12/93	ORC '17 INF NRC	'34	AWC '35	Yes
MG McClure, Robert Americal Div. (4/44–11/44)	9/15/96	ORC '17 INF NRC	'36	AWC '39	Yes
MG Arnold, William H. Americal Div (11/44–12/45)	1/18/01	USMA '24 INF	'38	No	Yes
BG Lough, Maxwell S.[q] Philippine Division (12/41–4/42)	9/15/86	'11 INF NRC	'24 HG	AWC '28	Yes

APPENDIX G

COMMANDING GENERAL COMPARATIVE DATA

CMDG GEN COMPARATIVE DATA	NUMBER	PERCENT
Graduated from or attended college	109	79
Graduate, C&GS	135	95
Graduate, SSC	98	71
GSC service	105	75
USMA graduate	70	49

APPENDIX H

CHRONOLOGY OF MILITARY SERVICE

ASSIGNMENT	DATES OF SERVICE
Co I, 2d Ind. INF	Feb. 1915–Mar. 1917
Army Service Schools	April 1917–July 1917
Fort Leavenworth, Kan.	
21st INF	July 1917–Feb. 1918
Calexico, Ca.	
5th DIV	Feb. 1918–Feb. 1920
Fort Lawton, Wash.	Feb. 1920–Aug. 1920
Infantry School (Instructor)	Aug. 1920–Sep. 1922
Fort Benning, Ga.	
Infantry School (Student)	Sep. 1922–May 1923
Camp Devens, Mass.	May 1923–Sep. 1923
Army Signal School	Sep. 1923–June 1924
Camp Alfred Vail, N.J.	
23d Infantry	June 1924–Feb. 1926
Fort Sam Houston, Tex.	
15th Infantry	May 1926–Apr. 1929
Tientsin, China	
Infantry School (Instructor)	Aug. 1929–Aug. 1932
Fort Benning, Ga.	
Command and General Staff School	Aug. 1932–June 1934
Fort Leavenworth, Kan.	
Washington National Guard (Instructor)	June 1934–July 1936
Spokane, Wash.	
Army War College	Sep. 1936–June 1937
Washington, D.C.	
Naval War College	July 1937–June 1938
Newport, R.I.	
Eighth Corps Area (G–3)	June 1938–Nov. 1942
Fort Sam Houston, Tex.	
COMSOPAC Staff	Dec. 1942–June 1943
Nouméa, New Caledonia	
Sixth Army	
Chief of Staff	June 1943–May 1944
CDG Gen., TORNADO Task Force	May 1944–June 1944
CDG Gen., CYCLONE Task Force	June 1944–Aug. 1944
6th INF DIV (CDG Gen.)	Sep. 1944–Mar. 1945

APPENDIX I

REGULAR ARMY PROMOTIONS

GRADE	TEMPORARY	PERMANENT
2nd. Lieut.		Mar. 21, 1917
1st. Lieut.		Apr. 15, 1917
Capt.	Aug. 5, 1917	Dec. 11, 1917
Maj.		Dec. 11, 1929
Lt. Col.		Jun. 12, 1939
Col.	Oct. 14, 1941	
Brig. Gen.	Apr. 26, 1943	
Maj. Gen.	Sep. 5, 1944	

Note: The WD biography of Edwin D. Patrick, HRC 201, Historical Records Branch, U.S. Army Center of Military History, Washington, D.C., was the source for the above information.

APPENDIX J

USNS *GENERAL EDWIN D. PATRICK*

USNS *General Edwin D. Patrick*
(Courtesy National Archives)

    The USNS *General Edwin D. Patrick* (AP–124), hereafter referred to as the *Patrick*, was one of eight troop transports (AP) of the "Admiral" class. Built at the Bethlehem–Alameda Shipyard in Alameda, California, in 1945, the ship was originally christened the *Admiral C. F. Hughes* (hereafter referred to as the *Hughes*). The ship's namesake had participated in the battle of Manila during the Spanish–American War, had served with the British Grand Fleet in World War I, and had subsequently served as Chief of Naval Operations.[1]

177

The "Admiral" transports displaced 20,120 tons when fully loaded, and were 609 feet long and $75^1/_2$ feet wide. Two General Electric turbo-electric engines powered them, developing 18,000 horsepower, and providing a cruising speed of nineteen knots and a cruising radius of 15,000 miles. Each ship's complement was made up of 37 officers and 330 enlisted men, and could carry up to 280 officers and 4,400 enlisted men.[2]

The *Hughes'* maiden voyage began at Los Angeles on March 13, 1945, destination Pearl Harbor. During the remainder of World War II, she operated in both the Atlantic and the Pacific Oceans, "calling at ports from Marseilles to Manila," including Guam, Leyte, Biak, Hollandia, and Yokohama.[3]

Early in 1948, the *Hughes* underwent modernization conversion at the Newport News Shipbuilding and Drydock Company, Newport News, Virginia. The navy transferred her and the other seven "Admirals" to the army for permanent peacetime use as army transports. All of these ships were rechristened in honor of deceased World War II generals, and they then became part of the "Generals" class of troop transports. The rechristening of the *Hughes* as the USAT *General Edwin D. Patrick* took place at Pier 2 East, Fort Mason Port of Embarkation, on Thursday, October 21, 1948, at 1300. A portrait of General Patrick was placed in the ship's wardroom.[4]

The *Patrick* continued in army service until March 1, 1950, when the navy reacquired her as the USNS *General Edwin D. Patrick*, assigned to the Military Sea Transport Service. During the Korean War the *Patrick* made more than two dozen round–trip voyages to the Far East: to American bases in Korea, Japan, Okinawa, the Mariana Islands, and the Philippine Islands, carrying more than 55,000 United Nations troops. She participated in the amphibious landings at Wonsan and Iwon, on the east coast of North Korea in late October 1950, and received three battle stars during the Korean war.

After the armistice in Korea in July 1953, the *Patrick* continued operating in the Western Pacific, steaming to the Far East some 110 times between 1953 and 1965.

On August 16, 1965, the *Patrick* left San Francisco, and, after stops at Pearl Harbor, Guam, and Manila Bay, docked at Cam Ranh Bay, and then continued on to Vung Tau, South Vietnam. She began another trip to South Vietnam on October 1, 1965, and during the first seven months of 1966 completed five additional Far East deployments, operating out of ports in South Vietnam, Okinawa, Korea, and Taiwan. She continued this duty during the remainder of 1966, arriving in San Francisco for the final time on December 31, 1966.[5] After overhaul early in 1967, the transport was placed in ready–reserve status as part of the Suisun Bay Reserve Fleet, Benicia, California, under control of the Maritime Administration, U.S. Department of Transportation.[6]

ENDNOTES

CHAPTER 1

1. I have extracted all of the following family history from Alma Patrick Kennedy, "Records and Recollections," TMs [Photocopy], April 1972, file of author. Alma Kennedy was Edwin Patrick's sister.

2. James M. McPherson, *"Battle Cry of Freedom" The Civil War Era* (New York: Oxford University Press, 1988), 582. Mrs. Kennedy's recounting of her father's wound problems during the remainder of his life provides a "textbook" description of chronic osteomyelitis with sequestrum formation.

CHAPTER 2

1. I have obtained most of the following information relating to Edwin Patrick's youth from two of his nieces, Mary Margaret Goffinet and Ruth Anne Werner, both of Tell City, Ind. They supplied letters to me, and Mrs. Werner allowed me to tape – record an interview with her in her home on May 29, 1990.

2. His family knew him as "Ed," but in the army he was known as "Pat."

3. Ruth Anne Werner, Tell City, to author, LS, November 10, 1991, file of author; Mary Margaret Goffinet, Tell City, to author, LS, November 9, 1991, file of author. Mrs. Werner is the daughter of Edwin Patrick's sister, Alma Patrick Kennedy; Mrs. Goffinet is the daughter of another sister, Alice Patrick Zoercher.

4. Ruth Anne Werner, of Tell City, interview by author, May 29, 1990, Tell City, tape recording, file of author; hereafter referred to as "Werner interview."

5. Werner to author.

6. Werner to author.

7. Werner to author.

8. Werner interview.

9. Werner to author.

10. Werner to author. The age at which Edwin Patrick sang in the church quintet is only approximate: I have a photograph of this quintet, supplied by Ruth Anne Werner, in which Ed, dressed as a policeman, appears to be approximately nine or ten years old. The church is now the Evangelical United Church of Christ.

11.   Goffinet to author.

12.   Goffinet to author.

13.   George J. Ress, Indianapolis, to Anna Patrick, Tell City, TLS [Photocopy], March 22, 1945, supplied by Thomas B. Patrick, file of author.

14.   Senior Class of 1912 of the Tell City High School, *The Rambler, 1912* (Tell City, Ind.: n.p., June 1912), 10. Of interest is the fact that of the thirteen men who graduated in that class, twelve would serve in World War I, and of these nine would serve as commissioned officers (*The Tell City News*, June[?] 1936); "Reminiscing," *The News*, May 4, 1989, 4A.

15.   File of Edwin D. Patrick, transcript from Indiana University [Photocopy], File 2466738, Records of the Adjutant General's Office, 1780s–1917, Record Group 94, National Archives, Washington, D.C.; ibid., A. P. Fenn to William C. Cox, TLS, November 13, 1916 [Photocopy]; "In Memoriam. . . ," *The November 1945 Indiana Alumni Magazine*, 17–18. Of interest is the fact that Patrick received the grades of "C" "C-" and "D" in mathematics, presaging his performance in the mathematics section of his examination for appointment in the Regular Army (see "Chapter 3").

16.   Goffinet to author; Werner interview.

17.   Patrick file, "Transcript from Indiana University," File 2466738, AGO, 1780s–1917, RG 94, NA.; "Office of the Secretary, Department of Law University of Michigan," TLS, October 10, 1916, ibid.

18.   The only information about Patrick's employment history appears in the Patrick file, "Form for Individual Record of Candidate," ibid.; Fenn to Cox, ibid. Mr. Fenn wrote this letter to support Patrick's application for a Regular Army commission. He also stated in the letter that Patrick loaned half of the money he had borrowed to "a school friend who was in like destitute circumstances." Patrick then repaid the entire loan to the bank, even though the friend to whom he had loaned half of it had not repaid him.

19.   Patrick file, Fenn to Cox, ibid.

20.   Patrick file, Cox to Secretary of War, TLS [Photocopy], November 15, 1916, ibid.; Cox to War Department, TLS, December 11, 1916, ibid..

21.   Patrick file, Louis Zoercher to the Adjutant General, TLS [Photocopy], September 22, 1916, ibid.

22.   Patrick file, Fenn to Cox, ibid.

23.   Paul D. Ramsey, Worshipful Master of Tell City Lodge #623, Free and Accepted Masons, to author, TLS, June 14, 1990; the *New York Times*, March 16, 1945, 15.

CHAPTER 3

1.   "Service File Cards" of Edwin D. Patrick, Indiana National Guard, INDANG, "Service File Cards," L Section, Archives Division, Indiana Commission on Public Records, Indianapolis; *The News* (Tell City, Ind.), October 13, 1982, 8B. Patrick's son, Thomas, stated that his father joined the National Guard to help him through school (Thomas B. Patrick, interview by author, September 18, 1990, The Woodlands, Tex., tape recording, in file of author; hereafter referred to as "Thomas B. Patrick interview").

2.   Maurice Matloff, ed., *American Military History* (Washington, D.C.: Office of the Chief of Military History, United States Army, 1969), 354–357.

3. Clarence C. Clendenen, *Blood on the Border: The United States Army and the Mexican Irregulars* (Toronto: Collier-Macmillan Ltd., 1969), 289–290.

4. "Service File Cards" of Edwin D. Patrick; Patrick file, Cox to Secretary of War, File 2466738, AGO, 1780s–1917, RG 94, NA.

5. *National Defense Act, Statutes at Large*, 39, Part 1, 166, 182 (1916). The National Defense Act of 1916 provided for, among other things, an increase in the peacetime strength of enlisted personnel in the Regular Army to a maximum of 175,000 over a period of five years. Vacancies in the grade of second lieutenant created or caused by this increase in the enlisted strength would be filled by appointment of officers, in order, from USMA graduates of the previous year for whom Regular Army vacancies had not existed, enlisted men, members of the Officers' Reserve Corps, commissioned officers of the National Guard, honor graduates of "distinguished colleges," and civilian candidates.

6. Patrick file, "Application for permission to take the examination for probationary 2nd Lieutenants' commission in U.S. Army," File 2466738, AGO, 1780s–1917, RG 94, NA.

7. Patrick file, "Summary of results of examination," File 2507137, ibid.

8. Patrick file, "Night Letter," ibid.

9. Patrick file, "Proceedings of a board of officers," File 2466738; "Physical examination," File 2507137, ibid.

10. Patrick file, "Night Letter"; "Summary of results of examination," ibid.

11. William J. Watt and James R. H. Spears, ed., *Indiana's Citizen Soldiers: The Militia and National Guard in Indiana History* (Indianapolis: The Indiana State Armory Board, 1980), 106, 119–20.

12. "Service File Cards" of Edwin D. Patrick.

13. Patrick file, Telegram of acceptance, File 2507137, and "Oath of Office," File 2560167, ibid.; "Service File Cards" of Edwin D. Patrick; War Department biography of Edwin Daviess Patrick, March 21, 1945, Center of Military History, United States Army, Washington, D.C., hereafter referred to as "WD biography."

CHAPTER 4

1. War Department, The Adjutant General's Office, Washington, *Army List and Directory, April 20, 1917* (Washington, D.C.: GPO, 1917), 46; *Commandants, Staff, Faculty, and Graduates of The Command and General Staff School, Fort Leavenworth, Kansas: 1881-1939* (Fort Leavenworth, Kans.: The Command and General Staff School Press, 1939), 5; WD biography.

2. J. W. McAndrew, Acting Commandant, Army Service Schools, "Address to the Second Class of Provisional Second Lieutenants, U.S. Army," address presented at the Army Service Schools, April 17, 1917 (Fort Leavenworth, Kans.: Army Service Schools Press, 1917), 3, 7; *Commandants, Staff, Faculty, and Graduates*, 6.

3. McAndrew, 4–5, 7–8.

4. Roger S. Fitch, *Estimating Tactical Situations and Composing Field Orders*, 2nd ed. (Fort Leavenworth, Kans.: Army Service Schools Press, 1917); Charles

Miller, *The Customs of the Service and Some Suggestions and Advice* (Fort Leavenworth, Kans.: Army Service Schools Press, 1917); Loren C. Grieves, *Outline of Lessons in Company Administration* (Fort Leavenworth, Kans.: Army Service Schools Press, 1917). It appears, from my study of the course materials obtained from the Combined Arms Research Library at Fort Leavenworth, that much of the course of study was theoretical in nature, with only a small amount of time devoted to practical application of the principles covered in the lectures.

5.   Patrick file, "Report of Preliminary Training," Army Service Schools, File 2466738, AGO, 1780s–1917, RG 94, NA.

6.   "Efficiency Report" File 2466738, AGO, 1780s–1917, RG 94, NA. This is the only extant "Efficiency Report" from Patrick's twenty–eight years of service. It covers the periods April 15 to July 12, when Miller rated Patrick, and July 11 to July 21, when Paige rated him. In this "Efficiency Report," Patrick's rank is indicated as "2d Lieut. (Prov.)," although both his War Department biography and the *Official Army Register* of January 1, 1945, confirm that he was promoted to first lieutenant on April 15, 1917. Capt. Edwin D. Patrick, "From Texas to China," *The Tell City News*, July 9, 1926, 1.

7.   "Efficiency Report."

8.   WD biography; War Department, The Adjutant General's Office, Washington, *Army Directory, September 1, 1917* (Washington, D.C.: GPO, 1917), 45; *Army Directory, October 1, 1917*, 49; *Army Directory, November 1, 1917*, 50; *Army Directory, December 1, 1917*, 52. The terms "temporary" and "permanent" when applied to military ranks refer respectively to the grades held during the temporary expansion of the standing peacetime army to wartime strength and to the highest grade authorized for the individual after demobilization and reduction of the wartime army to the authorized peacetime strength of the army.

9.   "World War I Strength Returns, MG Battalions, Company, Field & Strength Returns, 11th, 12th, 13th, & 14th Battalions," World War I Organization Records, 5th Division, RG 120, NA; American Battle Monuments Commission, *5th Division Summary of Operations in the World War* (Washington, D.C.: GPO, 1944), 1. "Appendix A" describes the organization and employment of divisional machine gun units in the AEF.

10.   Throughout this work, the times of the day will be given using the "military" or 24–hour clock system: times from one minute after midnight to noon are designated 0001–1200, and times from one minute after noon to midnight are designated 1201–2400. As examples, 11:00 A.M. would be 1100, and 4:00 P.M. would be 1600.

11.   "War Record, 14th Machine Gun Battalion, 5th Division," in "History," File 205–11.4, WW I, 5th Division, RG 120, NA; *5th Division Summary of Operations*, 4–5.

12.   The Society of the Fifth Division, *The Official History of the Fifth Division, U.S.A.* (Washington, D.C.: The Society of the Fifth Division, 1919), 57.

13.   *5th Division Summary of Operations*, 5; "War Record, 14th Machine Gun Battalion"; "Station List, Company A, 14th Machine Gun Battalion," File 205–10.7, WW I Org. Rec., 5th Div., 14th MG Bn., RG 120, NA.

14.   "WW I Strength Returns, MG Battalions," May 18, 1918.

15.   "WW I Strength Returns."

16. "WW I Strength Returns."; "Station List, Company A."

17. "Station List, Company A."

18. *5th Division Summary of Operations,* 6–8.

19. *History of the 5th Division,* 68–69.

20. *History of the 5th Division,* 70–75, 383; *5th Division Summary of Operations,* 8–9.

21. *5th Division Summary of Operations,* 9; "Station List, Company A."

22. *History of the 5th Division,* 77, 85.

23. *5th Division Summary of Operations,* 11.

24. *5th Division Summary of Operations,* 12.

25. *5th Division Summary of Operations,* 13; "Station List, Company A."

26. *5th Division Summary of Operations,* 13; *History of the 5th Division,* 85–86, 91, 93.

27. *5th Division Summary of Operations,* 93–96.

28. *5th Division Summary of Operations,* 97, 99.

29. *History of the 5th Division,* 101–8; *5th Division Summary of Operations,* 16–18.

30. *History of the 5th Division,* 106, 108.

31. *5th Division Summary of Operations,* 18-21; "Headquarters Orders, General Order No. 11," WW I, 5th Division, RG 120, NA.

32. *5th Division Summary of Operations,* 22; *History of the 5th Division,* 121.

33. Charles E. Zanzalari, Perth Amboy, N.J., to Thomas B. Patrick, LS [Photocopy], March 17, 1945, copy in author's files.

34. "Station List, Company A"; *History of the 5th Division,* 120; *5th Division Summary of Operations,* 23.

35. "Station List, Company A";*History of the 5th Division,* 129, 131, 133.

36. *History of the 5th Division,* 131–39; "Station List, Company A." For his actions, Woodfill received the Medal Honor.

37. *5th Division Summary of Operations,* 30–33; *History of the 5th Division,* 149.

38. *5th Division Summary of Operations,* 33–34; "Station List, Company A"; *History of the 5th Division,* 172, 383.

39. *5th Division Summary of Operations,* 37–38, 59–60.

40. *5th Division Summary of Operations,* 38, 40.

41. *5th Division Summary of Operations,* 39; "Station List, Company A"; "Report of Operations from October 25, to November 11, 1918, 14th Machine Gun Battalion," File 205–33.6, WW I Organization Records, 5th Division, "Reports of Op., Oct. 25–Nov. 11/18," RG 120, NA.

42. *History of the 5th Division,* 191.

43. "Station List, Company A."

44. *5th Division Summary of Operations*, 46–47.

45. *5th Division Summary of Operations*, 211–217; "Report of Operations, 14th Machine Gun Battalion."

46. *5th Division Summary of Operations*, 51–53; "Station List, Company A."

47. *5th Division History*, 259.

48. Headquarters Orders, WW I, 5th Division, RG 120, NA.

49. "Silver Star Citation" in file of World War I "Award Cards" at U.S. Army Reserve Personnel Center, St. Louis, Mo; copy in file of author. The Silver Star Citation was "a small silver medal worn on the ribbon of a service medal, but in 1932 it was replaced by a separate medal" (*American Armies and Battlefields*, 511). The complete citation appears as "Appendix B."

50. *5th Division in the World War*, 59.

51. "Station List, 14th MG Bn.," File 205–10.7, WW I, 5th Division, RG 120, NA; "WW I Strength Returns, MG Battalions, Field Return, July 13, 1919, Regimental Return, July 31, 1919," ibid. I have found no record of Patrick's activities or duties while in Oberkorn, except for a brief notation that he attended the Army Antitank School from February 2 until March 19, 1919 ("WW I Strength Returns, MG Battalions, Return, February 2, 1919," ibid.).

CHAPTER 5

1. "WW I Strength Returns, MG Battalions," World War I Organization Records, 5th Division, RG 120, NA. On January 20, 1920, a notation on Form 41 AGO indicated that Patrick was transferred to the "American Expiditionary [sic] Forces in Siberia per WD SO #10–0 dated Jan/13/1920." The War Department apparently rescinded this order, since Patrick never reported to the American forces in Siberia; no subsequent explanatory notation for this rescission is present in the "Strength Returns" for the battalion.

2. WD biography; *The Doughboy, 1923*, (Fort Benning, Ga.: Classes of 1923, The Infantry School, U.S. Army, n.d.). I have located no source material describing Patrick's activities at Fort Lawton, or any material describing the curriculum or Patrick's academic performance at the Infantry School.

3. WD biography.

4. Helen C. Phillips, *United States Army Signal School: 1919–1967*, (Fort Monmouth, N.J.: U.S. Army Signal Center and School, 1967), 35; Historical Office, U.S. Army Communications–Electronics Command, *A Concise History of Fort Monmouth, New Jersey* (Fort Monmouth, N.J.: n.p., July 1985), 9.

5. Phillips, 24, 26, 35. In the Department of Communication Engineering, Signal Corps officers completed 626 hours of study, whereas the others received 602 hours; in the Department of Applied Communications, Signal Corps officers took only 438 hours of instruction, as compared to the 582 hours required of the others. The former department covered the subjects "Electricity and Magnetism," "Wire Telegraphy and Telephony," "Pole Line Construction," "Storage Batteries and Charging Sets," and "Radio Telegraphy and Telephony"; the latter department was responsible for the subjects "Army Organization," "Technique of Field Wire Installations," "Message Centers," "Training Methods," "Code Practice," "Pigeons," "Combat Orders," "Signal Plans and Orders," "Signal Communication Tactics," and "Air Service Instructions."

6.   *San Antonio Evening News*, August 9, 1939, photocopy supplied by Thomas B. Patrick; "Fort Sam Houston Quartermaster Maneuver, 1925–1940, Maneuvers, May 1925," Records of the U.S. Army Continental Commands, 1920–1942, RG 394, NA. The Colorado River of Texas flows southeast from its origin approximately sixty miles southwest of Abilene, passing just south of Austin, and emptying into the Gulf of Mexico, approximately eighty-five miles southwest of Galveston.

7.   *San Antonio Evening News*, ibid.

8.   Edwin D. Patrick to Clara Patrick, TLS [Photocopy], June 2, 1925, file of author.

9.   *Tell City News*, May 29, 1925; Edwin Patrick to Clara Patrick, ibid.

10.   Edwin Patrick to Clara Patrick, ibid.

11.   *Tell City News*, ibid.; Edwin Patrick to Clara Patrick, ibid.

12.   *Tell City News*, ibid. Ulric subsequently took "Patrick" as his surname, but he is unsure if a formal adoption ever took place.

13.   Edwin Patrick to Clara Patrick.

14.   *Tell City News*, April 2, 1926, sec. 2, 1, 3.

CHAPTER 6

1.   Capt. E. D. Patrick, "From Texas to China," *The Tell City News*, April 2, 1926, sec. 2, 1.

2.   "From Texas to China," 3.

3.   "From Texas to China," 2; July 9, 1926, 4; February 11, 1927, sec. 2, 1.

4.   "From Texas to China," 9 July 1926, 1. Such friendships between general officers and those of lower grade were not uncommon in the army of that era; General Palmer alludes to this in the "Foreword," iv–v, and I discuss this more fully in "Chapter 23."

5.   "Texas to China," July 9, 1.

6.   "Texas to China," 4.

7.   *The Tell City News*, July 9, 1926, 4. Patrick's comments about the quality of U.S. Army transports are particularly interesting, since twenty–two years later another army transport would be rechristened the *USAT General Edwin D. Patrick* at Fort Mason, Ca., the same location where the Patrick family boarded the *Thomas*.

8.   Edwin Patrick, San Francisco, to Clara Patrick, Tell City, March 30, 1926, LS [Photocopy], author's file; *News*, ibid., 4. This is an example of how friendship with a senior officer could result in preferential treatment for a junior in the inter–war army.

9.   *News*, ibid. Unless otherwise indicated, this article by Patrick was the source of the following text.

10.   This stereotyping of non–Caucasians is an example of the racial prejudice common during the 1920s.

11.   *News*, February 11, 1927, sec. 2, 1. This article was the source of the following material, unless otherwise indicated.

12. Another example of Patrick's racial stereotyping.

13. *News*, ibid.; Glenn E. McClure, *Guam, Then and Now* (n.p., 1979), 6; Louis Morton, *The Fall of the Philippines* in *United States Army in World War II: The War in the Pacific* (Washington, D.C.: Center of Military History, United States Army, 1989), 77.

14. Capt. Edwin D. Patrick, "Guam to China," *The Tell City News*, March 25, 1927, 1, 4. This article was the source of the following material, unless otherwise indicated.

15. Still another example of Patrick's racial stereotyping. In the opinion of the author, Patrick's assessment of the fighting qualities of the Filipino soldier was not borne out by their conduct during the early days of World War II, when they fought gallantly alongside the American troops, and acquitted themselves admirably in resisting the Japanese occupation of the Philippine Islands.

16. "Guam to China"; Edwin Patrick, Tientsin, to Patrick family, Tell City, May 28, 1926, LS [Photocopy], file of author.

CHAPTER 7

1. This brief recounting of the history of United States–China relations has been taken from Dennis L. Noble, *The Eagle and the Dragon: The United States Military in China, 1901–1937* (Westport, Conn.: Greenwood Press, 1990), 4–35.

2. Noble, 4,6. Most favored–nation status "insured that any right, privilege, or concession extended in the future to any other nation would automatically accrue" to the United States; "extra-territoriality" allowed American citizens to reside in areas set aside in Chinese cities, where they would in essence form "foreign cities under foreign governments."

3. Noble, 6–8. The Arrow War, waged by the British and the French against China, grew out of the seizing of the *Arrow*, a Chinese ship under British registry, in Canton harbor, resulting in the imprisonment of the crew. The war was "a lopsided contest," and resulted in increased privileges in China for the British and the French, as well as the Americans and the Russians, who had joined in the negotiations in Peking in 1858. The Taiping Rebellion, an "uprising of peasants who were converts to their own forms of Christianity, ... was a mixture of anti–Manchu revolution and a religious crusade." Initially favorably acknowledged by Westerners, the Western powers soon viewed the rebellion with apprehension because of its emphasis on nationalism and religious fanaticism. Fearing a divided China, Britain and the other Western powers gave arms, naval support, and advice to the Manchus, contributing materially to the suppression of the rebellion by the ruling Manchus. This support, however, came with strings attached in the form of greater demands for more influence in China.

4. The Boxers were a secret society opposed to the Manchu Ch'ing dynasty. Eventually the society members became extremely xenophobic. Gaining the favor of the dowager empress, Tzu Hsi, the Boxers grew increasingly emboldened in their attacks on foreigners.

5. Noble, 30–31. In the early years of their duty in China, the troops of the 15th Infantry were to safeguard American lives and property, promote commerce, keep open the Peking–Tientsin railway, and oppose Japanese expansion in China.

6.   Noble, 31. Castner was echoing the observations and recommendations of his predecessor, Brig. Gen. William D. Connor.

7.   *News*, March 25,.1927, 4. The term "collies" is, I believe, a misspelling of the word "coolies."

8.   *News*. This initial compassion felt by Patrick for the Chinese laborer was of short duration. In his article for the *News* of March 27, 1927, Patrick stated that "now I'm hardened to it all and I don't think of feeling sorry for the rickshaw boys anymore."

9.   *News*, March 27, 1927. Noble renders the spelling of this Chinese warlord's name as "Chang Tso–lin."

10.   *News*, March 27, 1927.

11.   Edwin Patrick, Tientsin, to family, Tell City, LS [Photocopy], May 28, 1926, file of author. To assure his family that they were not spending all their money for servants, Patrick pointed out that "all five of them cost us less than one worthless negro girl cost us at San Antonio and they feed themselves, while we fed her and she ate more than we did (note here again Patrick's racial prejudice)." An article in *The Sentinel*, the weekly newspaper of the American Forces in China, September 24, 1926, 1041, 1043–1044, indicated that the average family had five servants, the total monthly cost for these servants being approximately $47.00 in American currency.

12.   Patrick to family, ibid.

13.   The description that follows was taken from *The Sentinel*, September 24, 1926, 1041–42, 1046–47.

14.   The designation of a military unit with the suffix "(-)" indicates that the unit at that time and at that location does not contain all of its normally assigned subordinate units. In the case of the 15th Infantry, it indicates that it was at less than full strength at Tientsin: its 1st Battalion was in Manila, and one company was habitually at Tongshan, 85 miles southeast of Tientsin, where it guarded the railroad shops of the Peking–Mukden railroad.

15.   Noble, 125, 127–28, 132–34.

16.   Noble, 87.

17.   *Sentinel*, December 23, 1927, 3–4.

18.   *Sentinel*, April 27, 1928, 1. On April 24, 1928, Camp Nan–Ta–Ssu was renamed Camp Burrowes in memory of 1st. Lieut. Robert M. Burrowes, a member of the 15th Infantry who died on February 14, 1928. Patrick became the first commander of Camp Burrowes.

19.   Noble, 90.

20.   *Sentinel*, September 24, 1926, 1047–48.

21.   Noble, 90.

22.   *Sentinel*, May 13, 1927, 11; October 7, 1927, 11–12; February 16, 1929, 1.

23.   *Sentinel*, September 10, 1926, 968; April 16, 1928, 1; December 22, 1928, 4.

24.   *Sentinel*, November 5, 1926, 1184; April 29, 1927, 1; May 20, 1927, 2; April 6, 1928, 1. Patrick celebrated his marksmanship score "by taking a dip in the surf, much to the relief of tent dwellers who had been checking up on him."

25. Edwin Patrick to Patrick family, Tell City, LS [Photocopy], July 10, 1926, file of author. Note again Patrick's racial stereotyping. Patrick informed his mother in this letter that "Nellie May says baby looks just like me. Isn't he beautiful?" A peculiarity of Patrick's handwriting was his habitual use of an "x" in place of a period. Possibly he acquired this habit during his World War I service, or while a student at the Army Signal School, when, in writing dispatches, he might have substituted "x's" for periods to indicate clearly the end of a sentence. E. Leslie Medford, Jr., Lieut. Col., USMC (Ret.), Stockton, Ca., informed me in an interview on November 16, 1991, that he used such a system in writing dispatches during his military service. In future quotations I shall substitute periods for Patrick's "x" 's." In his letters Patrick spelled his stepson's nickname variously as "Ricky," "Rickey," and "Rickie."

26. Edwin Patrick to Clara Patrick, Tell City, LS [Photocopy], June 23, 1927, file of author.

27. Edwin Patrick to Clara Patrick, ibid.; Edwin Patrick to Herbert Patrick, LS [Photocopy], June 23, 1927, file of author. The author was struck by Patrick's grasp of the situation in China at this time, predicting Chang Kai Shek's ultimate victory over the forces of Chang Tso Lin, but also presciently stating that "somebody else" would eject the Nationalists, as Mao Tse–tung and his forces were to do in 1949. Such insights into the political situation within China were apparently not commonplace among the officers in China, since Noble states that "the average soldier, sailor, or leatherneck, both officer and enlisted, had little comprehension of the Chinese domestic scene or, for that matter, little interest in what was happening" (xvi). Patrick also betrays the all–too–traditional American military belief in the relative inferiority of oriental soldiers vis–à–vis American soldiers, a view that was to have near-disastrous consequences in the early days of World War II and the Korean War, and during much of the Vietnam War.

28. Edwin Patrick to Patrick family, Tell City, LS [Photocopy], June 10, 1928, file of author.

29. *Sentinel*, November 12, 1926, 1215, 1216; November 19, 1926, 1242; November 26, 1926, 1268; February 18, 1927, 4; December 8, 1928, 7; Joseph W. Stilwell, Diary #29, March 10, 1929, in "Diaries, 1900–1946," Joseph W. Stilwell Collection, Hoover Institution on War, Revolution and Peace, Stanford, Ca.

30. *Sentinel* , February 18, 1927, 21, March 4, 1927, 6; Edwin Patrick to "Mama and folks," Tell City, ibid.; playbill for David Gray and Avery Hopwood, *The Best People*, photocopy furnished by Thomas B. Patrick.

31. *Sentinel*, May 27, 1927, cover page.

32. Edwin Patrick to Clara Patrick, Tell City, LS [Photocopy], June 23, 1927, file of author; *Sentinel*, April 27, 1928, 13.

33. *Sentinel*, February 9, 1929, 1; February 16, 1929, 1, 8; March 2, 1929, 1.

34. *Sentinel*, April 13, 1929, 10.

35. *Sentinel*, April 20, 1929, 2.

36. Finney, 13.

CHAPTER 8

1. WD biography; Thomas B. Patrick interview; Pogue, 247.

2.   Pogue, 247.

3.   Pogue, 250–51.

4.   Ed Cray, *General George C. Marshall: Soldier and Statesman* (New York: Simon & Schuster, 1990), 104–5; Pogue, 257. Company–grade officers include second lieutenants through captains.

5.   Pogue, 252–53.

6.   Pogue, 254.

7.   Pogue, 254–55.

8.   Pogue, 257–59.

9.   *The Doughboy* (Fort Benning, Ga.: The Infantry School, 1931, 1932), "Faculty" and "Second Section." Although the author has found no source materials indicating that Marshall specifically requested Patrick's assignment to the Infantry School, he thinks it to be logical that he did so. The two men had served together in China; Patrick had just completed a three–year tour of duty with troops, including time spent as a battalion commander; and Marshall knew Patrick, as attested by the latter's son, who stated that his parents had "a personal relationship" with Marshall (Thomas B. Patrick interview).

10.   Marshall to Heintzelman, December 18, 1933, George C. Marshall Files, quoted in Pogue, 259.

11.   Edwin D. Patrick, "The Training and Replacement of Infantry Signal Communication Personnel (Officers and Enlisted Men) in the Theater of Operations," a research paper for the Command and General Staff School, Fort Leavenworth, Kans. In the following chapter, I will enlarge upon this very thought–provoking paper.

12.   Patrick research paper, 14–16.

13.   George C. Marshall, Infantry School, to the Academic Department, Infantry School, TLS [Photocopy], May 5, 1931, Joseph Warren Stilwell Papers, Box 24, A–7, 1930–1931, Hoover Institution on War, Revolution and Peace, Stanford, Ca. Other officers listed in this letter of commendation are Lieut. Col. Stilwell, Maj. D. S. Wilson, Maj. H. R. Bull, Maj. E. G. Sherburne, Maj. C. F. Stivers, and Maj. L. F. Davidson; A–9, 1932–1933.

14.   Harriet E. Foley, Franklin, Ohio, to author, TLS, March 8, 1991, noting dramatic activities of the Patricks that are documented in materials in the E. Forrest Harding files of the Franklin Area Historical Society, Franklin, Ohio, file of author.

15.   Foley. Unfortunately, the reviewer and the publication in which the review appeared are not identified.

16.   Foley.

17.   WD biography; Pogue, 248; "Appendix F."

CHAPTER 9

1.   WD biography; Thomas B. Patrick interview.

2.   *Commandants, Staff, Faculty, and Graduates*, 6; Harry P. Ball, *Of Responsible Command: A History of the U.S. Army War College* (Carlisle Barracks,

Pa.: The Alumni Association of the United states Army War College, 1983), 29–30, 152, 183. In 1928, the Command and General Staff School course was expanded to two years, after the one–year course was found to be of "insufficient time to teach all that was necessary regarding the operation of the reinforced brigade, the division and the corps." Also, this two–year course, in addition to providing more thoroughly trained graduates, would produce fewer graduates, all of whom "could be admitted to the hallowed 'general staff eligible list,' avoiding the severe morale problem" experienced by the non–selected one–year graduates.

3. Nenninger, 59–60.

4. Nenninger, 61, 67. The five paragraphs in the operation order are "Situation," "Mission," "Execution," "Administration and Logistics," and "Command and Signal."

5. *Schedule for 1932–1933 First Year Course, The Command and General Staff School, Fort Leavenworth, Kansas, 1932* (Fort Leavenworth, Kans.: The Command and General Staff School Press, 1932), 3, 22–41; "Second-Year Class Schedule for 1933–1934," The Command and General Staff School, Fort Leavenworth, Kans., 3, 23–37.

6. *Annual Report of the Command and General Staff School, Fort Leavenworth, Kansas, 1933–1934* (Fort Leavenworth, Kans.: The Command and General Staff School Press, 1934), 2–3.

7. Edwin D. Patrick, "The Training and Replacement of Infantry Signal Communication Personnel (Officers and Enlisted Men) in the Theater of Operations," March 23, 1934, files of Combat Studies Institute, U.S. Army Command and General Staff College, Fort Leavenworth, Kans., 3. In World War I a field signal battalion, composed of three companies, was organized in each infantry division. One of these companies, an "outpost company," supplied a platoon to each infantry regiment to handle communications within the regiments. A platoon of infantrymen assisted these outpost platoons in each regimental headquarters. There were no organic signal personnel below division level.

8. Patrick research paper, 6, 10–11.

9. Patrick research paper, title page, 14–16, 24. One of Patrick's instructors made a written comment on the paper that this requirement was "very desirable, but impracticable," because it would occupy approximately 30 percent of the entire time available for instruction of these officers.

10. "Press Information 6th Inf Div, Roster, Officers Division, Headquarters, 6th Infantry Division," World War II Operations Reports, 1940–1948, RG 407, NA. Alfred L. Sanderson, Brig. Gen., USA (Ret.), Stockton, Ca., in a telephone interview by the author, November 16, 1991, confirmed that signal communications within the infantry division during World War II were organized as described above, and that the organization of division signal communications is essentially identical in today's army.

11. Rachel Crothers, *As Husbands Go* (New York: Samuel French, n.d.). Photocopy of playbill furnished by Thomas B. Patrick.

12. *Annual Report*, 4–5; WD biography; Edwin D. Patrick, Spokane, to his mother, Tell City, LS [Photocopy], July 6, 1934, file of author; Edwin D. Patrick, Spokane, to George C. Marshall, Chicago, LS [Photocopy], February 1935, Marshall Papers, Box 1, Folder 19, George C. Marshall Foundation, Lexing-

ton, Va., file of author. The letter to Marshall contains no clue as to the identity of "the Chief," but most likely he was the Chief of Infantry.

13. The author bases this description of the duties of an instructor on his ten years of service in the Missouri, Maryland, and California Army National Guard.

14. Virgil Field, *Official History of the Washington National Guard* (Camp Murray, Tacoma, Wash.: Headquarters Military Department, 1961–1965[?], 627.

15. Patrick to mother, July 6.

16. Patrick to Marshall, TLS, [Photocopy] October 31, 1935, Marshall Papers, Box 2, Folder 17, file of author.

17. Marshall to Patrick, TL, November 8, 1935, Marshall Papers, Box 2, Folder 18, file of author. This letter indicates to the author that Marshall had a genuine high regard for Patrick's opinions.

18. Infantry Washington," File 325.4, Army–NGB, State–Decimal File, 1922–45, Records of the National Guard Bureau, RG 168, NA; *Historical and Pictorial Review of the National Guard of the State of Washington, 1939* (Baton Rouge: Army and Navy Publishing Co., 1938 [sic], 11.

19. Patrick to his mother and his sister, Alma, Tell City, LS [Photocopy], 1935, file of author.

CHAPTER 10

1. Thomas B. Patrick interview; *The Tell City News*, June [?] 1936.

2. George S. Pappas, *Prudens Futuri: The US Army War College, 1901–1967* (Carlisle Barracks, Pa.: The Alumni Association of the US Army War College, 1967), 28.

3. Pappas, 28–30. Stetson Conn, "The Army War College, 1899–1940: Mission, Purpose, Objectives," December 1964, File 538, HRC 352, Army War College, Center of Military History, United States Army, Washington, D.C., 10–11.

4. Pappas, 123.

5. Army War College transcript of Patrick, Edwin D., Army War College Curricular Archives, File 6–1937–15, U. S. Army Military History Institute (USAMHI), Carlisle Barracks, Pa. All Army War College plans followed the War Department procedure of referring to war plans by color names rather than by the name of the country concerned, e.g., Green (Mexico), Orange (Japan), and Red Coalition (Britain allied with Mexico, Canada, and Japan). Each plan was predicated on a presumed attack against the United States and its possessions by the particular country or coalition (Pappas, 101–2; Ball, 227); Ball, 212–13.

6. Patrick transcript.

7. *Course at the Army War College, 1937 [sic]–1937. Conduct of War–Part II. Field Exercise. Jackson's Valley Campaign. Lectures by: Major Edwin D. Patrick, Inf. and Major Wendell L. Clemenson, Inf.* Army War College Curricular Archives, File 6–1937–15/K, USAMHI.

8. Playbill for *A Morning in A.W.C.*, photocopy provided by Thomas B. Patrick.

9.   WD biography; *Directory of Army War College Graduates* (Carlisle Barracks, Pa.: AWC Alumni Association, 1990), 91; "Appendix A." His academic record does not show any class standing.

10. *Directory of Army War College Graduates*, 91.

11. Ball, 172, 202; WD biography.

12. Thomas B. Patrick interview.

13. "Prospectus of the Naval War College Courses, Senior and Junior, 1938–39," U.S. Naval War College, July 1938, 10; Evelyn M. Cherpak, Head, Naval Historical Collection, Naval War College, Newport, R.I., to author, TLS, June 12, 1989, file of author. In this letter, Ms. Cherpak stated that although Patrick was a member of the Senior Class of 1938, the course of study for that class would have been the same as that described in the 1938–1939 prospectus cited above.

14. Prospectus, 1, 3.

15. Prospectus, 2.

16. Prospectus, 2.

17. Prospectus, 11–15, 21–22. These various problems appear to refer to the strategic and tactical problems and chart maneuvers to which I have previously alluded. The "quick decision" problems required the student to develop a solution to the problem that required instant decision and translation into effective action ("Prospectus," 1). Unfortunately, the Naval Historical Collection, the depository for Naval War College archives and manuscripts, does not contain any materials directly pertaining to Patrick, other than records indicating that he was a member of the Senior Class of 1938. However, his son recalls that his father "was busy all the time with the War College. He spent a lot of time working there. ... When he went to school he was kind of a workaholic" (Thomas B. Patrick interview).

18. Thomas B. Patrick interview.

19. WD biography; *Official Army Register*, 1945, 723. The General Staff Corps was established on February 14, 1903, by authority contained in the "General Staff Act" passed by Congress and signed by President Roosevelt. The officers of that corps would be responsible for preparing plans for the national defense and for wartime mobilization. In addition they were to render "professional aid and assistance to the Secretary of War, general officers, and other superior commanders," and to act as their agents in seeing that their orders were carried out. Officers eligible for this corps would be those "who had distinguished themselves in the school system and who had shown a 'high order of practical ability to command troops.' " Detail to the corps would be for a period of four years, and officers would serve either with the Army General Staff in Washington, or with general officer commands elsewhere (Ball, 67, 75, 82).

CHAPTER 11

1.   *San Antonio Evening News* , August 9, 1939, photocopy supplied by Thomas B. Patrick; Thomas B. Patrick interview; Ulric B. Patrick, interview by author, tape recording, Albuquerque, N.M., September 20, 1990, file of author. Fort Sam Houston is composed of several major areas: Quadrangle, the location of the Eighth Corps Area headquarters at that time, and several

posts named for the branches or duties of the troops occupying those areas, e.g., Staff Post, Infantry Post, Artillery Post. Since Patrick was a staff officer, he was quartered on Staff Post.

2. "Third Army Maneuvers, 1938, Fort F. E. Warren Concentration," Records of the U.S. Army Continental Commands, 1920–42, RG 394, NA. In reviewing the National Archives folder containing the documents pertaining to the Third Army Maneuvers, the author found the key documents describing the maneuvers to be missing. Attached as a cover sheet to the documents was a sheet of paper listing the enclosure numbers of the missing documents, with "Major Patrick" written above this list. I took that to mean that sometime after the maneuvers Patrick had signed out those documents for his review, and that he had never returned them.

3. WD biography; Matloff, *American Military History*, 419–20; Edwin Patrick, Fort Sam Houston, to his mother, LS [Photocopies], October 7, November 16, and December 23, 1940, file of author.

4. Patrick to his mother, November 16, 1940; John B. Wilson, comp., *Armies, Corps, Divisions and Separate Brigades in Army Lineage Series* (Washington, D.C.: Center of Military History, United States Army, 1987), 75.

5. Patrick to his mother, November 16, 1940, September 10, 1941

6. Patrick to his mother, LS [Photocopy], December 1 and December 6, 1941, file of author.

7. Patrick to his mother, December 24, 1941; WD biography.

8. Invitation to "Graduation of the Hospital and Recreation Corps– – –Gray Ladies" in Reid Hall, Station Hospital, Fort Sam Houston, 1500, February 6, 1941, Marshall Papers, Box 37, Folder 21, George C. Marshall Foundation, Lexington, Va. Marshall acknowledged receipt of this invitation in a reply addressed to Mrs. Patrick.

9. Camp Barkeley was built on a site southwest of Abilene that Patrick had surveyed and recommended as a prospective training site during his tenure as G–3, Eighth Corps Area (*Reporter-News*, Abilene, Tex., n.d., photocopy furnished by Thomas B. Patrick). The 90th Infantry Division, which Patrick was now joining, had fought on the flanks of Patrick's 5th Division during the St. Mihiel and Meuse–Argonne Offensives in World War I, when the divisions were part of I Corps and III Corps in those actions (*American Armies and Battlefields in Europe*, 109, 186).

10. George von Roeder, comp., *Regimental History of the 357th Infantry* (Weiden, Oberpfalz, Bavaria: Ferdinand Nickl Buchdruckerei, n.d.), 15.

11. von Roeder, 16. Patrick's emphasis on a high state of physical conditioning of his troops undoubtedly reflects his own experience as an officer in the 15th Infantry in China. His commander there, Brig. Gen. Castner, an "inveterate hiker," heavily stressed field marches, and insisted that his infantrymen be able to complete a fifteen–mile march "in heavy marching order" (Noble, 87-88). When the 357th entered combat on June 6, 1944, at Utah Beach, Normandy, it would do so as an infantry regiment.

12. Edwin D. Patrick, Nouméa, New Caledonia, to family, Tell City, LS [Photocopy], May 22, 1943, file of author.

13. von Roeder, 15, 17.

CHAPTER 12

1. John Miller, Jr., *Guadalcanal: The First Offensive*, in *United States Army in World War II* (Washington, D.C.: Historical Division, Department of the Army, 1949), 169.

2. Miller, 2–3, 14, 52.

3. Miller, 17, 19.

4. Miller, 348, 350.

5. Louis Morton, *Strategy and Command: The First Two Years* in *United States Army in World War II: The War in the Pacific* (Washington, D.C.: Center of Military History, United States Army, 1989), 257, 352–54, 360–61, 356.

6. Patrick, with his extensive experience as a combat officer in World War I, an infantry battalion commander in China, an instructor at the Infantry School, and a graduate of the Command and General Staff School, the Army War College, and the Naval War College, would rank high on the list of senior army officers whom Marshall would consider for such an assignment. Possibly Patrick's friendship with Marshall also played some role in Marshall's selection of Patrick for this assignment.

7. Samuel Eliot Morison, *The Struggle for Guadalcanal, August 1942–February 1943*, vol. 5; *History of United States Naval Operations in World War II* (Boston: Little, Brown and Company, 1984), 185–86.

8. Edwin Patrick, Nouméa, New Caledonia, to family, Tell City, LS [Photocopies], February 2, February 7, and March 1, 1943, file of author.

9. Miller, 222, 210, 212, 140–44, 180–83, 213.

10. Harmon did not greet Marshall's decision to assign army officers to Halsey's staff with enthusiasm, since he felt that his method of working with Halsey was entirely adequate. Possibly Harmon continued to work directly with Halsey, bypassing the army officers on Halsey's staff, accounting for the "duplication of an existing arrangement" to which Patrick referred (Morton, *Strategy and Command*, 361).

11. Edwin D. Patrick, Nouméa, to Lieutenant General Walter Krueger, APO 500, TLS [Photocopy], March 7, 1943, Folder 44, Krueger Papers, United States Military Academy Library, West Point, N.Y.

12. Krueger Papers, Box 7, Folder 44 (Krueger did not receive Patrick's March 7 letter until May 18); "General Orders, No. 25, Headquarters, Sixth Army, 21 June 1943," File 106–1.13, The Adjutant General's Office, World War II Operations Reports, 1940–1948, Sixth Army, RG 407, NA.

13. Edwin Patrick, Nouméa, New Caledonia to family, Tell City, LS [Photocopy], May 10 and May 22, 1943, file of author.

14. "General Orders, No. 25, 21 June 1943, Headquarters Sixth Army," File 106–1.13, AGO, WW II, Sixth Army, RG 407, NA; Krueger, 15; Krueger to Patrick, June 7, 1943.

CHAPTER 13

1. *The Sixth Army in Action: A Photo History, January 1943–June 1945* (Kyoto, Japan: 8th Information and Historical Service, United States Sixth Army, December 1945), 58.

2. *Sixth Army in Action*, 58; Krueger, 6.

3. Krueger, 6–7.

4. Krueger, 8.

5. Krueger, 10.

6. Krueger, 10; D. Clayton James, *The Years of MacArthur, Volume 2, 1941–1945* (Boston: Houghton Mifflin Company, 1975), 312–13.

7. Krueger, 10.

8. All code names for military operations will be spelled with capital letters.

9. Krueger, 15, 19–23.

10. Krueger, 24; Edwin D. Patrick, Brisbane, to family, Tell City, LS [Photocopy], June 30, 1943, file of author.

11. Patrick to family, August 4, 1943.

12. Krueger, 26–28.

13. Krueger, 27–28; *Sixth Army in Action*, 59.

14. Edwin D. Patrick to his family, LS [Photocopies], June 23, August 4, August 8, September 10, October 19, November 11, and November 21, 1943, file of author. Although Patrick retained only "pleasant" memories of his World War I experiences, one must seriously question the validity of these recollections. One of the "blessings" that our minds can impose on our memories is the suppression of those memories that are unpleasant and possibly painful, retaining for our recall usually only those memories that are less traumatic for us to bring back into our consciousness.

15. Patrick to family, September 19 and October 9, 1943.

16. Patrick to family, November 21, 1943.

17. Patrick to family, December 2, 1943. Cooper wrote a letter to Patrick's son, "Tommie," in which he told him that he had seen his father, who "was looking well."

18. George C. Marshall to Mrs. E. D. Patrick, El Paso, TL [Photocopy], December 23, 1943, Marshall Papers.

19. Krueger , 32–35.

20. Krueger, 29, 36–38.

21. Krueger, 38–39.

22. Krueger, 39. James indicates that MacArthur was well-satisfied with the results of DEXTERITY, remarking to Krueger that " 'this war had shown no finer victory.' " James also points out that "most authorities agree that it was well planned and executed," a compliment to Krueger, Patrick, and the Alamo Force staff, commanders, and troops. James goes on to quote the

"chief naval historian of the Pacific war," Samuel E. Morison, as admitting, despite doubts about the overall strategic value of the operation in the advance to the Philippines, that the operation was " 'well planned, well led and superbly executed.' " Still, James faults Krueger for his conduct of the Saidor operation, contending that his delay in allowing the Saidor force commander to move eastward toward Sio, and his failure to move far enough inland to block interior routes of withdrawal allowed eleven thousand to thirteen thousand Japanese troops to escape from the Huon Peninsula, thereby setting himself at odds with Krueger's evaluation of the success of the Saidor operation(345–47).

23.   Patrick to family, January 5 and January 27, 1944, file of author. One wonders if Patrick's lament was a reflection of Krueger's belief that the creation of Alamo Force by MacArthur "inevitably deprived Sixth Army of the credit for operations which in reality it conducted in the guise of Alamo Force" (Krueger, 10), or was a product of MacArthur's well-known penchant for having his name dominate all press releases emanating from SWPA, resulting in the relative anonymity of his subordinate commanders, particularly Krueger and Eichelberger (William M. Leary, ed., *We Shall Return! MacArthur's Commanders and the Defeat of Japan, 1942–1945* [Lexington, Ky.: The University Press of Kentucky, 1988], ix–x).

24.   Krueger, 29.

25.   Edward J. Drea, *MacArthur's Ultra: Codebreaking and the War against Japan, 1942–1945* (Lawrence, Kans.: University Press of Kansas, 1992), 98.

26.   Drea, xi–xii, 25. ULTRA was the code word the Allies used during World War II to denote information they obtained through "monitoring, intercepting, and decoding enemy radio communications"; "special intelligence" is synonymous with ULTRA. In the Pacific theater ULTRA referred to decrypted radio intercepts of Japanese military traffic; the special intelligence referred to as MAGIC consisted of intercepts of messages sent in the Japanese diplomatic codes. MacArthur's Central Bureau grew out of a cadre of cryptanalysts that he brought with him from the Philippines in 1942, along with some codebreakers from Washington. During the course of the war the bureau developed the capacity to read the highest-level secret communications of the Japanese army. The core of the Central Bureau was in Brisbane, but advance detachments followed closely behind MacArthur's advancing forces. By the end of the war, more than four thousand men and women were working in the bureau.

27.   Drea, 97–98.

28.   Drea, 98–99.

29.   Drea, 102–3.

30.   Krueger, 45–53; Drea, 103–4.

31.   Krueger, 52–53.

32.   Drea, 104.

33.   Drea, 53–54.

34.   Krueger, 56; *Sixth Army in Action*, 60; Drea, 97.

35.   Drea, 115.

36.   Krueger, 57–63.

37.   Drea, 116–17.

38.   Krueger, 74–75; *Sixth Army in Action*, 60–61.

39.   James, 452–53.

40.   Krueger, 75–76; Patrick to family, LS [Photocopy], August 8, 1944, file of
      author. I have found no records that indicate any increase in size of the
      Alamo Force staff to cope with their dramatically increased planning re-
      sponsibilities.

41.   The objective island was originally known as Insoemar Island and is one of
      the Wakde Islands. However, Alamo Force commonly referred to it as Wakde
      Island, and I will use that name in this manuscript.

42.   Krueger, 79–84.

43.   *Sixth Army in Action*, 61.

44.   Robert Ross Smith, *The Approach to the Philippines*, in *United States Army
      in World War II: The War in the Pacific* (Washington, D.C.: Center of Military
      History, United States Army, 1984), 237–38.

45.   "General Orders No. 78, 11 May 1944, Headquarters Sixth Army," File 106–
      1.13, AGO, WW II, Sixth Army, RG 407, NA.

46.   "Historical Report of Operations–Wakde–Sarmi—TORNADO Task Force, 25
      May to 12 June 1944," File 98–TF 9–0.3, AGO, WW II, Pacific Theater, RG
      407, NA.

47.   Patrick to family, LS [Photocopies], June 23, 1943 through April 6, 1944,
      file of author.

CHAPTER 14

1.   Edwin D. Patrick, New Guinea, to family, Tell City, LS [Photocopy], May [?]
      1944, file of author.

2.   Smith, 234–35, 237–38; Edwin D. Patrick to LTG Walter Krueger, TLS [Pho-
      tocopy], June 3, 1944, 1, George H. Decker Papers, Box: 6th Army 1943–
      1946, Archives, U. S. Army Military History Institute, Carlisle Barracks,
      Pa.; Drea, 133–34.

3.   Smith, 238–42.

4.   Smith, 243–45.

5.   Smith, 244; "Historical Report of Operations Wakde–Sarmi, Tornado Task
      Force," 2, File 98–TF–9–0.3, The Adjutant General's Office, World War II
      Operations, 1940–1948, Pacific Theater, RG 407, NA.

6.   "Historical Report, Wakde–Sarmi," 2.

7.   "Historical Report, Wakde–Sarmi," 2; Smith, 249–50.

8.   Smith, 250–51; Drea 133–34. Sibert, the commanding general of the 6th
      Infantry Division, took command of TORNADO Task Force on June 12. Since
      he did not favor mounting such an operation, he postponed it indefinitely
      ("Historical Report, Wakde–Sarmi," 4, File 98–TF–9–0.3, AGO, WW II, Pa-
      cific Theater, RG 407, NA).

9.   "Historical Report, Wakde–Sarmi," 3. These were undoubtedly troops of the
      223d Infantry that had passed south of and behind Herndon's line of ad-
      vance (Drea, 134).

10. Patrick to Krueger, June 3, 1944, 3; Smith, 252.

11. Patrick to Krueger, June 3, 1944, 3–4. Note that Patrick does not mention Herndon's withdrawal across the Tirfoam River as *the* reason for his relief of Herndon. Rather, he indicates that he doubted Herndon's ability from the beginning of their relationship. Possibly the withdrawal was the precipitating factor for Herndon's relief. Anthony Arthur [*Bushmasters: America's Jungle Warriors of World War II* (New York: St. Martin's Press, 1987), 109] states that "the fact that Sandlin was on the scene when Herndon left implied that the decision to remove Herndon had been planned earlier," appearing to substantiate Patrick's account of his reasons for Herndon's relief.

12. Leary, 65, 162.

13. Smith, 235, 246–47, 262–79; Drea, 133–34. That Herndon's concerns about the strength of the enemy forces facing him were valid is evidenced by the fact that subsequently the 6th Infantry Division and two regiments of the 31st Infantry Division would be required to destroy the Japanese forces in the Sarmi area, the operation not ending until September 2, 1944.

14. Arthur, 2, 110. Letters in the author's file from two former officers of the 158th Infantry, Herbert B. Erb and Hal Braun, former commander of Company B, 158th Infantry, state their belief that Herndon's withdrawal to the Tirfoam River was an appropriate decision, concurred in by all three of his battalion commanders (Erb to author, LS, July 12, 1989; Braun to author, TLS, April 27, 1989, both in file of author).

15. Arthur, 106–7.

16. Arthur, 109. Patrick recommended against reclassifying Herndon because of "his long service as commander of the 158th Infantry, also because quite recently two regimental commanders were disposed of without reclassification. From what I have been able to learn, Col. Herndon's record is no worse than theirs" (Patrick to Krueger, June 3, 1944, 3–4). Herndon later received "another responsible post command in the theater" (Smith, n., 34, 252).

17. One can only conclude that Patrick was still basing his actions on the faulty intelligence estimates. Apparently, those patrols had failed to detect any sizable Japanese forces in the area.

18. Smith, 253–58; Braun to author.

19. Smith, 258; "Historical Report, Wakde–Sarmi," 3-4.

20. "Historical Report, Wakde-Sarmi," 4.

21. "Historical Report, Wakde–Sarmi," 5; Smith, 261–62.

22. Smith, 262.

23. Erb to author.

24. Patrick to family, Tell City, LS [Photocopy], June 21, 1944, file of author; radiogram from Krueger to Patrick, Appendix G, G–7, "Congratulatory and Other Messages," in "World War II Correspondence," Box 25, Krueger Papers.

CHAPTER 15

1. Krueger, 106.

2. Krueger, 106–7.

3. Samuel Eliot Morison, *History of United States Naval Operations in World War II*, vol. 8, *New Guinea and the Marianas, March 1944–August 1944* (Boston: Little, Brown and Company, 1981), 135.

4.   Drea, 141; Smith, 398–400.

5.   Smith, 400.

6.   "Historical Report of the Noemfoor Operation, 22 June 1944 to 31 August 1944," 5–6, File 98–TF 11–0.3, Cyclone Task Force (Noemfoor Island), The Adjutant General's Office, World War II Operations Reports, 1940–1948 Pacific Theater, RG 407, NA; radiogram, [Photocopy], MacArthur to Chief of Staff, June 29, 1944, RG–4, USAFPAC, Correspondence, War Department, Archives, MacArthur Memorial, Norfolk, Va.

7.   Krueger, 108–9.

8.   Krueger, 109; Smith, 403.

9.   "Historical Report, Noemfoor Operation," 6.

10.   "Historical Report, Noemfoor Operation," 7–8.

11.   Drea, 141–42; Krueger, 107–9. Krueger based his estimate of the disposition of forces in the Kamiri area on the report from a reconnaissance team of Alamo Scouts sent to Noemfoor Island on the night of June 22–23. These scouts patrolled the island for two days, confirming the Japanese strength, general defensive dispositions, and the unmanned state of the coastal defenses.

12.   "Historical Report, Noemfoor Operation," 8–9.

13.   "Historical Report, Noemfoor Operation," 9–10; Smith, 410.

14.   Drea, 142; "Historical Report, Noemfoor Operation," 10.

15.   It is possible that fear that such a last minute delaying or postponing of the drop could have caused confusion within the airborne serial was the reason for not contacting the serial commander.

16.   Smith, 412–16.

17.   "Historical Report, Noemfoor Operation," 11–12.

18.   "Historical Report, Noemfoor Operation," 12–15.

19.   "Historical Report, Noemfoor Operation," 21.

20.   Morison, 136.

21.   S. D. Sturgis, Jr., Headquarters, Sixth Army, to Mrs. E. D. Patrick, Ruidoso, N.M., TLS [Photocopy], March 17, 1945, copy supplied by Thomas B. Patrick.

22.   Radiogram [Photocopy], MacArthur to CG, Alamo Force, July 4, 1944, Archives, MacArthur Memorial, file of author.

23.   Appendix G, "Congratulatory and Other Messages," "World War II Correspondence," Box 25, Krueger Papers.

24.   "Historical Report, Noemfoor Operation," 18.

25.   Patrick to family, LS [Photocopies], August 2 and 25, 1944, file of author. The citation for the Legion of Merit (Oak Leaf Cluster) appears as "Appendix C."

26.   Krueger, 135.

CHAPTER 16

1. Krueger, 114; Smith, *Approach to the Philippines*, 425–31.

2. Krueger, 118.

3. Drea, 142–43.

4. Krueger, 119–20.

5. Smith, *Approach to the Philippines*, 445.

6. Quoted by William M. Leary, "Walter Krueger: MacArthur's Fighting General," in Leary, ed., *We Shall Return!*, 70–71.

7. *The 6th Infantry Division in World War II, 1939–1945* (n.p.: May 1947; reprint, Nashville, Tenn.: The Battery Press, 1983), 57–59; Joseph A. Castagnetto, Alameda, Ca., interview by author, August 27, 1991, Alameda, tape recording, file of author, hereafter referred to as "Castagnetto interview."

8. *The 6th Infantry Division*, 59; Robert Ross Smith, *Triumph in the Philippines*, in *United States Army in World War II: The War in the Pacific* (Washington, D.C.: Center of Military History, United States Army, 1984), "Appendix A–5."

9. Bruce Palmer, Jr., Fort Walton Beach, Fla., to author, TLS, July 28, 1991, file of author; Bruce Palmer, Jr., The Fairfax, Va., interview by author, May 18, 1990, tape recording, file of author, hereafter referred to as "Palmer interview."

10. Palmer interview.

11. Palmer interview.

12. Patrick to family, Tell City, LS [Photocopies], October 7 and 15, November 11, and December 11 and 29, 1944, file of author.

13. *The 6th Infantry Division*, 59; Smith, *Triumph in the Philippines*, 56, "Appendix A–5."

14. Patrick to family, Tell City, LS [Photocopy], January 1, 1945, file of author. Apparently not all of the "Sightseers" enjoyed their New Year's meal as much as their commanding general did. The division history records that the *Calloway*'s sick bay was filled "to overflowing with the victims of food poisoning" after the New Year's day dinner (61).

15. Smith, *Triumph in the Philippines*, 56–57.

16. *The 6th Infantry Division*, 61–63.

17. Smith, *Triumph in the Philippines*, 76–80.

18. *The 6th Infantry Division*, 63–67; Palmer to author, July 28, 1991.

19. The designation for the day of the Lingayen Gulf landings.

20. *The 6th Infantry Division*, 67; Smith, *Triumph in the Philippines*, 80. The third regiment of Patrick's division, the 63d Infantry, was serving as I Corps reserve. ULTRA revealed to MacArthur that General Yamashita Tomoyuki, commander of the Japanese 14th Area Army headquartered in Manila, had correctly predicted that MacArthur's forces would land on both sides of Lingayen Gulf, but felt that meeting the Americans along the beachheads would result in the destruction of his army. Therefore he disposed his forces in the rugged hills inland to resist the American advance southward (Drea, 192).

21. Palmer to author, July 28, 1991.

22. *The 6th Infantry Division*, 67–69.

23. *The 6th Infantry Division*, 70.

24. *The 6th Infantry Division*, 70, 73–78.

25. Smith, *Triumph in the Philippines*, 85–87.

26. Smith, *Triumph in the Philippines*, 114–15, Map I.

27. Smith, *Triumph in the Philippines*, 115.

28. Smith, *Triumph in the Philippines*, 140–41. Throughout the Luzon campaign MacArthur and Krueger disagreed violently over Japanese strength on the island. Col. Horton White, Krueger's G–2, estimated that there were 234,500 Japanese on Luzon, whereas Willoughby, MacArthur's G–2, placed enemy strength at 152,500 (Smith, 141). The two commanders particularly differed over enemy strength to the east of Sixth Army. A captured enemy document, dated January 8, led Krueger to believe that an additional undetected and unsuspected force of at least corps size, code–named *Shimbu*, was present to the south and east of Manila. If true, White believed that there were 100,000 more Japanese troops on Luzon than Willoughby had estimated. The suspected presence of the *Shimbu* force undoubtedly accounted for Krueger's reluctance to move XIV Corps forward as rapidly as MacArthur desired (Drea, 194–95).

29. Smith, *Triumph in the Philippines*, 143.

30. The following account of the battle for the Cabaruan Hills is based on material in Smith, *Triumph in the Philippines*, 160–66, and in *The 6th Infantry Division*, 79–89.

31. Palmer to author, July 28, 1991.

32. Palmer to author, July 28, 1991. The author agrees with Palmer that Patrick should have paid closer heed to his regimental commanders' assessments of the enemy strength in the Cabaruan Hills. However, by pulling out the 20th Infantry elements to resume the advance southward, and replacing them with units from the 1st Infantry, which had met practically no resistance in its zone of advance, Patrick was able to reach the objective line on schedule. Reaching and securing this line was one of the major missions assigned to the 6th Division to support the XIV Corps' drive southward. By allowing an entire regiment to become engaged in the Cabaruan Hills, Patrick might not have reached the objective line on schedule, exposing XIV Corps' left flank to a possible enemy attack, which could have jeopardized the advance of that corps.

33. Joseph A. Castagnetto, interview by author, August 27, 1991, Alameda, CA, tape recording, file of author, hereafter referred to as "Castagnetto interview."

34. Krueger, 235, 239, 242.

35. The latter was the group that Krueger's G–2 had earlier identified, but of whose presence Willoughby was unaware (see n. 28, supra).

36. This account of the battles for Muñoz and San Jose and the seizure of Rizal and Cabanatuan is based on Smith, Triumph in *the Philippines*, 190–201, and on *The 6th Infantry Division*, 90–100.

37. Smith, *Triumph in the Philippines*, 195, n. 13, citing an interview with Col. George G. O'Connor, a former field artillery officer with the 6th Division, states that Maj. Gen. Charles E. Hurdis, who succeeded Patrick as division

commander, " 'felt that Patrick came to believe after the battle for Muñoz that in the light of the Japanese strength ultimately discovered there Colonel Ives's relief was regrettable and unjustifiable.' " Ives went on to command successfully a regiment of the 38th Division on Luzon, " 'reflecting the fact that General Krueger still had confidence in him.' "

38. Palmer to author, July 28, 1991.

39. The following abbreviated summary of the capture of Manila is based on Krueger, 246–51, and on Smith, *Triumph in the Philippines*, 211–308.

40. ULTRA was able to provide no information on enemy strength in Manila or of the enemy's intentions regarding its defense (Drea, 197).

41. Krueger, 262.

42. Smith, *Triumph in the Philippines*, 309–31.

43. Smith, *Triumph in the Philippines*, 331-34; Krueger, 269.

                                   CHAPTER 17

1. Smith, *Triumph in the Philippines*, 361–66.

2. Drea makes no mention of any ULTRA in the campaign against the *Shimbu* Group east of Manila.

3. Smith, *Triumph in the Philippines*, 367–71.

4. Smith, *Triumph in the Philippines*, 371–72; *6th Division in World War II*, 107.

5. The following account of the attack against the Shimbu line is from Smith, *Triumph in the Philippines*, 371–84, and *6th Division in World War II*, 107–14.

6. Krueger, 277.

7. John D. Humphrey, Tupelo, Miss., to author, LS, June 2, 1989, file of author. Both Col. Humphrey and Gen. Palmer have told the author that they believe the Japanese had observed Generals Hall and Griswold at the battalion OP, and that during the night of March 14 had infiltrated a machine gunner through the American lines to occupy a "spider hole," from which he would have a good field of fire toward the OP, in the event any senior officers came forward to the OP again.

8. Humphrey to author, LS, June 2, 1989, November 4, 1991, file of author; Bernard J. Macauley, M.D., Gerald, Mo., to Col. James L. Massey, Fort Sam Houston, Tex., TLS, May 4, 1946, Box 10, File 3, Krueger Papers; James Young, Jr., Salina, Kans., to Col. James L. Massey, Fort Sam Houston, Tex., TLS, May 5, 1946, Box 10, File 3, Krueger Papers.

9. Walther A. Huchthausen, Philippine Islands, to wife, LS [Photocopy], March 16, 1945, file of author, furnished by Chaplain Huchthausen's daughter, Mrs. Christa Mueller, Newport News, Va.

10. Young to Massey, May 5, 1946; "Historical Report of Action Against the Enemy–Luzon Campaign–54th Evacuation Hospital, 25 November 1944–30 June 1945," File MDEH–54–0.3, World War II Operations Reports, 1940–1948, Medical, RG 407, NA.

11. Macauley to Massey, May 4, 1946; "Historical Report, 54th Evacuation Hospital," WWII, Medical, RG 407, NA.

12. Young to Massey, May 5, 1946.

13. Young to Massey, May 5, 1946.

14. Young to Massey, May 5, 1946; Macauley to Massey, May 4, 1945; "Morning Report," 54th Evacuation Hospital (SM), March 15, 1945, [Photocopy], National Personnel Records Center, St. Louis, Mo., file of author.

15. C. P. Hall, XI Corps, to Mrs. Nellie M. Patrick, TLS [Photocopy], March 17, 1945, copy supplied by Thomas B. Patrick; Palmer to author, LS, February 23, 1991, file of author.

16. Henry L. Stimson, Washington, D.C., to Nellie M. Patrick, El Paso, Tex., TLS, [Photocopy], April 10, 1945, furnished by Thomas B. Patrick, file of author.

17. G. C. Marshall, Washington, D.C., to Mrs. Edwin D. Patrick, Ruidoso, N.M., TL, [Photocopy], March 15, 1945, Marshall Papers, file of author.

18. Douglas MacArthur, SWPA, to Nellie M. Patrick, Ruidoso, N.M., TLS [Photocopy], April 4, 1945, furnished by Thomas B. Patrick, file of author.

19. Walter Krueger, 6th Army, to Nellie M. Patrick, Ruidoso, N.M., TL [Photocopy], March 17, 1945, Box 9, Folder 55, Krueger Papers.

20. Hall to Mrs. Patrick.

21. Brig. Gen. S.D. Sturgis to Mrs. E. D, Patrick, Ruidoso, N.M., TLS [Photocopy], March 17, 1945, copy supplied by Thomas B. Patrick, in file of author.

22. Sam Tron, Detroit, to Mrs. Patrick, LS [Photocopy], March 14, 1949, copy supplied by Thomas B. Patrick, file of author.

23. Charles E. Zanzalari, Perth Amboy, N.J., to Thomas B. Patrick, LS [Photocopy], March 17, 1945, copy supplied by Thomas B. Patrick, in file of author.

24. George J. Ress, Indianapolis, to Anna Patrick, Tell City, TLS [Photocopy], March 22, 1945, copy supplied by Thomas B. Patrick, file of author.

25. "General Orders, 1942–1945, File 98–USF1–1.13 (49036), AGO, WW II, Pacific Theater, RG 407, NA. The entire citation appears in "Appendix D."

26. " 'Johnny Doughboy' Honored by AA at Armstrong Field," *The Fort Bliss News*, June 21, 1945, 1; "Citation for Distinguished Service Medal (Posthumous)," n.d., copy furnished by Thomas B. Patrick. The entire citation appears in "Appendix E."

27. *Indianapolis Star*, June 13, 1948, 11; *Indianapolis News*, June 30, 1948, sec. 2, 11.

CHAPTER 18

1. Leary, ed., *We Shall Return!*, Russell F. Weigley, *Eisenhower's Lieutenants* (Bloomington, Ind.: Indiana University Press, 1981).

2. Robert H. Berlin, "United States Army World War II Corps Commanders: A Composite Biography," *The Journal of Military History* 53 (April 1989): 147–67.

3. Gary Wade, "World War II Division Commanders" (Fort Leavenworth, Kans.: Combat Studies Institute, U.S. Army Command and General Staff College, Report No. 7, 1990).

4. Leslie Anders, *Gentle Night: The Life and Times of Major General Edwin Forrest Harding* (Kent, Ohio: The Kent State University Press, 1985); Michael T. Booth and Spencer Duncan, *Paratrooper: The Life of General James M. Gavin* (New York: Simon & Schuster, 1994); J. Lawton Collins, *Lightning Joe: An Autobiography* (Baton Rouge: Louisiana State University Press, 1979); Ernest N. Harmon, *Combat Commander: Autobiography of a Soldier* (Englewood Cliffs, N.J.: Prentice-Hall, 1970); Robert A. Miller, *Division Commander: A Biography of Major General Norman D. Cota* (Spartanburg, S.C.: The Reprint Company, Publishers, 1989); Frank James Price, *Troy H. Middleton: A Biography* (Baton Rouge: Louisiana State University Press, 1974); Matthew B. Ridgway, *Soldier: The Memoirs of Matthew B. Ridgway* (New York: Harper & Brothers, 1956).

5. As "Appendix F," I have compiled a list of the 140 men who commanded infantry, armor, and airborne divisions in World War II combat. This table contains the data that I have used in arriving at the conclusions that appear in the remainder of this chapter.

6. Among the "handful" were Robert S. Beightler, Leonard F. Wing, Raymond McLain, and Charles C. Haffner.

7. Edward M. Coffman and Peter F. Herrly, "The American Regular Army Officer Corps Between the World Wars," *Armed Forces and Society* 4 (November 1977): 55, 59.

8. Coffman and Herrly, 63.

9. "Appendix G."

10. Charles E. Kirkpatrick, "Orthodox Soldiers: Army Formal Schools Between the Two World Wars," a paper presented at the 1990 Annual Meeting of the Organization of American Historians, and the Society for History in the Federal Government, March 23-25, 1990, 8-11, file of author.

11. Kirkpatrick, "Orthodox Soldiers," 11, n. 30.

12. "Appendix G."

13. Kirkpatrick, "Orthodox Soldiers," 14-15, n. 41.

14. "Appendix G"; "Appendix F."

15. "Appendix G."

16. "Appendix F."

17. Kirkpatrick, "Orthodox Soldiers," 24.

18. Charles E. Kirkpatrick treats at length the influence of senior officers in the career development of junior officers in "Filling the Gaps: Reevaluating Officer Professional Education in the Inter-War Army, 1920-1940," a paper presented at the 1989 American Military Institute Annual Conference, April 14-15, 1989, file of author. See also Kenneth A. Jolemore, "The Mentor: More Than a Teacher, More Than a Coach," *Military Review* 66 (July 1986): 5-17.

19. Kirkpatrick, "Orthodox Soldiers," 19, n. 53.

20. Kirkpatrick, "Orthodox Soldiers,".

21. See Weigley, 1060–61.

22. Kirkpatrick, "Orthodox Soldiers," 22.

23. See rosters of Patrick's classes at the Infantry School, the Command and General Staff School, and the Army War College; Patrick's correspondence with Marshall, Krueger, and his family; and author's interviews of his sons, Thomas B. Patrick and Ulric B. Patrick.

24. Palmer interview.

25. Werner interview; Patrick File, Fenn to Cox, November 13, 1916.

26. Palmer interview.

27. Castagnetto interview.

28. Humphrey to author, June 26, 1990.

29. Castagnetto interview.

30. Ulysses Grant, *Personal Memoirs of U. S. Grant*, vol. 1 (New York: Charles L. Webster & Company, 1885; a facsimile edition of the original 1885 edition, New York: Bonanza Books, n.d.), 345 (page reference is to facsimile edition); Palmer interview; transcript of oral history interviews with Bruce Palmer, Jr., in 1975–1976, by Lieut. Col. James E. Shelton and Edward P. Smith, 101, Bruce Palmer, Jr., Papers, Archives, U.S. Army Military History Institute, Carlisle Barracks, Pa., hereafter referred to as "oral history interviews of Bruce Palmer, Jr."; Russell K. Brown, *Fallen in Battle: American General Officer Fatalities From 1775* (Westport, Conn.: Greenwood Press, 1988), 99–100, 117–18, 153.

31. "Tripp Soldier Recalls Activity of General Killed in Europe [sic]," newspaper article [Photocopy] from an unidentified newspaper, copy furnished by Thomas B. Patrick, file of author.

32. Palmer to author, July 28, 1991; oral history interviews of Bruce Palmer, Jr., 338.

33. Palmer interview.

34. Palmer to author, July 28, 1991, 6, file of author.

35. Oral history interviews of Bruce Palmer, Jr., 338. Humphrey to author, June 26, 1990, file of author.

36. Floyd H. Simmons, Reno, Nev., former battalion commander, 6th Infantry Division, to author, LS, November 11, 1991, file of author; Palmer to author, July 28, 1991, 6.

37. Roy Clark, Bandon, Oreg., to author, TL, May 10, 1989, file of author.

38. Schaal newspaper interview.

39. Brown, *Fallen in Battle*, xi.

40. Bernard J. Macauley, M.D., Gerald, Mo., to Colonel James L. Massey, Fort Sam Houston, Tex., TLS [Photocopy], May 4, 1946, Box 10, File 3, Krueger paper.

APPENDIX A

1. *United States Army in the World War, 1917–1919*, vol. 1, *Organization of the American Expeditionary Forces* (Washington, D.C.: Historical Division, Department of the Army, 1948), 341, 344, 348–50; Wendell Westover, *Suicide Battalions* (New York: G. P. Putnam's Sons, 1929), 22.

2. The Diagram Group, *Weapons: An International Encyclopedia from 5000 BC to 2000 AD* (New York: St. Martin's Press, 1980), 214–15; Westover, 22. The U.S. Army had been slow to pay attention to the machine gun as an infantry weapon. In 1910 John M. Browning had produced a prototype of the recoil–operated machine gun that would become the M1917 later used in France. However, the U.S. Army refused to look at it until February 1917, but still made no decision on adopting the weapon. In May 1917 the army finally adopted the gun and ordered it into production. The Browning M1917 weighed only 41 pounds and had a rate of fire of 450–600 rounds per minute. Until July 1918, American units in France used French machine guns and automatic rifles. Divisions sailing for France after that date carried the Browning M1917 water–cooled machine gun and Browning M1918 automatic rifles, although these weapons were not used in combat until September, because of Pershing's fear that the Germans might capture and copy them [Ian V. Hogg, *The Encyclopedia of Infantry Weapons of World War II* (Northbrook, Ill.: Book Value International, 1977), 40, 79; Russell F. Weigley, *History of the United States Army* (New York: The Macmillan Company, 1967), 363–64].

3. "Station List, Company A"; The Society of the First Division, *History of the First Division during the World War, 1917–1919* (Philadelphia: The John C. Winston Company, 1931), 427.

4. *History of the First Division*, 427, 430.

5. *History of the First Division*, 403.

6. Captain H. Douglas, *Machine Gun Manual: A Complete Manual to Machine Gunnery* (New York: Military Publishing Co., n.d.), 107–8; Westover, 153.

7. Westover, 152; Douglas, 108.

APPENDIX C

1. Photocopy furnished by Thomas B. Patrick. Unfortunately, I have been unable to locate a copy of the citation for Patrick's first Legion of Merit, awarded for his "work as Chief of Staff 6th Army for almost a year" (Patrick, APO 442, to family, Tell City, LS [Photocopy], August 2, 1944).

APPENDIX D

1. "General Orders, 1942–45" File 98–USF1–1.13 (49036), AGO, WW II, RG 407, NA.

APPENDIX E

1. Photocopy furnished by Thomas B. Patrick.

APPENDIX F

a.   Unless otherwise indicated, biographical data were compiled from the *Official Army Register, 1 January 1945* (Washington, D.C.: GPO, 1945) and the *Official Army Register, 1 January 1946* (Washington, D.C.: GPO, 1946). Commission "source" indicates either the service academy from which the officer graduated or the component in which he first received a commission; if no source is shown, the officer most likely received a direct appointment. The divisional command data and dates of command, unless otherwise indicated, were taken from Shelby L. Stanton, *Order of Battle: U.S. Army, World War II* (Novato, Ca.: Presidio Press, 1984), 46–186. Information about the deaths of the three division commanders who died during combat actions was found in Brown, *Fallen in Battle*, 99–100 (Patrick), 117–18 (Rose), 153 (Wharton).

b.   Killed in action or died of combat wounds.

c.   Graduate of land–grant college. The Morrill Act of 1862 provided for the donation of public lands to the several states, the proceeds of which were to support colleges emphasizing instruction in agriculture and the mechanical arts, and including "military tactics." These latter studies enabled graduates to compete for Regular Army commissions, and were the forerunner of the Reserve Officer Training Corps program, authorized in the National Defense Act of 1916. See *Encyclopedia Britannica*, 1966 ed., s.v. "Land Grant Colleges and Universities," by Lloyd E. Blauch; Maurice Matloff, *American Military History* (Washington, D.C.: Office of the Chief of Military History, 1973), 290, 367.

d.   Commissioned from enlisted ranks of the Regular Army.

e.   Date of relief from divisional command obtained from Brian Garfield, *The Thousand–Mile War: World War II in Alaska and the Aleutians* (Garden City, N.Y.: Doubleday & Company, Inc., 1969), 232.

f.   Date of assumption of divisional command obtained from Garfield, *The Thousand–Mile War*, 232; date of relief from divisional command deduced from WD biography of Charles H. Corlett, HRC 201, Historical Records Branch, U.S. Army Center of Military History, Washington, D.C.; commisioned from enlisted ranks of Regular Army.

g.   Date of assumption of divisional command obtained from WD biography of Charles H. Corlett.

h.   Killed in action; graduate of land–grant college; biographical data from *Official Army Register, 1 January 1944* (Washington, D.C.: GPO, 1944).

i.   Who's Who in America, vol. 24, 1946–1947 (Chicago: The A. N. Marcus Co., 1946), 165 (Beightler), 2594 (Wing), 1586 (McLain), 957 (Haffner).

j.   *Who's Who in America*, 309; *Official Army Register*, 1946, "Retired List."

k.   *Official Army Register*, 1946, "Retired List."

l.   *Official Army Register*, 1937; *Who's Who in America*, 1627.

m.   *Official Army Register*, 1945.

n.   Date of birth from *Who's Who in America*, 1251.

o.   *Official Army Register*, 1945, "Retired List."

p.   *Official Army Register*, 1944.

q.   Brown, 215; captured in the Philippine Islands in April 1942; prisoner of war until his release in August 1945.

r.   Berlin, "World War II Corps Commanders," 152.

s.   Although Maj. Gen. Robert Eichelberger, I Corps commander, had relieved Harding on December 2, 1942, as commander of the three regiments of the 32nd Division then engaged in New Guinea, Harding continued to serve "on paper" as division commander in Australia until February 1943. After Harding's departure, the three-regiment combat force was commanded successively by Brigadier Generals Albert W. Waldron and Clovis E. Byers, and finally, by Eichelberger himself; however, none of these officers was ever designated as division commander [Anders, 268; John Francis Shortal, *Forged by Fire: Robert L. Eichelberger and the Pacific War* (Columbia, S.C.: University of South Carolina Press, 1987), 47, 51-52, 57].

APPENDIX J

1.   Edgar Schergens, Editor Emeritus, "In Honor of Maj. Gen. Edwin D. Patrick," *The News* (Tell City), July 28, 1986, 4–5; "The Story of U. S. Naval Ship Gen. Edwin Patrick," n.p., n.d., photocopy supplied by Ethel E. Simianer, Cedar Lake, Ind., file of author.

2.   Raymond V. Blackman, ed., *Jane's Fighting Ships, 1969–70* (New York: McGraw Hill Book Company, n.d.), 508; "Transport Named," *The Sightseer*, National Association of the Sixth Infantry Division, 11 (September–December 1948): 3.

3.   Schergens, "The Story of the Patrick."

4.   "Transport Named," 1, 3. Fort Mason is the same Port of Embarkation from which Patrick and his family sailed for China in 1926.

5.   *Dictionary of American Naval Fighting Ships*, vol. 3 (Washington, D.C.: Navy Department, Office of the Chief of Naval Operations, Naval History Division, 1968); Schergens, 5.

6.   *Jane's Fighting Ships*. In July 1990, the author, with his wife and daughter, received permission to visit the *Patrick*. The ship is now "mothballed," with no power or electricity. Using flashlights, and with Mr. Ingram and Mr. Valdez acting as guides, the author revisited the troop compartment in which he was quartered in May 1950; the ship's laundry, where he had operated a "mangle" (a steam–pressing device to press bedsheets); and the galley, where he had the "privilege" of performing "K.P."

BIBLIOGRAPHY

PRIMARY SOURCES

ARCHIVAL MATERIAL

"14th M.G. Bn., 1917–1918, Officers' Returns, Rosters & Monthly Reports WW I Strength Returns, MG Battalions, Co., Field & Strength Returns, 11 Bn., 12 Bn., 13 Bn., & 14 Bn." World War I Organization Records, 5th Division. Record Group 120. National Archives. Washington, D.C.

"14th M.G Bn., Operations Maps." File 205–32.6. World War I Organization Records, 5th Division. Record Group 120. National Archives. Washington, D.C.

Course at the Army War College, 1936–1937. Field Exercise (Administrative). Subject: A Strategic and Tactical Study of Civil War Campaigns with Visits to Various Scenes of Action. File 6–1937–15. Army War College Curricular Archives. U.S. Army Military History Institute. Carlisle Barracks, Pa.

Course at the Army War College, 1937–1937. Conduct of War–Part II. Field Exercise. Jackson's Valley Campaign. Lectures by Major Edwin D. Patrick, Inf. and Major Wendell L. Clemens, Inf. File 6–1937–15/K. Army War College Curricular Archives. U.S. Army Military History Institute. Carlisle Barracks, Pa.

"General Orders, No. 25, Headquarters, Sixth Army, 21 June 1943, 11 May 1944." File 106–1.113. The Adjutant General's Office, World War II Operations Reports, Pacific Theater, 1940–48. Record Group 407. National Archives. Washington, D.C.

"General Orders," File 98-USF1–1.13 (49036), 1942–45. The Adjutant General's Office, World War II Operations Reports, 1940–

1948, Pacific Theater. Record group 407. National Archives. Washington, D.C.

"Headquarters Orders. General Orders 11." World War I Organization Records, 5th Division. Record Group 120. National Archives. Washington, D.C.

"Historical Report of Operations—Wakde–Sarmi—TORNADO Task Force, 25 May to 12 June 1944." File 98–TF9-0.3. The Adjutant General's Office, World War II Operations Reports, 1940–1948, Pacific Theater. Record Group 407. National Archives. Washington, D.C.

"Historical Report of the Noemfoor Operation, 22 June 1944 to 31 August 1944." File 98–TF 11-0.3, CYCLONE Task Force. The Adjutant General's Office, World War II Operations Reports, 1940–1948, Pacific Theater. Record Group 407. National Archives. Washington, D.C.

"Historical Report of Action Against the Enemy—Luzon Campaign—54th Evacuation Hospital, 25 November 1944-30 June 1945." File MDEH–54-0.3. The Adjutant General's Office, World War II Operations Reports, 1940–1948, Medical. Record Group 407. National Archives. Washington, D.C.

"Infantry, Washington" File 325.4. Army—NGB. State—Decimal File, 1922–1945. Records of the National Guard Bureau. Record Group 168. National Archives. Washington, D.C.

"Maneuvers, May 1925. Fort Sam Houston Quartermaster Maneuver, 1925–1940." Records of the U. S. Army Continental Commands, 1920–1942. Record Group 394. National Archives. Washington, D.C.

"Patrick, Edwin D. Army War College Transcript." File 6–1937–15. Army War College Curricular Archives. U.S. Army Military History Institute. Carlisle Barracks, Pa.

"Patrick, Edwin D." File 2466738. Records of the Adjutant General's Office, 1780s–1917. Record Group 94. National Archives. Washington, D.C.

"Press Information 6th Infantry Div., Roster Officers Division Headquarters." 6th Infantry Division. The Adjutant General's Office, World War II Operations Reports, 1940–1948. RG 407. National Archives. Washington, D.C.

"Reports of Operations from October 25th, to November 11, 1918, November 16, 1918." Major Tom Fox, Brigade Machine Gun Officer, Ninth Infantry Brigade to the Commanding General, Ninth Infantry Brigade. TLS. File 205–33.6. World War I Organization Records, 5th Division, "Reports of Op, Oct. 25–Nov. 11/18." Record Group 120. National Archives. Washington, D.C.

"Service File Cards of Edwin D. Patrick, Indiana National Guard." "INDANG Service File Cards," L Section, Archives Division, Indiana Commission on Public Records. Indianapolis, Ind.

"Station List, 14th M.G. Bn." File 205–10.7. World War I Organization Records, 5th Division. Record Group 120. National Archives. Washington, D.C.

"Third Army Maneuvers, 1938, Fort F. E. Warren Concentration." Records of the U.S. Army Continental Army Commands, 1920–42. Record Group 394. National Archives. Washington, D.C.

"War Record, 14th Machine Gun Battalion, 5th Division." File 205–11.4 "History, 14th MG Bn." World War I Organization Records, 5th Division. Record Group 120. National Archives. Washington, D.C.

PERSONAL MANUSCRIPT COLLECTIONS

Decker, George H. Archives, U.S. Army Military History Institute. Carlisle Barracks, Pa.

Harding, E. Forrest. Franklin Area Historical Society. Franklin, Ohio.

Krueger, Walter. United States Military Academy Library. United States Military Academy. West Point, N.Y.

MacArthur, Douglas. Archives, MacArthur Memorial. Norfolk, Va.

Marshall, George C. George C. Marshall Foundation. Lexington, Va.

Palmer, Bruce, Jr. Archives, U.S. Army Military History Institute. Carlisle Barracks, Pa.

Stilwell, Joseph Warren. Hoover Institution on War, Revolution and Peace. Stanford, Calif.

LETTERS AND CORRESPONDENCE

Braun, Hal, Hollywood, Calif., to author. TLS, April 27, 1989. File of author.

Clark, Roy, Bandon, Oreg., to author. TL, May 10, 1989. File of author.

Erb, Herbert B., Col., USA (Ret.), San Francisco, to author. LS, May 3, July 12, 1989. File of author.

Goffinet, Mary Margaret, Tell City, to author. LS, November 9, 1991. File of author.

Hall, C. P., Maj. Gen., USA, APO 471, to Mrs. Nellie M. Patrick, Ruidoso, N. Mex. TLS [Photocopy], March 17, 1945. Copy supplied by Thomas B. Patrick. File of author.

Huchthausen, Walther, Chaplain, 6th Infantry Division, Philippine Islands, to wife. LS [Photocopy], March 16, 1945. Copy supplied by Chaplain Huchthausen's daughter, Christa Huchthausen Mueller, Newport News, Va. File of author.

Humphrey, John D., Col., AUS (Ret), Tupelo, Miss., to author. LS, June 2, June 16, 1989; TLS, June 26, 1990; November 4, 1991. File of author.

MacArthur, Douglas, Gen., USA, SWPA, to Mrs. Edwin D. Patrick, Ruidoso, N.Mex. TLS [Photocopy], April 4, 1945. Copy supplied by Thomas B. Patrick. File of author.

Palmer, Bruce, Jr., Gen., USA (Ret.), Fort Walton Beach, Fla., to author. LS, February 23, 1991; TLS, July 28, 1991. File of author.

Patrick, Edwin D., Fort Sam Houston, to Clara Patrick, Tell City. TLS [Photocopy], June 2, 1925. File of author.

_____, San Francisco, to Clara Patrick, Tell City. LS [Photocopy], March 30, 1926. File of author.

_____, Tientsin, to Patrick family, Tell City. LS [Photocopies], May 28, July 10, 1926; December 30, 1927; June 10, 1928. File of author.

_____, Tientsin, to Clara Patrick, Tell City. LS [Photocopy], June 23, 1927. File of author.

_____, Tientsin, to Herbert Patrick, Tell City. LS [Photocopy], June 23, 1927. File of author.

_____, Spokane, to his mother, Tell City. LS [Photocopy], July 6, 1934. File of author.

_____, Fort Sam Houston, Tex., to his mother, Tell City. LS [Photocopies], October 7, 1940; December 1, December 6, December 24, 1941. File of author.

_____, Waco, Tex., to his mother, Tell City. LS [Photocopy], September 10, 1941. File of author.

_____, Nouméa, New Caledonia, to his family, Tell City. LS [Photocopies], February 2, February 7, February 21, March 1, April 20, May 6, May 10, May 22, 1943. File of author.

_____, APO 442, to family, Tell City. LS [Photocopies], June 30, August 4, August 8, September 10, September 19, October 9, October 19, November 11, November 21, December 2, 1943; January 5, January 27, May[?], June 21, August 2, August 25, 1944. File of author.

_____, APO 6, to family, Tell City. LS [Photocopies], October 7, October 15, November 11, December 11, December 29, 1944.

_____, APO 6, to family, Tell City. LS [Photocopy], January 1, 1945.

Ress, George J., Indianapolis, to Anna Patrick, Tell City. TLS [Photocopy], March 22, 1945. Copy supplied by Thomas B. Patrick. File of author.

Simmons, Floyd H., Reno, Nev., to author. LS, November 11, 1991. File of author.

Stimson, Henry L., Washington, D.C. [?], to Mrs. Nellie M. Patrick, El Paso, Tex. TLS [Photocopy], April 10, 1945. Copy supplied by Thomas B. Patrick. File of author.

Sturgis, S. D., Brig. Gen., USA, APO 442, to Mrs. E. D. Patrick, Ruidoso, N. Mex., TLS [Photocopy], March 17, 1945. Copy furnished by Thomas B. Patrick. File of author.

Tron, Sam, Detroit, Mich., to Mrs. Patrick. LS [Photocopy], March 14, 1949. Copy supplied by Thomas B. Patrick. File of author.

Werner, Ruth Anne, Tell City, to author. LS, November 10, 1991. File of author.

Zanzalari, Charles E., Perth Amboy, N.J., to Thomas B. Patrick. LS [Photocopy], March 17, 1945. Copy supplied by Thomas B. Patrick. File of author.

INTERVIEWS

Castagnetto, Joseph A. Interview by author, August 27, 1991, Alameda, Calif. Tape recording. File of author.

Palmer, Bruce, Jr., Gen., USA (Ret.) Interview by author, May 18, 1990, The Fairfax, Fort Belvoir, Va. Tape recording. File of author.

Patrick, Thomas B. Interview by author, September 18, 1990, The Woodlands, Tex. Tape recording. File of author.

Patrick, Ulric B. Interview by author, September 20, 1990, Albuquerque, N. Mex. Tape recording. File of author.

Werner, Ruth Anne. Interview by author, May 29, 1990, Tell City. Tape recording. File of author.

UNPUBLISHED MANUSCRIPT

Kennedy, Alma Patrick. "Records and Recollections." April 1972. TMs [Photocopy]. File of author.

NEWSPAPERS

The Fort Bliss News (Fort Bliss, Tex.), June 21, 1945, 1.

Indianapolis News (Indianapolis, Ind.), June 30, 1948, sec. 2, 11.

Indianapolis Star (Indianapolis, Ind.), June 13, 1948, 11.

The News (Tell City, Ind.), October 13,1982; May 4, 1989.

Reporter–News (Abilene, Tex.), n.d.

San Antonio Evening News (San Antonio, Tex.), August 9, 1939.

Schergens, Edgar. "In Honor of Maj. GEN Edwin D. Patrick." *The News* (Tell City), July 28, 1986, 4–5.

The Sentinel (Tientsin, China), September 10, September 24 , November 5, November 12, November 19, November 26, 1926; February 18 , March 4, April 29, May 13, May 20, May 27, October 7, December 23, 1927; February 24, April 6, April 27, December 8, December 22, 1928; February 9, February 16, March 2, April 13, April 20, 1929.

The Tell City News (Tell City, Ind.), May 29, 1925; April 2, April 9, April 16, July 9, 1926; February 11, March 25, 1927; June[?] 1936.

OTHER

"158th RCT Operations Report, Sarmi–Wakde Campaign, May 11–June 21, 1944." Copy furnished by Herbert B. Erb, Col., USA (Ret.), San Francisco.

The Adjutant General's Office. *Official Army Register, 1 January 1937* . Washington, D.C.: GPO, 1937.

_____. *Official Army Register, 1 January 1944*. Washington, D.C.: GPO, 1944.

_____. *Official Army Register, 1 January 1945*. Washington, D.C.: GPO, 1945.

_____. *Official Army Register, 1 January 1946* . Washington, D.C.: GPO, 1946.

Annual Report of the Command and General Staff School, Fort Leavenworth, Kansas, 1933–1934. Fort Leavenworth, Kan.: The Command and General Staff School Press, 1934.

Commandants, Staff, Faculty, and Graduates of The Command and General Staff School, Fort Leavenworth, Kansas: 1881–1939. Fort Leavenworth, Kan.: The Command and General Staff School Press, 1939.

The Doughboy. Fort Benning, Ga.: The Infantry School, U. S. Army, 1923.

_____. 1931, 1932.

Historical Office, U. S. Army Communications—Electronics Command. A *Concise History of Fort Monmouth, New Jersey.* Fort Monmouth, N.J.: n.p., July 1985.

Krueger, Walter. *From Down Under to Nippon: The Story of Sixth Army in World War II.* Walter Krueger, 1953; reprint, Washington, D.C.: Zenger Publishing Co., Inc., 1979.

National Defense Act. Statutes at Large. Vol. 39, Part 1 (1916).

·*Papuan Campaign: The Buna–Sanananda Operation, 16 November 1942–23 January 1943.* Washington, D.C.: Historical Division, War Department, 1945; reprint, Center of Military History, United States Army, 1990.

"Prospectus of the Naval War College Courses, Senior and Junior, 1938–39." U. S. Naval War College, July 1938. Newport, R.I.

von Roeder, George. *Regimental History of the 357th Infantry.* Weiden, Oberpfalz, Bavaria: Ferdinand Nickl Buchdruckerei, n.d.

Schedule for 1932–1933 First Year Course, The Command and General Staff School, Fort Leavenworth, Kansas, 1932. Fort Leavenworth, Kan.: The Command and General Staff School Press, 1932.

"Second–Year Class Schedule for 1933–1934." The Command and General Staff School, Fort Leavenworth, Kan.

Senior Class of 1912 of Tell City High School. *The Rambler, 1912.* Tell City, Ind.: n.p., 1912.

"The Story of U. S. Naval Ship Gen. Edwin D. Patrick." n.p.: n.d. Copy supplied by Ethel E. Sinianer, Cedar Lake, Ind. File of author.

"Transport Named." *The Sightseer*, 11 (September-December 1948): 1, 3. National Association of the Sixth Infantry Division.

Wade, Gary. "World War II Division Commanders." Fort Leavenworth, Kan.: Combat Studies Institute, U.S. Army Command and General Staff College, Report No. 7, 1990.

War Department. The Adjutant General's Office, Washington. *Army List and Directory, April 20, 1917.* Washington, D.C.: GPO, 1917.

_____. *Army Directory, September 1, 1917.* Washington, D.C.: GPO, 1917.

War Department. *Army Directory, October 1, 1917.* Washington, D.C.: GPO, 1917.

War Department. *Army Directory, November 1, 1917.* Washington, D.C.: GPO, 1917.

_____. *Army Directory, December 1, 1917.* Washington, D.C.: GPO, 1917.

"War Department Biography of Edwin Daviess Patrick." Washington, D.C.: March 21, 1945. HRC 201, Historical Records Branch, Center of Military History, United States Army. Washington, D.C.

World War I "Award Cards." "Silver Star Citation" awarded to Patrick, Edwin D., Capt., 14th MG Bn. Hqrs. Ninth Inf. Brig., 31st Dec. 1918. U.S. Army Reserve Personnel Center. St. Louis, Mo.

SECONDARY SOURCES

UNPUBLISHED MANUSCRIPTS

Conn, Stetson. "The Army War College, 1899–1940: Mission, Purpose, Objectives." December 1964. File 538. Center of Military History, United States Army. Washington, D.C.

Patrick, Edwin D. "The Training and Replacement of Infantry Signal Communications Personnel (Officers and Enlisted Men) in the Theater of Operations." March 23, 1934. Combat Studies Institute, U.S. Army Command and General Staff College, Fort Leavenworth, Kan. TMs [Photocopy]. File of author.

BOOKS AND OTHER PUBLISHED MATERIALS

A History of the 90th Division in World War II, 6 June 1944 to 9 May 1945. n.p. n.d.

American Battle Monuments Commission. 5th Division Summary of Operations in the World War. Washington, D.C.: GPO, 1944.

American Battle Monuments Commission. American Armies and Battlefields in Europe: A History, Guide, and Reference Book. Washington, D.C.: GPO, 1938.

Anders, Leslie. Gentle Knight: The Life and Times of Major General Edwin Forrest Harding. Kent, Ohio: The Kent State University Press, 1985.

Arthur, Anthony. Bushmasters: America's Jungle Warriors of World War II. New York: St. Martin's Press, 1987.

Ball, Harry P. Of Responsible Command: A History of the U.S. Army War College. Carlisle Barracks, Pa.: The Alumni Association of the United States Army War College, 1983.

Blackman, Raymond V., ed. *Jane's Fighting Ships, 1969–1970*. New York: McGraw Hill Book Company, n.d.

Brown, Russell K. *Fallen in Battle: American General Officer Fatalities From 1775*. Westport, Conn.: Greenwood Press, 1988.

Clendenen, Clarence C. *Blood on the Border: The United States Army and the Mexican Irregulars*. Toronto: Collier–Macmillan Ltd., 1969.

Cray, Ed. General *of the Army George C. Marshall: Soldier and Statesman*. New York: Simon & Schuster, 1990.

The Diagram Group. *Weapons: An International Encyclopedia from 5000 BC to 2000 AD*. New York: St. Martin's Press, 1980.

Dictionary of American Fighting Naval Ships. Vol. 3. Washington, D.C.: Navy Department, Office of the Chief of Naval Operations, Naval History Division, 1968.

Directory of Army War College Graduates. Carlisle Barracks, Pa.: AWC Alumni Association, 1990.

Douglas, Captain H. *Machine Gun Manual: A Complete Manual to Machine Gunnery*. New York: Military Publishing Co., n.d.

Drea, Edward J. *MacArthur's Ultra: Codebreaking and the War against Japan, 1942–1945*. Lawrence, Kan.: University Press of Kansas, 1992.

Encyclopedia Brittanica. 1966 ed. S.v. "Land–Grant Colleges and Universities," by Lloyd E. Blauch.

Field, Virgil. *Official History of the Washington National Guard*. Camp Murray, Tacoma, Wash.: Headquarters, Military Department, 1961–1965[?].

Fitch, Roger S. *Estimating Tactical Situations and Composing Field Orders*. Fort Leavenworth, Kan.: Army Service Schools Press, 1917.

Garfield, Brian. *The Thousand-Mile War: World War II in Alaska and the Aleutians*. Garden City, N.Y.: Doubleday & Company, Inc., 1969.

Grant, Ulysses S. *Personal Memoirs of U. S. Grant*. Vol. 1. New York: Charles L. Webster & Company, 1885; a facsimile of the original 1885 edition, New York: Bonanza Books, n.d.

Grieves, Loren C. *Outline of Lessons in Company Administration*. Fort Leavenworth, Kan.: Army Service Schools Press, 1917.

Harrison, Gordon A. *Cross-Channel Attack*. In *U.S. Army in World War II: The European Theater of Operations*. Washington, D.C.: Office of the Chief of Military History, United States Army, 1951.

Historical and Pictorial Review of the National Guard of the State of Washington. Baton Rouge: Army and Navy Publishing Co., 1938.

Hogg, Ian V. *The Encyclopedia of Infantry Weapons of World War II*. Northbrook, Ill.: Book Value International, 1977.

James, D. Clayton. *The Years of MacArthur, Volume 2, 1941–1945*. Boston: Houghton Mifflin Company, 1975.

Leary, William W. *We Shall Return! MacArthur's Commanders and the Defeat of Japan*. Lexington, Ky.: The University Press of Kentucky, 1988.

Matloff, Maurice, ed. *American Military History*. Washington, D.C.: Office of the Chief of Military History, United States Army, 1969.

McAndrew, J. W. *Address to the Second Class of Provisional Second Lieutenants, United States Army.* Fort Leavenworth, Kan.: Army Service Schools Press, 1917.

McClure, Glenn E. *Guam, Then and Now.* n.p.: 1979.

McPherson, James M. *Battle Cry of Freedom: The Civil War Era.* New York: Oxford University Press, 1988.

Miller, Charles. *The Customs of the Service and Some Suggestions and Advice.* Fort Leavenworth, Kan.: Army Service Schools Press, 1917.

Miller, John, Jr. *Guadalcanal: The First Offensive.* In *United States Army in World War II: The War in the Pacific.* Washington, D.C.: Historical Division, United States Army, 1949.

Morison, Samuel Eliot. *History of United States Naval Operations in World War II.* Vol. 5, *The Struggle for Guadalcanal, August 1942–February 1943.* Boston: Little, Brown and Company, 1984.

————. History of United States Naval Operations in World War II Vol. 8, *New Guinea and the Marianas, March 1944–August 1944.* Boston: Little, Brown and Company, 1981.

Morton, Louis. *The Fall of the Philippines.* In *United States Army in World War II: The War in the Pacific.* Washington, D.C.: Center of Military History, United States Army, 1989.

————. *Strategy and Command: The First Two Years.* In *United States Army in World War II: The War in the Pacific.* Washington, D.C.: Center of Military History, United States Army, 1989.

Noble, Dennis L. *The Eagle and the Dragon: The United States Military in China, 1901–1937.* Westport, Conn.: Greenwood Press, 1990.

O'Loughlin, W. J. *Notes on Messing Organizations*. Fort Leavenworth, Kan.: Army Service Schools Press, 1917.

Pappas, George S. *Prudens Futuri: The U. S. Army War College, 1901–1967*. Carlisle Barracks, Pa.: The Alumni Association of the U. S. Army War College, 1967.

Phillips, Helen C. *United States Army Signal School: 1919–1967*. Fort Monmouth, N.J.: U. S. Army Signal Center and School, 1967.

Pogue, Forrest C. *George C. Marshall: Education of a General, 1880–1939*. New York: The Viking Press, 1963.

Shortal, John Francis. *Forged by Fire: Robert L. Eichelberger and the Pacific War.* Columbia, S.C.: University of South Carolina Press, 1987.

Smith, Robert Ross. *The Approach to the Philippines*. In *United States Army in World War II: The War in the Pacific*. Washington, D.C.: Center of Military History, United States Army, 1984.

_____. *Triumph in the Philippines*. In *United States Army in World War II: The War in the Pacific*. Washington, D.C.: Center of Military History, United States Army, 1984.

The Society of the Fifth Division. *The Official History of the Fifth Division, U.S.A.* Washington, D.C.: The Society of the Fifth Division, 1919.

The Society of the First Division. *History of the First Division during the World War, 1917–1919*. Philadelphia: The John C. Winston Company, 1931.

Stanton, Shelby L. *Order of Battle: U. S. Army, World War II*. Novato, Ca.: Presidio Press, 1984.

The Sixth Army in Action: A Photo History, January 1943–June 1945. Kyoto, Japan: 8th Information and Historical Service, United States Sixth Army, December 1945.

The Sixth Infantry Division in World War II, 1939-1945. n.p.: May 1947; reprint, Nashville, Tenn.: The Battery Press, 1983.

Watt, William J., and James R. H. Spears, ed. *Indiana's Citizen Soldiers: The Militia and National Guard in Indiana History*. Indianapolis: The Indiana State Armory Board, 1980.

Weigley, Russell F. *Eisenhower's Lieutenants*. Vol. 2, *The Campaign of France and Germany, 1944-1945*. Bloomington: Indiana University Press, 1981.

Westover, Wendell. *Suicide Battalions*. New York: G. P. Putnam's Sons, 1929.

Who's Who in America. Vol. 24. Chicago: The A. N. Marcus Co., 1946.

Wilson, John B., comp. *Armies, Corps, and Separate Brigades*. In *Army Lineage Series*. Washington, D.C.: Center of Military History, United States Army, 1987.

ARTICLES

Berlin, Robert H. "United States Army World War II Corps Commanders: A Composite Biography." *The Journal of Military History* 53 (April 1989): 147–167.

Coffman, Edward M. and Peter F. Herrly. "The American Regular Army Officer Corps Between the World Wars." *Armed Forces and Society* 4 (November 1977): 55–73.

"In Memoriam ...," The *November 1945 Indiana Alumni Magazine*, 17–18.

Jolemore, Kenneth A. "The Mentor: More Than a Teacher, More Than a Coach." *Military Review* 66 (July 1986): 5–17.

Nenninger, Timothy K. "Creating Officers: The Leavenworth Experience, 1920–1940." *Military Review* 69 (November 1989): 58–68.

OTHER

Kirkpatrick, Charles E. "Filling the Gaps: Reevaluating Officer Professional Education in the Inter–War Army, 1920–1940." A paper presented at the 1989 American Military Institute Annual Meeting, April 14–15, 1989. File of author.

_____. "Orthodox Soldiers: Army Formal Schools between the World Wars." A paper presented at the 1990 Annual Meeting of the Organization of American Historians, and the Society for History in the Federal Government, March 23–25, 1990. File of author.

ACKNOWLEDGMENTS

I wish to thank the following individuals, who, without exception, responded promptly and graciously to the requests that I made for information and assistance:

Governmental Agencies:

Dorothy M. Flowers, Freedom of Information Act Inquiry Office, Army Reserve Personnel Center, St. Louis, Missouri.

Edward J. Drea, Ph.D., Lieutenant Colonel Clayton R. Nevell, and Major Charles E. Kirkpatrick, Center of Military History, U.S. Army, Washington, D.C.

Charles D. Johnston, Maritime Administration, who very kindly made arrangements for my wife, my daughter, and me to visit the "mothballed" USNS *General Edwin D. Patrick*, and Mr. Ingram and Mr. Valdez, who accompanied us on our tour of the ship in the Suisun Bay Reserve Fleet, Benicia, California.

Michael Knapp, National Archives, Washington, D.C.

David L. Petree, Director, and William Seibert, Senior Archivist, National Personnel Records Center, St. Louis, Missouri.

J. L. Mooney, Ships' Histories Branch, Naval Historical Center, Washington, D.C.

Evelyn M. Cherpak, Head, Naval Historical Collection, Naval War College, Newport, Rhode Island.

Major Michael D. Hess and Corporal Michael K. Pinasey, Civil Military Affairs, Sixth Infantry Division (Light), Fort Richardson, Alaska.

Carol J. Morrison, Librarian/Archivist; Karla C. Norman, Assistant Archives Librarian; and Elizabeth R. Snoke, Librarian, Combined Arms Research Library, U.S. Army Command and General Staff College, Fort Leavenworth, Kansas.

Marilyn J. Kruk, Editor/Archivist, U.S. Army Communications–Electronics Command, Fort Monmouth, New Jersey.

Major Scott Johnson, Deputy Secretary, and Betty Collins–Van Sickle, Donovan Technical Library, U.S. Army Infantry School, Fort Benning, Georgia.

Richard J. Sommers, Ph.D., Archivist–Historian; David A. Keough, Assistant Archivist–Historian; and Pam Cheney, U.S. Army Military History Institute, Carlisle Barracks, Pennsylvania.

Kathy R. Coker, Ph.D., Deputy Command Historian, U.S. Army Signal Center, Fort Gordon, Georgia.

Major William Woodward, Command Historian, Washington Army National Guard, Camp Murray, Washington.

Richard Boylan and David Giordano, Washington National Records Center, Suitland, Maryland.

Judith A. Sibley, West Point Manuscript Librarian, United States Military Academy, West Point, New York.

Thomas D. Lund, Indiana Commission on Public Records, Indianapolis, Indiana.

Noralee Young, Reference Librarian, Indiana Division, Indiana State Library, Indianapolis, Indiana.

Individuals and Non–Governmental Agencies:

Leslie Anders, Ph.D., Central Missouri State University, Warrensburg, Missouri, biographer of Major General Edwin Forrest Harding. Professor Anders directed me to the repository of General Harding's papers at Franklin, Ohio. General Harding was a professional associate and friend of General Patrick.

Edward J. Boone, Jr., Archivist, MacArthur Memorial, Norfolk, Virginia.

Joseph A. Castagnetto, Alameda, California, aide–de–camp to General Patrick while he commanded the Sixth Infantry Division. Mr. Castagnetto provided many personal insights into the life and career of General Patrick from the perspective of a close junior associate and a combat–seasoned infantryman.

Herbert Erb, Colonel, USA (Ret.), San Francisco, California. Colonel Erb, now deceased, was a member of the 158th Regimental Combat Team, which General Patrick commanded on New Guinea. He provided a great deal of personal information about the New Guinea campaigns, as well as a copy of the "Operations Report" of the 158th Regimental Combat Team in the Wakde–Sarmi operation.

Richard Flanders, Secretary–Treasurer, National Association of the Sixth Infantry Division, Minneapolis, Minnesota.

Harriet E. Foley, Franklin Area Historical Society, Franklin, Ohio, who diligently searched the files, papers, and records of the late Major General Edwin Forrest Harding, and provided me with playbills and other memorabilia relating to General and Mrs. Patrick's amateur dramatic activities

Mary Margaret Goffinet and Ruth Anne Werner, Tell City, Indiana, nieces of General Patrick, who kindly allowed me access to letters, photographs, and other memorabilia of their uncle, and shared reminiscences about him and his family. I have particularly appreciated their continuing interest and encouragement in this project.

John D. Humphrey, Colonel, AUS (Ret.), Tupelo, Mississippi, a former member of the 1st Infantry Regiment, who provided an eyewitness account of General Patrick's wounding.

Leonard A. Humphreys, Ph.D., Lieutenant Colonel, USA (Ret.), Professor of History, University of the Pacific, Stockton, California, who encouraged me to pursue graduate studies in history prior to embarking on a second career in military history after my retirement from the practice of medicine.

John N. Jacob, Archivist–Librarian, George C. Marshall Foundation, Lexington, Virginia.

John L. Johnson, Colonel, USA (Ret.), Curator, Arizona National Guard Historical Society, Phoenix, Arizona.

Christa Mueller, Newport News, Virginia, daughter of Chaplain Walther A. Huchthausen, who was attached to the 1st Infantry Regiment at the time of General Patrick's wounding. Mrs. Mueller provided me with a copy of a letter that her father had sent to her mother, in which he described the wounding of Patrick and the death of Colonel Rees, commander of the 1st Infantry Regiment.

John R. O'Dell, Ph.D., Associate Professor, School of Engineering, University of the Pacific, Stockton, California, who provided invaluable assistance in unraveling the mysteries of my computer and its software.

Bruce Palmer, Jr., General, USA (Ret.), The Fairfax, Fort Belvoir, Virginia. General Palmer, who served as General Patrick's chief of staff during his command of the Sixth Infantry Division, very kindly hosted my wife and me at his home, where he graciously submitted to a long interview in which we discussed his remembrances of Patrick. In this interview, and in a subsequent letter, General Palmer shared his opinions of General Patrick's abilities as a division commander, his command and leadership qualities, his relationships with staff and subordinate commanders, and his potential to have risen to higher grade and command if he had not died. General Palmer's contributions to this book cannot be overemphasized: his experience at all levels of command, during three wars, in a military career spanning forty-two years, beginning when he became a cadet at the United States Military Academy in 1932, has enabled him to provide, from a unique perspective, a critical analysis of General Patrick as a division commander. I am deeply indebted to General Palmer for his assistance, support, and encouragement.

Mr. and Mrs. Thomas B. Patrick and their son Edwin D. Patrick II, The Woodlands, Texas. Mr. and Mrs. Patrick were very gracious hosts of my wife and me during our visit to The Woodlands. Tom, General Patrick's youngest son, allowed me to examine his father's memorabilia, and allowed me to record an interview, in which he provided many reminiscences of and insights into his father. In addition, he provided photocopies of much of the material in his possession.

Ulric B. Patrick, stepson of General Patrick, Albuquerque, New Mexico. "Ric" kindly invited my wife and me to his home, and allowed me to examine memorabilia, documents, and photographs in his possession. He also consented to grant me a very helpful interview.

Paul D. Ramsey, Worshipful Master of Tell City Lodge #623, Free and Accepted Masons, Tell City, Indiana.

Edgar Schergens (deceased), former Editor Emeritus, *The News*, Tell City, Indiana.

Ethel Simianer, Cedar Lake, Indiana, who was a passenger on the USNS *General D. Patrick* in 1953, and who supplied me with a document giving the history and a description of the ship.

Staff of the Tell City Library, who kindly supplied photocopies of pertinent issues of *The Tell City News* in their library holdings.

INDEX